Also by Ben Bassham:

Conrad Wise Chapman, Artist and Soldier of the Confederacy,
Kent, Ohio: The Kent State University Press, 1998.

The Lithographs of Robert Riggs, with a Catalogue Raisonné,
Philadelphia: The Art Alliance Press, 1986.

The Theatrical Photographs of Napoleon Sarony, Kent,
Ohio: The Kent State University Press, 1978.

Books edited:

*Ten Months in the Orphan Brigade: The Civil War Journal of Conrad
Wise Chapman,* Kent, Ohio: The Kent State University Press, 1999.

Abel Warshawsky, *Memories of an American Impressionist,*
Kent, Ohio: The Kent State University Press, 1980.

Exhibition catalogues:

Conrad Wise Chapman in Mexico, San Diego:
The Timken Art Museum, 1997.

John Taylor Arms, American Etcher, Madison,
Wis.: The Elvehjem Art Museum, 1974.

A LOCAL KID

(DOES ONLY O.K.)

Growing Up in Rogers, Arkansas 1945-1960

BEN L. BASSHAM

iUniverse, Inc.
Bloomington

A Local Kid (Does Only O.K.)
Growing Up in Rogers, Arkansas 1945-1960

iUniverse books may be ordered through booksellers or by contacting:

iUniverse
1663 Liberty Drive
Bloomington, IN 47403
www.iuniverse.com
1-800-Authors (1-800-288-4677)

Because of the dynamic nature of the Internet, any Web addresses or links contained in this book may have changed since publication and may no longer be valid. The views expressed in this work are solely those of the author and do not necessarily reflect the views of the publisher, and the publisher hereby disclaims any responsibility for them.

Any people depicted in stock imagery provided by Thinkstock are models, and such images are being used for illustrative purposes only.

Certain stock imagery © Thinkstock.

ISBN: 978-1-4759-2833-4 (sc)
ISBN: 978-1-4759-2834-1 (e)

Printed in the United States of America

iUniverse rev. date: 6/11/2012

"I don't want to be a big star. I just want to twinkle a little."

John Lowenstein, Cleveland Indians outfielder, 1970-1977

For our daughters Claire and Marianna

and

For Bill and Phyllis

and

To the memory of

Patricia Ann Mathew and Edgar C. Bassham

PREFACE

━━━►◆◄━━━

Several years ago, while visiting our daughters in Boston, I found myself scrambling to make last-minute arrangements for a flight to my home town of Rogers, Arkansas. My sister Phyllis, who was facing open-heart surgery, had been anxiously awaiting word from the Cleveland Clinic on the date scheduled for her operation. She and I had made plans some time in advance for me to fly to Rogers and drive her to my home in Kent, located some forty miles south of Cleveland, and then help her through the whole pre-op registration process. Following her surgery, she would then have a couple of weeks' recovery at our home to get back on her feet.

The Clinic had been vague about dates, only suggesting that the surgeon might get around to her case early in February, 2004. When the summons eventually came on a Friday, it read like an order from a kindly, benevolent dictatorship: Be at the Clinic on Monday morning at 8:00 a.m. sharp. Period. So said the world's premier authority on heart surgery, the renowned savior of kings, sheiks, ayatollahs, and, we certainly hoped, sister Phyllis.

I boarded a plane at Boston's Logan airport and headed for Rogers, 1300 miles to the west. Most of my fellow passengers on the leg from Boston to Newark appeared headed for the sands and sun of the Caribbean, for they were a raucous bunch, already in their sandals and perhaps on their fourth Coronas before our 737 had even risen above the clouds. When a group of partying Red Sox fans bound for a week's relief from a bleak New England winter make nuisances of themselves, it's best to shut up, get out of the way, and hope for calmer and quieter skies ahead.

With relief in Newark I climbed aboard a half-full commuter jet, a plane of exotic origins, an Embraer, I think, from Brazil, with single seats on one side and rows of two on the other, and with neatly upturned wingtips, like

1

clever origami creations in aluminum. The day was gorgeous, the weather cold, and the skies clear all the way to the Mississippi and beyond. The ordeal of navigating American airports only a few months after 9/11 was behind me, and I sat back to enjoy one of the most relaxing, and memorable, flights of my life. Sharing the plane with only a handful of fellow passengers made it easy for me to slip into the fantasy that this was *my* jet, ordered up just for this trip.

What would you guess the odds would be of finding a direct flight from Newark, New Jersey, to the upper left corner of Arkansas in 2004? Pretty good, as it happens. When I experienced my first plane trip in the early 1960s, in a DC3 that was a good many years older than I was at the time, flights flew in and out of the Fayetteville airport some 25 miles to the south of Rogers. Then my home town's population numbered perhaps fewer than 5,000, and Bentonville, the county seat some nine miles to the west, was even smaller. On both sides of old Highway 71 between the two towns were mostly woods and open farm land. But four years into the new century, everything had changed. Prosperity and wealth on a scale we could not have dreamed of when I was a kid had come to my home town and to the entire region. Now Rogers and Bentonville had essentially grown together; indeed, the whole region— encompassing Fayetteville, home of the University of Arkansas; Springdale, headquarters for Tyson Foods, the world's second-largest marketer of processed chicken; and Lowell, where J.B. Hunt, America's biggest publically-traded trucking company has its offices— constitutes a major metropolitan area and an economic powerhouse.

A good part of the world's business is now conducted in what fifty years ago were sleepy backwater towns where the most exciting events took place at Friday night football games or on Saturdays when the Razorbacks were playing at home. The only business around then that had any national profile to speak of was Daisy Air Rifle, a company that moved to Rogers in the mid-1950s. I can remember how we used to wonder when the rest of the world was going finally to include our little town. When will we get our own McDonald's, our first Holiday Inn, our big Penney's store? Finally, when I was far away and not looking, we got them, and more.

The airport I flew into—Northwest Arkansas Regional—was built in 1998 not to fly out frozen chickens but to accommodate the thousands of business people who needed to get to Bentonville, for, as everyone who has ever been passed by one of their big semi-trailer trucks knows by now, Bentonville is the home of Wal-Mart, the world's largest retailer, America's largest grocer, and the main engine for the area's astounding growth. Sam Walton opened his first Wal-Mart in Rogers in 1962 and insisted thereafter on keeping his company's corporate headquarters in Bentonville. And today, doing business with Wal-Mart means coming to Bentonville; Wal-Mart does not come to you.

All this has resulted in huge amounts of money circulating and re-circulating through the region's commercial arteries, the evidence of which may be seen in burgeoning housing developments chock full of McMansions, up-scale shopping malls nearly as big as Disney World, professional-grade golf courses that have attracted LPGA tournaments, Mercedes and Range Rovers 'til they're in the way, and non-denominational churches the size of airplane hangars. I exaggerate only a bit.

And 2011, thanks to the riches of Sam's daughter Alice Walton, whose net worth surpasseth all understanding (estimated in 2010 at $22 billion), the Crystal Bridges Museum of American Art, an institution expected to take its place among the country's most important art collections, opened in a picturesque and woodsy valley in Bentonville. With an $800 million endowment from the Walton's family foundation and cash from Alice's bottomless purse to use, Crystal Bridges, in throwing its weight around in the art market and outbidding America's other museums, can boast a collection that will be a major tourist attraction and still another reason for people to settle in the region.

My dad, a carpenter for most of his ninety-nine years, lived long enough to witness and be delighted by these astounding developments, for he appreciated growth and progress and always wanted things to get bigger, always bigger. Dad had a ground-level grasp of economics: Larger and better meant jobs, paychecks, and food on the table. My brother Edgar —"Bud" to our family— also lit many candles at the altar of progress. After retiring in the late 1990s, he returned to his home town and on my occasional visits liked nothing better than to chauffeur me around for hours and brag about how new streets, suburban housing developments, shopping centers, schools and fire stations were pushing out into and filling up the old farmlands. And like millions of other loyalists he would bristle at any criticism or slight directed at Wal-Mart, the company that had put Arkansas on the world stage while transforming his old home town into a model of American prosperity.

By 2010 the population of Rogers, which numbered only a few thousand or so when Bud left town around 1950, was pushing 56,000 and growing fast. (City officials in the south take a special pride in posting signs that boast of census figures much as western towns like to cite their elevations above sea level.) But with growth and affluence have also come the inevitable problems. Streets and highways—especially those linking Rogers and Bentonville—are jammed to capacity and beyond, and the relatively new Interstate 540 between Rogers and Fayetteville, a work-in-progress that will eventually join Interstate 44 in Missouri and I-40 in central Arkansas, is a raceway crowded with motorists who behave as if they're driving on the old brick oval at the Indianapolis Speedway.

The towns in the area have felt the pressure of keeping up with the growth by building schools and making sure that safety forces and other municipal services are up to par. And, the people of northwest Arkansas have been introduced to another kind of change: ethnic and racial diversity. While the number of African-Americans in my home town has increased only slightly from the zero that lived there when I did, the influx of Spanish-speaking workers drawn to jobs in Tyson's plants has been huge. That most business and church signs are bilingual is a symbol of change that still puzzles and, in many cases, irritates some of the town's old-timers.

I was not exactly an eye-witness to or a participant in the colossal changes to once-sleepy, small-town Rogers. Following graduation from high school in 1960 I studied briefly at the University of Tulsa before getting a degree from the University of Arkansas. Before my parents moved to Oklahoma in 1964, I worked summer jobs in Rogers to pay for a part of my tuition and other college expenses, but I never saw myself returning there to live. Even as an undergraduate I knew I wanted to do "okay," expand my horizons, to become a college professor, and that ambition meant graduate study and, after that, going to wherever the jobs were. In the spring of 1964 a small miracle occurred: the University of Wisconsin Department of Art History accepted me into its program and offered me a generous scholarship. In a medieval manuscript illustration I've seen, the hand of God extends downward from a cloud and lifts a lost soul up into heaven. So it was with me, a wretched sinner saved!

So began also the process of putting Rogers and my past behind me, and it was with considerable reluctance that over the years I made the long, and expensive, return trips to Arkansas and then Oklahoma to visit family members still living there. After my mother's death in Tulsa in 1967, Dad moved back to Rogers, and was somewhat puzzled that I didn't move back, too. He had a difficult time with my long absences. Why would I ever want to live anywhere else but Arkansas, he wondered? Why didn't I get a job teaching at the University of Arkansas? And I would say that it doesn't work that way and explain that academic positions are as scarce as hen's teeth, that even if there were to be an opening at Fayetteville I'd have to compete for it, etc., etc. Still, he just couldn't figure it out. And, on top of it all, I'd met and married Carlyn, a *Yankee*, even though she was a wonderful example of the race, and I had *chosen* to live in the North, a decision still considered a betrayal on the part of any southern-born son. Unlike most of the graduates in my high school class, I had, as Arkansas-born novelist Charles Portis put it so nicely in his novel, *The Dog of the South*, "achieved escape velocity."

(A good example of how some Southerners still hate the north because, damn it to hell, they made General Lee surrender back in 1865 is the conversation I had with a relative some years ago, just in a shoot-the-bull sort of a way, that it was interesting that no one had ever ventured to open a ski slope near the town of Bella Vista, a resort community just a few miles north of Bentonville. There's not much snow in northwest Arkansas winters, but it does get cold and you can make all the snow you need, and the hills bordering the town would be perfect for skiing. My kinsman thought a second, then said, "Nobody'd come." I asked, "Why wouldn't they?" "Because skiin's a *Yankee* thing," he said, and he didn't mean that in the nicest way.)

Indeed, southerners are a proud lot who resist and resent people coming down from Up North and beginning any sentence with "Wouldn't it be better if you would...?"

Dad came to see us twice in Ohio before his death in 2000, but his heart was never in it. He was antsy to get back on that plane and go home. On his first visit I picked him up at the Cleveland airport for the 45-mile drive to Kent. Tired from his flight, he was uncharacteristically quiet as he looked out the window at the northeast Ohio landscape. Then, out of nowhere he offered up this unanswerable observation: "This is the goddamned sorriest looking country I've ever seen in my life!" In other words, it wasn't Arkansas.

But time passed, and as the decades have slipped by, my feelings about Rogers and the South in general have changed. It seems that the South is joining the rest of the country. For example, the deeply ingrained racism that pervaded Arkansas in my early years, when segregation was the order of the day and no black students were allowed to room in dormitories at the University of Arkansas or to play on any of its athletic teams, had begun the slow, as-yet-uncompleted process of fading away. And then, wonder of wonders, we actually had a man from Arkansas, Bill Clinton, a bad boy but a pretty good president, elected for two terms. Indeed, the state was getting its act together and gaining greatly in stature.

So by the time I made the trip to Rogers in February of 2004 I'd mellowed a bit and even was beginning to feel a bit sentimental about the "old days" back home. And of course, this trip was a dutiful one. Family is family. And, yes, Phyllis came through the surgery in fine shape.

As my plane on that February day entered its approach pattern, we flew over the original, downtown Rogers –*my* Rogers, not all that new stuff to the west and the south—at perhaps 3,000 feet, and I had a panoramic view from my window. The sun was setting and the raking light on this sparkling, clear winter day appeared to set off every detail of the town in sharp relief. There was the Harris Hotel, perhaps Rogers's most distinguished edifice; the steeple of the venerable Methodist Church; the old city hall and fire station; the Frisco rail tracks, the two-story brick shops and office buildings lining Walnut Street. And I could see Lake Atalanta and the hills as they fell away to the east. Beaver Lake, the reservoir that had drowned my beloved White River in the early 1960s, stretched out on its north-south axis just beyond the outskirts of downtown, so close, though in my boyhood it had been a long and exhausting bike ride away. Although the view couldn't have lasted more than a few seconds, I had nevertheless in that brief time a comprehensive glimpse of the town in which I had spent my early years. Rogers was spread out below me like one of those maps that form the end papers in a child's book, like in *Treasure Island*. In my mind's eye, I could see the dotted lines for trails I'd explored and the X's marking the locations of favorite haunts and important places. And the town seemed so *small*, so compact, so just the right size for a boy to grow up in.

Everyone has had that experience of one or another of the senses—taste or smell— setting off an instantaneous and mysterious flight to the past, the experience lasting only a second or so, but very real, and one that leaves you such a delicious feeling that you regret it can't last longer, or can't be summoned at will. That moment on the plane as we passed over dear old Rogers was one such moment for me. It kindled an unbidden but powerful sense of affection for the old place. It was as if I could see the Rogers of 2004, the so-called "historic district," and at the same time the Rogers that was, with the old high school on Walnut and the First Presbyterian Church just a couple of blocks to the east, the old cafes and the ice cream parlor and other gathering spots, the marquee on the Victory Theater, when it was the center of our social life—the sorts of landmarks that live only in grainy old black-and-white photographs at the town's historical museum.

My Rogers, like all towns and cities, resembles a *palimpsest*, a fancy, unfamiliar word that embodies a useful concept: Like a child's slate tablet on which one can write, erase, and write some more *ad infinitum,* the ground that a town stands on may be marked on and may be changed indefinitely by each generation, by each lot's owner. People do what they have to do in each generation's brief window onto the world. Buildings rise and are torn down or burned and then replaced; towns evolve, or, in drastic cases are abandoned and then disappear.

I prefer the Rogers of 1955 to today's version. My late sister Patsy told me once that as one gets older change becomes increasingly harder to accept; change might even rise to the level of aggravation, she'd said. So it had become for me.

Recently I spoke with Kenneth Petway, a long-time Rogers resident who had been a pharmacist at and then the owner of the Rexall Corner Drugstore where I worked when I was a teenager. He had read an early draft of the chapter in which I lamented the modernization of his store in the early 1960s, a process that spelled the doom of the beautiful, old-fashioned, dark-wood paneling and beveled glass cabinets of the old interior. "I had to do that to sell merchandise," Kenneth said. And with that dash of cold water truth Kenneth brought home to me how reality trumps sentiment every time. Of course, a town must change, but we can still regret it.

So it was perhaps on that February, 2004 trip "home" that my desire to write a book about growing up in Rogers was born, or perhaps more honestly, finalized, since I had been thinking about such a project for a long time.

This is not a history of Rogers, nor is it a work of non-fiction that is the product of a lot of research (though I did from time to time call on everyone's new pal, Wikipedia, the online resource that will henceforth make it unnecessary for undergraduates to enter the campus library). I did use authoritative sources to check dates and to flesh out my references to music, movies, and key historical events. But for the most part I have relied on my memory, and if I've made mistakes along the way I ask the reader's forgiveness.

It is not even strictly speaking an autobiography or that exalted literary critter, the memoir. In the introduction to his short and selective biography of Franklin D. Roosevelt (*That Man*), Robert H. Jackson, a U.S. attorney general and associate justice of the Supreme Court, said with a chilling tone of finality that only people who have done significant things in their lives or were witnesses to important moments in history and have valuable observations about those experiences to contribute to the historical record should take up pen or word processor to write a memoir. Those guidelines, then, would look with favor on a memoir by Lee Harvey Oswald but keep me on the outside looking in.

Well, I'm just going to forget that I read that. Or more precisely, I'm going to dodge Jackson's admonition and call this book a series of "remembrances," a nifty distinction contributed by my friend and Rogers citizen David Stiegler. What I present here is a series of remembrances grouped together in related but intentionally independent essays, arranged more or less chronologically, that muse on my family and our life in Rogers.

I have made a fuss about the old town's landmarks, past and present, but what I really wish to return to in these pages is the life I lived there up to age 18, the good times enjoyed with the many friends still dear to me even though I haven't seen some of them for more than fifty years. And I want to pay homage to the men and women of Rogers who helped me to grow up.

One of those men was one of Rogers's most colorful characters, the cattlemen and all-around entrepreneur, Rex Spivey, for whom my brother Bill and I worked in the early 1960s. After a stint in the oil fields of the Middle East, Spivey settled east of Rogers, where he built a huge house and kept a small herd of steers. Spivey took an interest in me and often asked me about how I was doing in my studies at the University of Arkansas. One of his sternly offered bits of advice has never left me and has been at least in part co-opted as the title for this book: "Study hard and make something of yourself," he told me. "This town is not well served when a local kid does only O.K."

The reader will learn soon enough that during the years I was growing up in Rogers, I did "only O.K." in the workplace, in school, in music, and on a few football fields and basketball courts. Like the kids of Garrison Keillor's "Lake Wobegon" I was only "above average." But I have never stopped trying to "make something" of myself. And, notwithstanding the lackluster record of my teenage years, that ambition began in Rogers, where it was nurtured and encouraged by people whom I wish to pay tribute to in this account.

Writing a book about one's life and times is an ego trip to a greater or lesser extent, and it was with some irony in mind that I chose to publish it with a vanity press, an act that was strictly *verboten* in the academic world I inhabited for thirty years. But now, having arrived at my three score years and ten, I insist here on being free to do what I want. You will perhaps excuse the vanity of this effort when I tell you that I fully recognize how self-indulgent I have been in its creation.

For, as most women, especially wives, know so well, inside most men, regardless of their age, there is a small boy standing out at the end of a diving board yelling, "Mommy, Mommy! Look at me!"

And with this caveat: Memory plays tricks, does it not? Facts are facts, to be sure, but then this really isn't a book about facts, but one about recollections, feelings, and random, often vaguely expressed thoughts about the past and the characters who dwell there. As Joyce Carol Oates notes in her novel *Marya: A Life* (1986), "A little truth goes a long way." So it may have to be with this book.

Although I depended largely on my own memory as the source for the chapters that follow, I have come to believe that it usually requires five or more seventy-year-old minds to equal the mental faculties of one healthy and fully intact adult brain, so the recollections of friends and relatives in my "researches" for this book were a great help. I'm especially grateful to my brother Bill and my sister Phyllis for reading early drafts of this book and assisting their little brother by supplying anecdotes and details he had long forgotten— or in a few interesting cases, never knew. My classmate from grade school through college, David Stiegler, whose command of names and knowledge of Rogers history is truly amazing, filled in many blanks for me, and he also provided room and board on my trips back to Rogers.

The unofficial town historian Gary Townzen was generous with tips, and James F. Hale's picture books on the history of my home town proved to be invaluable. Doris Moser and her son David loaned me pictures taken in the mid-fifties when Robert Moser was the pastor of the Presbyterian Church and they helped me identify my Sunday school classmates in those photographs. Kenneth Petway contributed his recollections of my days at Rexall, and Don Garrison supplied interesting memories from our time as reporters at the old *Rogers Daily News*. I'm also grateful to John Burroughs of the Rogers Historical Museum for locating photographs and making them available to me. Joan Bender, a friend and classmate at Rogers High School and a volunteer at the museum, was also a great help with photographs as well as the ongoing (to me) mysteries of the computer. (Incidentally, Joan and I were born on the same day, March 10, 1942.) LaVonne Clark, the widow of "Cactus" Clark, and her daughter Sharon loaned me wonderful photographs of Cactus and his brother, "Buddy," dating from the early years of the Lakeside Café. Chris Hackler and his brother Tim provided interesting material about their dad Joe Bill Hackler, and a long interview with Kathleen Huber Garvin was especially informative. I also touched base with Mrs. Betty Sutton, our choir director at the Presbyterian church and the accompanist and arranger of songs for our all-guy quartet, "The Four Lettermen," so that we could reminisce together. Thanks, too, to Judy Gundlach, for lending me the photo of her late husband, Maxie, who was probably the best musician to ever call Rogers home. My friends Mike and Diane Sperko were also a big help in getting illustrations ready for publication. I am especially grateful to have worked with Dave Myers, who created the cover design and with Joanna Hildebrand Craig who performed superb work as the copyeditor.

The advice and encouragement of my long-time colleagues, John Hubbell, director emeritus of the Kent State University Press, and Emeritus Professor of English Bill Hildebrand, both fellow members of the Old Boys Book Club, did much to keep me writing during the three years I worked on it.

And, my sincere gratitude to Pat Nash and Sally Yankovich, friends from our days together in the Honors College at Kent State University, who often came to my rescue as I fought the never ending battle with word processing in the production of this manuscript.

Finally, thanks to my dear wife Carlyn for her love and encouragement during the years I was at work on this book.

1

———⬗———

MY FAMILY'S OZARK ORIGINS

EVERYONE HAS TO START SOMEWHERE, and my starting point was Fort Smith, Arkansas, where I was born on March 10, 1942. I have a birth certificate to prove it, and this document is duly signed, dated, and authenticated by an odd-looking blotch, a mark looking something like a bug splatter on a windshield, that is my footprint. I was a *big* baby (8 lbs. 11 oz.) with a big head (it's still big: I take a 7 7/8 hat size). My brother Bill remembers me, not unaffectionately, as "just a *big* 'ol baby."

I was the first in our family born in a hospital, my siblings who preceded me having all been home deliveries. Founded as a military post in 1817, Fort Smith is located on the Arkansas state line and was then and remains today no great shakes as a big town/small city, but it does have a colorful history and I've always believed that a place with historical significance has a certain *shine* to it. In the nineteenth century, the Indian Territory—later Oklahoma—lay just across the Arkansas River from Fort Smith and evildoers unlucky enough to be captured there had to stand before Judge Isaac Parker, the famous "Hanging Judge" who during his twenty-plus years on the bench sent 79 people to the gallows. From Fort Smith also, Mattie Ross and Rooster Cogburn set out in pursuit of Ned Chaney in the classic western novel, *True Grit,* by Arkansas-born and educated Charles Portis, who still lives in Little Rock. So, as birthplaces go, a baby could do worse than to be born in Fort Smith, Arkansas.

Thirty miles north of Fort Smith is Mountainburg, the Basshams' home town, a tiny, one stop-light, blink-and-you-miss-it hamlet set in the hills and hollows of the Boston Mountains about 40 miles south of Fayetteville, home of the state university. Since we didn't own a car in those days, getting to and from the "big city" must have posed some interesting problems. But when you don't have, as Momma often said, "you make do."

I was the fifth child and third son of Benjamin Edgar Archibald Bassham (Dad's mother loved names and was generous with them) and Sarah Elizabeth Young. Six years separate me from the next oldest in the birth order, so I must have been a bit of a surprise. And a war baby to boot, conceived before Pearl Harbor and born in what was perhaps the country's darkest period, just after entering the war.

We were a big family by today's norms, but a small one compared to those of Dad's and Momma's. My oldest brother, Bill, or William Howard (named after our maternal grandfather) was born in 1929. Edgar Carlson, known all his life to us as "Bud," came the next year, and was followed by Patricia Ann ("Patsy") in 1933, and Phyllis Kay in 1936. The years in which this family was started straddle the end of the Roaring Twenties, years of relative (if delusional) prosperity for many Americans, followed in short order by the Crash of 1929 and the years of misery known as the Great Depression, arguably the worst period in American history, worse even than the war years that followed them. Just when everything seemed to be going great guns in the 1920s and the American economy could do no wrong, the bottom fell out of everything. In 1932 the unemployment rate was 25 percent; in a two-year period 5,000 banks failed. The United States itself seemed to be on the verge of failure. And on top of the grinding economic hardships came the terrible heat waves, droughts, and agricultural disasters of the 1930s, a period aptly labeled the Dust Bowl Years, when bad farming techniques combined with awful weather to wreck the lives of thousands in the American South and Middle West. My family stayed put to wait out the crisis but many farm people didn't, pulling up stakes and heading west in search of work.

But hard as life could be then, almost everyone within shouting distance of Mountainburg and across the country was in the same boat, and our parents' extended families must have been a welcome source of support.

There's a picture of us kids that has survived showing all of us arrayed on a long, white Adirondack-style garden bench with me, the little unanticipated bundle, front and center. (Fig. 1) They all doted on me, the newcomer, and in many ways have continued to do so in all the years since. I was both a plaything for them, and, because Momma was probably literally worn out by babies by this time, a responsibility as well. My sisters, bless their souls, did much to help raise me.

Fig. 1. Patsy, Bill, anonymous mutt, Me, Bud, and Phyllis. c. 1943.

My dad was born in 1901 in Salem in north central Arkansas just below the Missouri state line. Throughout his life he retained a sentimental attachment to the Salem area and liked visiting there to see how time and age had treated the town and his boyhood acquaintances. His family had settled in the Mountainburg area in the second decade of the century. He told me once that his family arrived in Mountainburg in a wagon and I believe it. You could probably have counted the automobiles in Arkansas in those days on your fingers.

The name Bassham may seem an unusual one but Basshams are not rare, either in the United States or in England, where the name may have originated; it very probably derives from the English town of Barsham in Norfolk. There were about a dozen Basshams listed in the London phone book when I studied there in 1967-68, and there are hundreds across America today. There's even another Ben Bassham ("Bamboo Ben," a popular maker of swimming pool cabanas) in the parallel universe of San Diego, California. In addition to Basshams there are Bashams, for in our own family tree the second letter "S" seems to come and go for no apparent reason. Pronunciations of the name are of even more bewildering variety. Dad pronounced it "BASS-HAM," as in the fish and the joint of pork, with equal emphasis on both syllables. I have preferred "BASH-em" and find that people I've met for the first time, store clerks and salespeople, for example, say it that way, too. A professor of mine at Wisconsin persisted in calling me "BASS-em," which, paired with Ben, made me sound like a foreign student from the Middle East. When, in 1969, another university called in search of an instructor in their Department of Art History, Dr. James Watrous said, "Well, we've got this Ben BASS-em," and the guy on the other end of the line said, "Actually, we were looking for an American to fill the position." But that may not be as silly as it sounds since another theory has it that the name comes from the Arabic "Bassam," meaning "the one who smiles."

Basshams, whether English, Arabic, or of the one or two S types, came to the 'States as early as 1806 and, along with the thousands of other poor Scots-Irish immigrants moved westward deep into the South, across Virginia (where an ancestor served as a lieutenant in Lee's army) and into Tennessee, Mississippi, Arkansas, and Texas. (Not long ago, the discussion in my men's book club turned to the concept of the Jews as a "people." How is it, I asked rhetorically, that the Jews can call themselves a "people" and we Scots-Irish cannot? Aren't we a "people," too? Yes, a friend snarked, "You're called 'white trash'." Ouch!)

Dad's father was John Frederick Howard Bassham, his mother's name was Hettie Marie (Robertson). I don't know much about Grandpa Bassham, and I sorely regret now that I never asked to be told about him. Nor do I recall having heard Dad volunteer any information about him. My sister Phyllis, who took care of Dad during his declining years, got the distinct impression that there was no love lost between him and his old man. Perhaps Dad harbored some deep grudge that arose from his father's early demise around 1918, a victim, probably, of the world-wide influenza epidemic, a sudden death no doubt and one that left Dad, the oldest of the boys, as his family's chief bread-winner. In Salem John Frederick Bassham had been a lawman, perhaps a sheriff, but after the move to Mountainburg he made his way as a "trader," who traded "pocket to pocket." My brother Bill also thinks Dad's father had a weakness for gambling, and if so, the picture that emerges is one of a somewhat shady character. In the only photograph I've seen of him, he's posed with a baseball team he is said to have sponsored, the team in the rather comical, fussy uniforms of the period.

And as for those ancestors who preceded Grandpa Bassham, or my mother's distant forbears for that matter, I haven't the foggiest notion. Although I've seen genealogical charts and a family tree researched diligently by my brother Bud, those names mean nothing to me and I have no interest in learning more about them. Biologist Richard Dawkins, author of *The Selfish Gene*, has the novel, if cold, notion that people are, at base, little more than disposable carriers and potential transmitters of genetic information, and, if successful in carrying out the procreative function, achieve the only form of immortality available to us. Given this hard-eyed view of humanity's purpose, I thank my great-great-great-grandparents for doing their part.

Dad's family was huge. Grandma Hettie gave birth to a baby almost every year of her marriage until her husband's death. First was Ruth, then Dad, followed by Fred, Dave, Helen, Dick, Don, and Harry. (Fig. 2) Another daughter, Carmen, died in infancy. (Why "Carmen? Such an exotic name among all these American standard-issue types.)

Fig. 2. Dad's family at a Mountainburg Reunion, c. 1962
(Standing, left to right) Dad, Fred, Dave, Dick, Harry, Don
(seated) Dave's wife Jessie, Grandma Hettie, Ruth.

The Bassham family lived in a big (though probably not big enough for this brood), raw-looking house on the edge of a steep hillside at the end of a very rough gravel and dirt road, a road like probably 98 per cent of the roads in the state back then. The house had a tin roof, a kitchen equipped with a wood stove, and an outhouse out back. And hot! In the summers there's no house hotter than one with a tin roof; but also no more pleasant sound than the rain falling on that tin. (Mark Twain had an upstairs room of his Hartford mansion fitted out with a tin roof to remind him of his Missouri boyhood.) We still have a photograph of this homestead and I have a few spooky memories from my only visit there one summer when I was around 12 or 13. The place seemed *so* far back in the woods and the way there bore a greater resemblance to a dry, rocky creek bed than a road. I was paying a visit to Grandma Hettie along with one of my California uncles—Dick or Don, I forget which— and his family, that included a teenage daughter who whined the whole trip, no doubt wishing she was back on the beach in La Jolla.

One evening on this same trip we visited other relatives in the area, a very "country" older couple connected somehow to my uncle. They invited us to stay for supper, and I suppose no one could come up with a reason to decline. I recall vividly we were served the best they could offer— pork sausage patties and Kool-Aid— in their backwoods house that had no electricity or screens on the open windows. As we ate our supper by the light of a kerosene lantern, a moth about the size of a large frying pan, attracted by the lantern's flame, flapped in to join us, and my cousin from the West Coast went into hysterics. "Oh, Gawd," she balled, "why do bugs have to be so UG-G-G-GLY!"

I spent an uneasy night in Grandma Hettie's old house. I must say that snakes and spiders were a bit on my mind. The next morning, other kinfolks arrived, and Grandma conjured up a huge breakfast on that ancient wood stove and laid it out on a picnic table outside under the trees. I can still see that feast of made-from-scratch biscuits, ham, bacon, gravy, and an enormous platter of fried eggs. We were joined by Grandma's second husband, a plump, elderly man turned out in a straw hat and his best suit of bib overalls.

Another memory of Grandma Hettie is when in the late 1950s she arrived in Rogers one cold winter day with Uncle Harry and his wife, Lois, to pay us a visit on their way to north central Arkansas, where the family, it seemed, just *might* still hold title to land that contained possibly rich coal deposits. Everyone was uncommonly serious and close-mouthed about this, as you might imagine would be the case among people who throughout their lives had had little "extry", but who might, by the grace of God, be looking at a possible windfall. But these prospects led to nothing.

And I also remember her funeral in 1962, which occasioned the gathering in Mountainburg of the entire clan, West Coast contingent and all. It was an agonizing ordeal for me then, because even as a young man—I was in college at Fayetteville at the time—these affairs were both spooky and embarrassing for me. The weeping and wailing made for a dramatic spectacle. At one point one of my uncles was so overcome that he embraced his mother's body and practically lifted it to a sitting position in the coffin. James Harry, my cousin who, like me, boasted a Southern "double name" (as in Ben Lloyd, Jim Bob, Joe Bill, etc.) was there with his wife, who sang "Beyond the Sunset," a great old gospel number. For years afterward I avoided funerals when I could, unable to bring myself to view the deceased lying in state.

Of all these aunts and uncles on Dad's side of the family I really got to know only Fred and Harry. I have no memories at all of his sisters, and Dick and Don rolled the dice after World War II and headed out to San Diego to the Promised Land, where they landed "steady work"— Dad's words for the American Dream— as skilled workers in auto body shops, where they stayed, prospered, and thereafter ceased to figure in my life. Dad, Fred, and Dave became carpenters, and Harry, the "baby" took over a small grocery/ general store in Mountainburg, made a good living, and became a pillar of that small community.

Dad, Fred, Dave, and Harry were all good-looking, personable men, and could even exhibit on occasion that rare quality, charm. Dad, in fact, would no doubt have made a successful salesman. Dad always said he had to go to work full-time to help his family when his own dad died of the flu; as the eldest son, he must have felt the weight of that responsibility. And he retained that "first-in-the-birth-order" mentality throughout his long life; he was seemingly always getting people "lined out," as he put it.

While I don't know much about my father's family and its origins, when it comes to my mother's people, I'm afraid I know even less. Momma was born in 1909 and grew up in a large family in Mountainburg. Her mother was born Sarah Emeline Blevins; her father's name was William Howard Young. I knew my maternal grandparents only a little, and only after they were moved to Rogers to live out their days in the Wilmoth Convalescent Home on the east side of town. Family members must have shared the cost of the Youngs' room and board expenses. Bill tells me that Grandma Young drew an old-age "pension" from the state of Arkansas in the grand sum of $2 a month, while her husband, because he was blind, received twice that amount, $4.

Momma would take me to visit my grandparents from time to time, mostly on Sundays. How I dreaded those trips to that awful place. "Convalescent" was of course the euphemism that everyone agreed on then, for there was not much in the way of convalescing that went on there; everyone who entered there did so on a one-way ticket. (We call such places "nursing homes" today and even that is only a marginal improvement. But both were advances over the nineteenth-century's insistence on calling them "old peoples' homes.") The place was dark, smelly, and airless as most such establishments tend to be. To soften the blow for young people the "home" provided huge peppermint sticks for the old people to treat us with.

Grandma and Grandpa Young were scary people to me. Grandpa was almost completely blind and had been sightless since a boyhood bout with measles, during which illness his eyes were treated with a solution of blue vitriol (copper sulfate), then a home remedy for maladies of all sorts, which left his eyes badly burned. But not all the Bassham brood found Grandpa Young as scary as I did. His children and grandchildren were devoted to him. My sister Phyllis fondly recalls taking the old man by the hand and guiding him down the hill to Mountainburg, where he could sit on a store's front porch and chew the fat with some of the town's other old-timers.

But think of it. A young man marries and sires nine children without the sense of sight. Then try to imagine the marriage and life my grandmother experienced. How could the family have possibly put food on their table? The answer seems to be that Grandma Young and her kids fended for themselves, keeping a garden, raising corn, milking the cow, gathering eggs, and killing a chicken from time to time, all the while the lot of them sharing the same outhouse and sleeping each night under the tin roof of a small farmhouse.

Sadly, it also appears that Grandma Young's marriage had been an arranged one. Some clue of what that life might have been like for her is suggested in an anecdote passed down by one of the Young daughters. My mother, still in her mid-teens, longed to join her sister Ethel, my uncle Fred, and my dad on an outing of some kind. "She's in love," another sister observed. "Love!"

Grandma Young said bitterly. "What do we know about love? My daddy gave me to Bill Young when I was fifteen years old!"

But gentleness and an enduring stoicism, not bitterness, were the hallmarks of Grandma Young's character. Not surprisingly, Momma and her sisters (and my two sisters) worshipped her like a saint, and my vague recollections of her also support a belief that she must have been a sweet and kind lady. Lord knows she had had her share of suffering in her days.

Our mother had two brothers, Clarence and Harlan, and a sister, Agnes, who died early in their lives. Harlan succumbed to diphtheria in childhood and Clarence was killed in a car crash while driving drunk over the mountains north towards Fayetteville sometime during the late 1930s. Most tragic of all, Agnes, a tall, be-speckled beauty, died following a botched abortion at about age twenty-four. And all this happened in the so-called "good old days."

But six siblings, all girls, survived to maturity, indeed, to old age (with the exception of my mother, who passed away at age 58), and they had their own adventures, some of which are still vivid in my memory. They were a veritable garden of sisters, beginning with Florence, then Lilly, followed by Rose, Esther, Ethel, and Sarah, my mother. (Fig. 3)

Fig. 3. The Young family, c. 1925. Standing, left to right: Florence, Clarence, Ethel, Rose, Sarah, Esther. Seated: Grandma Young, Lilly, Grandpa Young,

The sisters grew up close but parted as they married and moved away to parts of the "four-state area"—Arkansas, Oklahoma, Kansas, and Missouri—which was as far as I, as a boy, could imagine the world extending. (It wasn't until I was in college I ventured out into no man's land by traveling to Madison, Wisconsin, with a college roommate for Christmas.)

I imagine that our mom and dad probably first laid eyes on one another in the late teens. Somehow the Bassham and Young families discovered each other, and initially Dad began squiring around Sarah's sister Ethel. He said once that he remembered seeing our mother, eight years his junior, looking at him through the Young family fence.

In the early 1920s Dad and his brother Fred went out West to find work on the railroads, not, undoubtedly, as brakemen or engineers but probably as laborers on construction gangs. (In 1993 when I stopped by to see him in Rogers on the way home from my first big trip out west I told him that I'd had a beer in the famous bar of the Brown Palace Hotel in Denver. He quickly responded, "Oh, yeah, right there on 17th Street!" And this after a passing of some seventy years!)

It was no doubt on one of his returns to Arkansas that he saw our mother again, now all grown up. Ethel was now history, at least as the object of his romantic intentions (Ethel would marry Fred, so my mother's sister was also her sister-in-law). He and Momma got married in 1928. (Fig. 4)

The newlyweds moved to Sand Springs, Oklahoma, a town adjacent to Tulsa, and there, in 1929, Bill and, one year later, Bud were born. When the family returned to Mountainburg in 1931 Dad bought a horse and became a one-horse farmer as well as a carpenter, now his chosen (or perhaps his default) profession. The next year Franklin D. Roosevelt challenged Herbert Hoover for the presidency, the economy was in chaos, and life must have looked pretty bleak for a young couple with two little boys. On the upside, if it can be called that, our mother and father had never had much, so they did not have too much to lose. By farming Dad could at least try to feed his family. And he looked for work constantly. He once told me a crude joke that seems to capture the dispiriting character of those early years of the decade. A young man applies for a job and the foreman tells him, "I'd never hire you. You have bad breath." And the desperate applicant replies, "You'd have bad breath, too, if you had to kiss every ass in the county to get a job!"

Fig. 4. Ben and Sarah Bassham in Sand Springs, Oklahoma, c. 1928.

So it must have been. From these times Dad developed the central theme in his life's philosophy: The most important thing in life is a job and not just a job but "steady work" (Dad always pronounced it "study work"). He was sincerely thankful for (and recalled fondly) the Civilian Conservation Corps. the New Deal government program that put millions of young men to work building structures in parks, planting trees, fighting forest fires, and, later, constructing military barracks. The men lived in camps and received room (in barracks or in tents) and board and were paid about $30 a month (most of which had to be sent home to the worker's family). According to the program's official history, most of the boys and men gained weight on Uncle Sam's three-meals-a-day bounty. The CCC provided useful work but also valuable experience. Dad worked as a carpenter and in the early 1940s became the boss of large work gangs engaged in the construction of Camp Crowder, near Neosho, Missouri, and Fort Chaffee in Fort Smith, Arkansas. (Fig. 5) It was there he put to use his mastery of "lining out" workers, that is, assigning all the responsibilities for completing large construction projects.

Fig. 5. Dad in his Civilian Conservation Corps days, c. 1938.

Dad's work on CCC projects and the programs of our activist government in Washington during the Great Depression in general deepened his devotion to FDR and set the whole family on the path to a lifelong dedication to the

Democratic Party. Surprisingly radical in his political leanings from his early years (in 1924 he cast his first vote in a presidential election for "Fighting Bob" LaFollette), Dad viewed Republicanism as the party of the smug and comfortably well-off, and, in league with most of Arkansas' working people, did his part to keep the GOP from gaining power in the state. Allegiance to the Democrats would be such an unquestioned article of faith in my family that I felt not the least bit odd when I enthusiastically backed Adlai Stevenson in both his campaigns for the White House in the fifties, despite the obvious fact that his blueblood style and his egghead image stood in such spectacular contrast to our humble working-class way of life. That Arkansas ultimately moved into the Republican camp during the Reagan years still strikes me as a political development as odd and unexpected as the fall of the Soviet Union.

An excellent work ethic and an admirable sense of responsibility to his family were among my Dad's best attributes, and he carried the burdens of these pressures pretty well. Indeed, he appeared actually to like working hard and seeing a project done well. His bosses got good value out of him for the piddling sums they paid. Not that he was an especially good carpenter—his son Bill and his grandson Howard far surpassed him in the excellence of their cabinetry and finish work. (I think Dad must have realized that exacting carpenter work was not one of his strong suits. Upon finishing something he would often announce, "Good enough for a town this size." I must have heard that a thousand times.) But Dad knew how to lay out a plan and see it through from blueprints, framing, roofing to the final details; he could see the big picture. And, he knew how to handle men on the job. I learned from him, through a process of osmosis if nothing else, the importance of doing a job well and an intolerance for leaving a project unfinished.

It also helped that he had few bad habits, unless the ability to use profanity with abandon is counted as a bad habit. On Dad's lips cussing achieved a level of mastery that can only be described as performance art. When angry, which was often, he could blister the air with words that I am loath to lay down on these pages. Momma used to say that when my Dad said "shit" you could just smell it. And in my teens, when I was momentarily besotted with Presbyterianism, his foul and imaginative taking of the Lord's name in vain filled me with forebodings (or perhaps the secret wish) that the mouth of Hell would open up and suck him into its depths.

Dad did not drink, neither did he smoke. Both indulgences marked a person as either rich—because only the wealthy could spend money on booze without dipping into the funds for food and rent— or "no damned good" or both. Notwithstanding Uncle Clarence's untimely end which had been hastened by alcohol, beer, wine, or the hard stuff did not figure in my family's life back then. It was an expensive and debilitating luxury that common folks frowned on.

Actually, a drink now and then might have helped. Dad was a tightly wrapped package of nerves that would regularly come undone in violent and frightening outbursts of temper directed at one or more of us kids, or in red-faced, teeth-clenching displays of fury directed at our mother. As the oldest and thus the son loaded with the most responsibility, Bill regularly caught it. And my turn came soon enough as I also received my share of Dad's beltings across my butt and his scary tongue-lashings; those awful moments are still branded onto my memories of him.

The tensions of job and family life—compacted as we were in tiny houses where we shared one bathroom (or outhouse) took its toll on his body. He suffered from chronic heartburn and indigestion, whether from diet or nerves I can't say. He adored fatty foods and ate a greasy diet to his final age of 99. Even though he chewed Tums like candy, constantly, he persisted in returning to the table in the evenings for another dose of bacon drippings on his green beans.

Dad did not see military duty during the war; he was too old and was already doing valuable war work at home. But his brother Harry did serve. Married to my Aunt Lois, the cute, petite daughter of Mountainburg's sheriff, and already a father by the war's outbreak, Harry bought some land and, according to family lore, sought to make himself useful in Uncle Sam's eyes as a farmer rather than a soldier. But he was drafted anyway and spent much of the war stuck on some tiny atoll in the Pacific. Old photographs prove, however, that he looked great in Army khaki, and he was rightly proud of his service. Some years later his son, James Harry, did the family proud again by piloting B-52s and rising to the rank of major general in the Air Force Reserves.

Mountainburg was home for the my first three years of life, but, much as I'd like to say that I remember learning to walk and talk and listening to FDR's fireside chats on the radio and discussing the latest news from the Russian front and being shocked when we dropped atomic bombs on Hiroshima and Nagasaki, I must admit that I have almost no memories of those times whatsoever, and what memories I have are elusive and unreliable. A British painter once remarked that one's past life is "little better than a remembered dream." I don't subscribe to that rather gloomy take on our personal histories; our memories are important, indeed indispensable in shaping our sense of self. But memories are malleable things, subject to our own editorial spin and easily melded with the shared recollections of those close to us. For a long time I thought my earliest memory was this: We are living in Mountainburg. It is winter because snow is falling, the flakes illuminated by the light of a powerful outdoor floodlight so that they look like a meteor shower falling in parallel, diagonal lines. I see the snow then I see Dad walking away to a barn or some other outbuilding. It's not much, and probably a false blip on my memory radar; and we wouldn't have had a powerful floodlight in any case.

If my infant brain was not yet sufficiently developed to store impressions for posterity, the few baby pictures of me that have survived give evidence that in all other ways I was a thriving toddler: my cheeks, arms, legs, and torso filled to capacity with fat until I began to resemble a pink putto in a Baroque ceiling painting. And with my cue ball head I possessed a striking resemblance to a very young Winston Churchill. I am told that I was a particularly cute and adorable baby, and, while that may seem like faint praise, I'll take it, because all babies are not cute and adorable.

And with that meager recital of the Mountainburg years, we leave the place because the Basshams left the place. In August of 1945, with the wars in Europe and the Pacific over and a new day, the future, dawning, the Bassham family packed up all its belongings, the whole "kitty kaboodle," as Aunt Ethel might have termed it, and moved about seventy miles north to Rogers.

2

SMALL-TOWN U.S.A.—ARKANSAS STYLE

WHEN I WAS GROWING UP in the 1950s, the motto embossed on our license plates boasted that Arkansas was the "Land of Opportunity." Today, fifty-plus years later, plates call Arkansas the "Natural State," the projected identity having segued from those postwar, up-by-our-bootstraps years to something more eco-conscious and trendy but still unabashedly positive. I will not argue with the Natural State assertion: It is a lovely place in many ways, as retirees from the North have discovered after moving there. But back then some of us teenagers—already dreaming of launching ourselves out into the world and becoming indispensable to its happiness and betterment—got much snide merriment out of that "opportunity" slogan. We looked around us at those drab and old-fashioned storefronts, the miles of unpaved roads, worn-out school buildings, and underpaid teachers and wondered, "Opportunity for whom?" Undoubtedly, things later on worked out handsomely for Sam Walton, the Tyson's chicken empire, and Bill and Hillary Clinton, but as we came of age in the years immediately following World War II, some of us projected lives lived elsewhere, and preferably far from our Arkansas roots.

Dad saw it differently in 1945. For him there were no more beautiful words than *opportunity* and *progress*. Most of all, with six mouths plus his own to feed, he loved the word *job*— both as employment and the work itself. But there were precious few utterances of these words in Mountainburg in 1945. Dad's work during the war had required long commutes and weeks away from home. (Phyllis remembers a bus trip Momma, she, and I took to see Dad when he was busy building barracks in Missouri.) So Dad and his brother Fred probably talked seriously before the war's end about the need to go where they could make a living. Why they settled on Rogers I don't know; I wish now I'd had a long talk with Dad about that. But Rogers was agreed on, and Uncle Fred and Aunt Ethel moved there first, joined there by my brother Bill, who sought summertime work in Rogers before the rest of the family made the move in August of 1945.

Rogers, much bigger than tiny Mountainburg, promised a wealth of opportunities. The end of World War II brought a sense of hope that, at the very least, normal life would resume. The optimistic dared to think that things might be even better than they'd been in the prewar years. Hundreds of thousands of American servicemen would now be demobilized and return to civilian life, get married, and buy a home. Construction would presumably enter a boom period. The U.S. economy rebounded more quickly than those of our wartime allies. In the late 1940s, Detroit once again began turning out automobiles instead of tanks and planes, and building materials were again going to construct houses, not barracks. (But the switchover from national life dedicated to military purposes to civilian consumption was spotty, inconsistent, and not immediate. Elmer Novotny, the director of the School of Art at Kent State when I arrived there in 1970, told me that he built his house and studio in part with lumber salvaged from ammunition crates he obtained somehow from the nearby Ravenna Arsenal.)

At the beginning of our new lives in Rogers, Dad and his brother Fred may have had an understanding that they would be a kind of team. They placed an ad in the *Rogers Daily News* notifying the town that they were skilled carpenters and were prepared to make their services available to the public. If they started out as a brother act, however, the partnership didn't last. Dad, the oldest, was probably too bossy for Uncle Fred, who always seemed to have a more laid-back approach to work. Fred, a fairly good cabinet maker, would probably rather have been fishing than working. Dad put it more uncharitably: Fred, in his opinion, "didn't have no ambition."

Our move to the big city, which is how we thought of it, was not unanimously positive in the Bassham household. Phyllis, only eight at the time, resisted it vociferously and went along kicking and screaming. It was probably from this period that her older brothers, in a rare display of wit, christened her "Teargas" for her frequent crying spells. Recently Phyllis told me that after arriving in Rogers and settling into a rented house on B Street on the east (and "wrong") side of the tracks in a rundown neighborhood that

Uncle Fred dubbed "Snuff Hollow," a kind of straw vote was taken to see who wanted to return to Mountainburg. More tears surely followed, for Phyllis voted in the minority.

But who could return to Mountainburg after they'd seen Rogers? Situated on a plateau from which the land fell away in rolling hills to the four cardinal points of the compass, the town must have seemed enormous to us kids. With its neat grid of streets—numbered running north-south and named pleasantly after trees for the intersecting east-west thoroughfares—Rogers was small-town America right out of MGM family fare. (Some of the tree monikers still seem somewhat exotic for an Ozark town—cypress? Olive? Surely these species thrive hundreds, if not thousands, of miles from northwest Arkansas.) To the north farmlands stretched to the Missouri border, perhaps 25 miles away. You could visit the Elkhorn Tavern north of Rogers, and we school kids were bused to that area to walk over the Pea Ridge battlefield, a lesson I wasn't prepared to relish. To me the Civil War was creepy, like those brown photographs of gaunt, ugly ancestors staring out of oval frames; the dead past didn't interest me in those days. Eight miles to the west was Bentonville, the county seat and home of our athletic archrivals, the Bentonville Tigers. Some forty miles west of little Bentonville was the Oklahoma border. To the south, and separated from us by farming country, was Springdale, already then the chicken capital of America. (Once, at a gathering of Presbyterians from Rogers and surrounding towns, a Springdale pastor bragged about the growing population of his town and mentioned a figure of, say, 10,000. Bob Moser, our minister, quipped aloud, "How much of that is poultry?") Still farther to the south stood Fayetteville, which all of us persisted in pronouncing "FED'vil," home of the University of Arkansas, the storied Razorbacks, and tough high school football and basketball teams that usually got the better of us Mountaineers. Fayetteville, a college town, also stood for a heightened sophistication that put poor Rogers in the shade.

Draw a circle with its center at the intersection of Walnut and Second streets and make its radius about 20 miles: The world beyond this area was all but irrelevant to us as kids. (Fig. 6) It just didn't matter. And if we traveled there it was usually as athletes representing Rogers High School, and then we saw little beyond a town's gym or football field.

Fig. 6. Aerial view of Rogers, Arkansas. Courtesy
of the Rogers Historical Museum

We cherished the familiar. Walnut Street, which ran through the middle
of town, was interrupted by a stoplight at Second Street, and then proceeded
east a few blocks before dipping abruptly down a steep, winding hill to a valley
that cradled our principal recreational amenity, Lake Atalanta, a man-made
fishing lake with a bait shop and boats to rent. (Why this small body of water
was christened with the name of an Amazon-like Greek princess known for
slaying bears and anything else that got in her way remains a deep mystery to
me.) Nearby were a public swimming pool, Lakeside Café (Fig. 7), a roller-
skating rink, a miniature golf course, and two tarry tennis courts. Many were
the times I would fly on my bike down that steep road to the lake and then,
sunburned and exhausted, push the bike back up that hill.

Most of the buildings downtown were two-story brick structures which
housed businesses that were locally owned mom-and-pop affairs or branches
of regional chains. We had a Rexall drugstore, as well as two other drugstores,
and if we needed tires or other stuff for our cars, we went to Western Auto
or to Oklahoma Tire and Supply. For clothes we went to Stroud's or Hunts'
department stores, where we could deal in cash or put purchases on charge
accounts, a practice that is as obsolete today as the telegraph. If we wanted

electronic products, like the new black-and-white television sets that come in cabinets as big as chifforobes—we Basshams got our first one around 1952—we went to Rogers Radio and Electric. Beaulieu's (pronounced BOWL-yer's) Hardware on First Street was one of my favorite places; they sold World War II army surplus rifles (including a German Mauser) that I could drop by and fondle. Another was Russell's Five-and-Dime, a magical place for a kid and overseen by its friendly owner, Max Russell, who was always glad to pass the time with a kid, especially when the kid had change to rattle in his pockets. (My favorite item among the thousands in his store were the little wax bottles containing a few drops of sweet liquid; once that was polished off you could chew the wax for hours.) Russell's emporium was unique in possessing two store-front entrances, one on Walnut, another on First Street.

Fig. 7. The Lakeside Cafe, pool, and Lake Atalanta.
Courtesy of the Rogers Historical Museum.

And, again quite different from today's small-town scheme, Rogers had a busy bus station where Greyhound Scenicruisers and the more modest Arkoma buses made frequent arrivals and departures. (Fig. 8) A visit to the bus station was hazarded only when absolutely necessary, however, for the place possessed a distinct air—as in *smell*—of the disreputable about it, as if it were linked, at least by association, with the sinful world beyond the Rogers city limits. But perhaps that unique bouquet was only a compound of diesel fumes and the depot's unsavory restrooms.

Fig. 8. Greyhound Bus Station. Courtesy of the Rogers Historical Museum

There was a selection of eateries in town, including a cafe that was my favorite during my teens, the Snack Shack on Second Street near the Rogers (later the Rose) Pharmacy. My favorite, that is, until I broke a tooth there on a rock lurking in a bowl of chili. Another popular dining venue, although mainly for those of my sisters' generation, rather than kids like me, was Jack's Drive-In, located a couple of blocks north of the intersection of Highways 62 and 71. The place was mobbed after Friday-night football games when jocks and bobby-soxers congregated there. Before the advent of fast-food franchises—and Rogers' first was a Dairy Queen at Poplar and Highway 71—whose products have been taste-tested by focus groups to the ultimate in flavor and uniformity, you learned only by trial and error who had good food and who didn't. Jack's was good, hence its popularity. At the other end of the spectrum was the food at Rife's, across the street from the high school, where a hamburger cost a nickel—*a nickel!*—and at that was overpriced. Rumors among us kids had it that the patties were made of sawdust, or perhaps floor sweepings, or worse.

Although it lacked architectural distinction, the Coke bottling plant on Poplar Street held a certain fascination for us kids; its enormous plate-glass window allowed us to gaze in wonder at the complex machinery that carried gleaming green bottles whizzing and looping past on their way to receiving that fizzy dark-brown liquid known fondly as Coke' Cola, which was brewed, as we all know, by following a mysterious recipe the company treated like a state secret. Occasionally a man dressed in a pin-striped shirt bearing the company logo would sit at a folding chair and seriously inspect the bottles sweeping by. We joked, but only half in jest, that that was the job we wanted when we grew up because it involved no real work at all—our notion of the ideal occupation—*and* you could drink as much free Coke as you wanted.

West of the high school was a splendid array of the town's "mansions," which, for the most part, were two-story affairs with generously proportioned porches, balustrades, columns in the various Greek orders, and glazed entrances that glittered in the sun. These were the homes of the "quality" of Rogers, past and present. Some of them were built of brick when brick in a little southern town signified wealth, that the owners within were "high-toned." Many small towns still sport such magnificent residences, even if today the largest of them might serve as a funeral home or attorney's office. But these grand homes are now conspicuously missing from Rogers, having been demolished to make way for strip malls (one of which boasted the first of Sam Walton's discount stores).

Rogers also had a handful of car dealerships right downtown, not banished to its edges, as they are today. Their showrooms, ornamented with fabulous Fords, Buicks, Packards, and Chryslers, each of them with a distinctive, instantly recognizable style that changed annually, added a touch of glamour to our lives and earned their owners enough money to become our town's aristocracy. David Stiegler, my friend since grade school, loved to visit the auto showrooms and pester the salespeople for all the brochures and "literature" on the latest models. (David tells me that he still has all those brochures packed away somewhere.) Eventually I caught the same collecting bug.

Like all Bible Belt towns, our downtown was once graced with lovely and architecturally interesting churches. But as the city's population grew, congregations decided to build new houses of worship on the southwest edge of town. There, with more room both for the buildings and the parking lots, huge complexes dwarfing the old-fashioned "home" churches in town and costing God only knows how much went up in the eighties and nineties, one after the other. Only the Gothic-style Methodist church, with its original stained-glass windows, still stands on Third and Poplar streets to remind us what Rogers's big old churches were like. And like the other really important churches in Rogers at one time, it was built of brick. (My high school friend John Dacus, whose father owned Dacus Drugs, when filling out registration materials at the University of Arkansas responded to the item "church preference" by filling in "red brick.")

Our own Presbyterian church, a smallish cube of a building on North Fourth and Walnut, with its sanctuary painted an airy robin's-egg blue and its pipe organ so good that music students from the university would come to practice on it, was torn down sometime in the 1980s. (Fig. 9)

Fig. 9. First Presbyterian Church, mid-1950s. Courtesy of Mrs. Doris Moser.

Rogers was a railroad town from its origins (named, in fact, after a Frisco Railroad executive) and still had passenger train service in the late forties and early fifties. (Fig. 10) Among my earliest memories were the evenings when Dad took me by the hand to walk the short distance from B Street to the train station to watch the enormous locomotives at the depot. These giant black and oily machines created a storm of smoke and a lot of noise for a little boy to take in. I can still see and feel that station, with its brick platform and its iron-wheeled Railway Express carts used to carry luggage and freight. It was no doubt little changed from how it had been in the nineteenth century.

Fig. 10. The Frisco Depot. Courtesy of Rogers Historical Museum

Travelers stepping down from those trains could stop over at the nearby Harris Hotel (formerly the Lane Hotel), a surprisingly stately Italianate affair embellished with traces of both Spanish and Moorish touches. (Fig. 11) The place was billed with some justification as the "Palace of the Ozarks." There, oddly enough, controversial author Henry Miller, who wrote the once-banned novels *Sexus* and *Plexus*, was a guest. Other American celebrities who took rooms there were Amelia Earhart, Jack Dempsey, and Will Rogers, who stayed there when he and his wife, Rogers's own Betty Black, returned to her hometown. And none other than Tyrone Power stayed at the hotel in 1939 while filming "Jesse James" near Rogers.

Not to say that the hotel was filled with tourists, but if travelers did come to Rogers there were plenty of marvelous things that we, at the time, didn't think were extraordinary because we'd grown up seeing them as simply part of the background for our lives.

Most remarkable of all these wonders were the strange sights of Monte Ne, the remains of a tourist attraction developed around 1900 by William Hope Harvey, one of the many delightful eccentrics who added pepper to the otherwise dull stew of American political and economic history.

Fig. 11. The Harris Hotel in 2010.

Nicknamed Coin Harvey because of his fervent lifelong crusade for the adoption of both silver and gold as America's legal tender, he became disillusioned with politics and turned to the creation of a resort that consisted of rustic hotels situated on a lagoon on which one could ride in comfort on actual gondolas. Harvey, it is said, devised the name "Monte Ne" by combining the Spanish for "mountain" and the Cherokee word for "water." We kids, speaking in our native Arkansanese, called it simply "MOTT-nay," but we knew it mainly as the Pyramids. (Fig. 12)

Long before we kids began making our treks to Monte Ne, Henry Miller paid a visit and wrote a lengthy description of what he saw there in his essay "Arkansas and the Great Pyramid." While in Rogers, Miller obtained a copy of *The Pyramid Booklet*, a pamphlet in which Harvey set forth his plans for a structure that would symbolize the passing of a culture brought down by greed and corruption. Harvey had intended to erect a pyramid that would stand 130 feet tall on a 40-square-foot base. At its summit was to be placed a plate made of "the most enduring metal known" that would bear the inscription, "When this can be read, go below and find a record of and the cause of the death of a former Civilization." In its base there was to be a time capsule containing books that would presumably offer both an account of the causes of America's collapse as a well as rebukes to the benighted times in which he lived. But the pyramid was never built. The cost of its construction was estimated by Harvey to be about $75,000, and he ran out of money and in the end had to settle for a mere tomb to serve as a resting place for himself and his son.

Given the dimensions set forth in the booklet, Harvey's edifice would have been a very elongated pyramid or an oddly proportioned obelisk, a squat version of the Washington Monument. But the site became known as the Pyramids, and that name extended also to the peculiar and ancient-seeming amphitheater at the southern end of the lagoon, a semi-circular arrangement of chairs and couches rendered in concrete, their "cushions" plumped up to invite the tired visitor to sit and to direct his eye toward a kind of dais surrounded by the lagoon's shallow waters. Miller heartily approved of Harvey's outsized ambition, and, no big fan of American culture himself, he found the strange structures of Monte Ne delightful. We kids never grew tired of the novelty of this odd place, a true work of "outsider art" before its time, though the term had not yet been invented and definitions of art had not then been stretched so thinly.

Fig. 12. The Pyramids, Monte Ne, 1950s.
Courtesy of the Rogers Historical Museum

Located only a few miles southeast of town on unpaved Highway 94, Monte Ne was a destination for us kids that had a payoff at its end. Whether on bicycle or in the cars we began driving at sixteen, the road took us downhill through a cool hollow lined with natural springs, where we could stop for a drink on a hot day. We might also turn into the exclusive Joyzell Girls' Summer Camp for a swim in the icy waters of its spring-fed pool, where I learned to swim. I recall one of those boyhood excursions one summer when my friends and I were accompanied by our very game family dog, Jack, a vague version of a fox terrier, who trotted all those miles to Monte Ne and back on his short legs only to suffer the indignity of being mauled there by a gigantic, muscular boxer belonging to the old resort's owner. Before we could remove his attacker Jack was unmistakably heard to say through his barks, "Help me! Help me!" (I still have affidavits from my buddies to confirm that Jack was, verifiably, the first talking dog in the Ozarks.)

When Jack accompanied me and my friends on such "bike hikes," it was because on those days he had nothing better to do, such as follow Dad to work, for there was no question that he was definitely Dad's dog. We always seemed to have had one mutt or another during my boyhood, but Jack stands out among all of them and was clearly the best loved. He was a little black-and-white guy that possessed enormous energy—he could jump three feet or more from a standing stop—and staying power. And he knew his place in the family scheme of things. He was not allowed in the house, and he learned not to expect to be fed some fancy, balanced diet of expensive dog food. He was fed table scraps, and always by Dad, the ultimate master. Jack also slept outside in summer and in the garage during cold weather. He never missed a workday and seemed always delighted to jump into Dad's car or pickup for another day in the construction business. One winter morning I put on Dad's work boots to go out to perform one of my chores, burning the trash in the backyard (there's a custom we've put behind us!), and Jack, thinking it was just another workday, jumped into the bed of our truck, ready to go.

Jack was not a source of unalloyed pleasure, however. He had the disgraceful habit of squatting in the driveway and intently licking his private parts for seemingly hours at a go, and he did so without the least trace of embarrassment or awareness of how annoying it was to us kids. He was rather like someone sitting next to you in an airport terminal who is deeply into a cell phone conversation of amazing intimacy but whose behavior lets you know that at that precise moment you simply don't exist, you don't matter. Jack's attitude seemed to be, "Stick around if you must, but it's mine, and by God I'll lick it if I want to." Very sadly, Jack died a painful death after some wicked kid or vindictive neighbor—may the guilty party burn in hell forever—fed him something that contained ground glass. When poor Jack died, Dad was more broken up than he had ever been by a death in the family.

On a later occasion, when I was more interested in girls than in bicycling companions, the Pyramids was the destination for a fall hayride. Once, after arriving at the park-like grounds bordering the lagoon, a gang of us built an enormous bonfire right there on the grass to roast our hotdogs and marshmallows. This soon drew the furious attention of the property owner, the father of our classmate Lynn McWhorter, who directed us to put out the fire and to get lost, in that order.

By the 1950s, the boarded-up hotels at Monte Ne had begun to sink into ruin, and the gondolas, like Harvey himself, were long gone. When Beaver Dam was built in the early sixties, the new reservoir began to fill the valleys and hollows and eventually crept into Monte Ne. Today, Harvey's pyramids have been swallowed up by Beaver Lake and are only visible during times of drought. A nice bit of Rogers' history has largely disappeared.

Another of our town's attractions, albeit one shared by many neighboring communities, was an indispensable and cherished part of our young lives. I refer to the beautiful White River, which flowed north out of the Boston Mountains and through seemingly limitless reaches of forestland into Missouri before heading east back into Arkansas to its mouth at the Mississippi. Such untamed rivers, commonplace in America when I was a boy, are today a rarity and require the protection of the states or the federal government. A slow-moving, gentle stream during dry spells, with broad swatches of gravel bars on the inward shores of its curves and stretches of white water where the stream flowed downgrade through what Uncle Fred called "riffles," White River was bounded by picturesque limestone bluffs or bordered by dense canebrakes as it meandered through the countryside. To get a sense of the charm and beauty the White River once had, one must travel to the Buffalo River, one of its tributaries, which flows through north-central Arkansas and is today supervised by the National Park Service. What is cherished today was taken for granted, or worse, in the fifties. The White was ideally suited for the overnight float trips favored by my brother Bill, our family's avid fisherman.

Like Monte Ne, but of a more adventurous character, the White River drew us kids to its warm swimming holes in summer months. There we could also while away an afternoon in a borrowed flat-bottomed boat of a design configured to perform in the river's shallow waters. We enjoyed the short jaunts along the jarring gravel Prairie Creek Road to the iron truss bridge, from which we'd drop the biggest rocks we could carry or, around July 4th, the dangerous and forbidden cherry bombs that would sink before exploding like little depth charges. This same road, growing ever more threatening to our balding tires, took us eventually to the home of Uncle Fred and Aunt Ethel, where they had raised their rambunctious and outdoorsy young sons, Marshall and Dave, in a log cabin close to the river, a cabin designed and built by Uncle Fred. There, surrounded by the attributes of the sporting life— rifles, fishing rods, and mounted fish trophies—Uncle Fred read his favorite magazines, *True* and *Argosy*, and spent every free moment on the river. On overnight stays at the cabin, I'd accompany Dad and his brother in search of frogs, which they'd freeze in the bright beam of a flashlight and "gig" with a kind of spear to collect the poor creatures' legs for the frying pan. And in the mornings I'd take baths in the river with cousins and brothers, who'd always bring along a bar of Ivory, that miraculous floating soap. To go farther east from Uncle Fred's, an adventure seldom dared, meant entering lands that were truly terra incognita, mysterious and unsettling. Go far enough to the east and perhaps one could come to the edge of the world.

Though usually gentle and ideally scaled for human use, the White River could become a beast in times of flood, when it would inundate low-lying woods and turn the bottomlands into broad lakes. Then its waters would move along at a frightening pace, carrying deadwood and even whole trees along on its chocolate-brown surface and would seem to emit a deep sigh, a vibration at the lowest range of human hearing. Viewed close up, from its slick, muddy banks under massive, dripping cottonwoods or from perspectives higher up on its flanking cliffs, the flooded river was both fascinating and menacing. More than once I've been disturbed by dreams of the White River as a brown monster sliding past and growing larger.

Perhaps it was inevitable that the dark side of the river's split personality would attract the attention of an Arkansas congressman eager to join his fellow seekers of pork and see that money got pitched to the Corps of Engineers so they could build still another dam on a river that already, by 1960, had seven downstream from Rogers. Flood control, hydroelectric power, and recreational use served as the conventional rationale. (See Marc Reisner's book *Cadillac Desert* for an intelligent treatment of the dam-building epidemic that seized America in the twentieth century.) I am surely in the minority when I say that the coming of Beaver Dam in 1960—even though it brought some jobs to the local economy, provided recreation opportunities galore, gave a boost to the real estate business by creating overnight lakeside lots, caused marinas to pop up here and there, and brought bait shops and fast-food restaurants to former farmland and wooded hillsides—was a net loss. Such is progress, I realize, but I miss the river and question whether, on balance, its containment and development were worth it. Today, in extended periods of dry weather, the lake's receded waters reveal an ugly bathtub ring above its shoreline and the sad remains of rotted tree trunks where there was once wilderness. Not a pretty sight, and a bad bargain in exchange for waterskiing and evening cruises on martini barges.

Though far more conventional architecturally than Monte Ne, back in town our high school building a couple of blocks west of the downtown on Walnut Street competed with the Harris Hotel for the status of Rogers's classiest structure. (Fig. 13) Built in 1911, Rogers High School was a rather rickety and untrustworthy structure by the mid-fifties (if enough of us bounced our feet in unison on the study-hall floor we could make the second floor shake ominously). But with its white stone moldings set off against the red brick walls, it was an edifice we took a measure of teenage pride in. It was a handsome building, designed as it was by an architect of talent, A. O. Clark, who also drew up the plans for the Victory Theater and other prominent buildings in town. Now long gone, its site marred by a homely modern building, Rogers High School was for six years (Rogers did not have a middle school, so the high school housed grades seven through twelve) the center of the most important events in our lives. That no major structural collapse or fire claimed any lives during that period was a blessing.

Add to the scene a town hall that also housed the police station, jail, and firehouse (with a World War I period howitzer deployed nearby); a cute little public library that would not have been out of place at Colonial Williamsburg; two movie theaters (plus the drive-in on the way to Bentonville); an ice cream parlor that featured a virtually unlimited variety of choices; and a real estate office in a tiny building shaped like an apple, and you have the makings of a nearly perfect small-town U.S.A., Arkansas style.

Fig. 13. Rogers High School. Courtesy of the Rogers Historical Museum

For a southern, or at least mid-South, small town there was something missing, however. Rogers had no "minorities" (a word we would not have used, much less understood, then). None whatsoever. Oh, there was the Greek fussbudget who owned the Candy Kitchen across the street from the Victory Theater and who was always shouting, "If you want to read the comic book, buy it!" But other than him, there was just us WASPs of varying income levels. Apparently the town was like that because that's the way we wanted it. (Probably that's the way African-Americans, Jews, and other minority groups wanted it, too.) There were some Catholics in our midst (many Catholic Republicans made the move down from Michigan with Daisy Air Rifle), but they weren't "like us." They had mysterious forms of worship embellished—in *Latin*, no less—with who-knows-what sort of strange mumbo-jumbo. Then there was the Catholics' sheep-like allegiance to Rome, with its pope with his fancy robes and all that incense that you could see on television on Christmas Eve. Not to mention the priests, who'd supposedly taken a vow of chastity, which of course made them even more suspect. This is the kind of talk and rumor-mongering I heard in town and at work as late as my senior year in high school. But I knew a few Catholics among my classmates—Leann Dean and John Martfeld, for example—and I don't recall that they were ever singled out or discriminated against because of their faith.

I would not come into contact with African-Americans, either in school or on the high school athletic fields, for the first 18 years of my life. There were no blacks in Rogers. There was an urban legend that persisted in those years that blacks were not allowed to be in Rogers after sundown. (Or what? Would they have been run out of town? Beaten up? Lynched? Their fate, should they presume to show their faces in town, was just left to our vivid imaginations.) The nearest black community, Tin Cup, was located in Fayetteville, and, because Fayetteville's schools were segregated back then, the black students who lived there were bused to and from Fort Smith, some seventy miles away. And in Fayetteville, specifically the university, that presumed citadel of reason, no black students were allowed to live in dormitories with white students, and none played on any Razorback team or on any team in the Southwest Conference. Arkansas basketball games were so white you needed sunglasses to watch them. I recall one classmate, a guy who transferred to Arkansas when James Meredith integrated the University of Mississippi, saying through clenched teeth that blacks would live in any dorm he'd room in "over my dead body." Oh, how I wished I'd remarked then, "That would be the scenic route."

When I was a senior at the university, I lived with three other guys in a house on Storer Street, located just a few houses down from a building that housed a number of African-American coeds, with whom we were on at least a head-nodding, "good morning" social basis. In time, some black students attended one or more beer parties at our place. One of them, a kid with the unfortunate name of Seaman (which I always felt compelled to spell out when referring to him), became a regular at these parties. That winter each of my housemates, on separate occasions, was attacked and beaten by townies while walking home at night. I was the only one of us spared this indignity.

I must confess that while I am not ashamed of it, neither am I proud that I had little or nothing to do with bringing about progress in race relations on our campus during those very early years of the civil rights movement. Hans Hermann, a graduate student visiting from Tübingen, Germany, who became a good friend, demonstrated against segregation during his two years in America, thereby doing more than we Arkansas natives did to call attention to our awful racial injustice. The only moment I spoke up was when, in an ROTC class, I objected to our instructor's attempts to demean campus protestors like Hans, pointing out that one of the jobs of the military is to protect our rights to peaceably assemble. But that wasn't much.

It's fair to say that growing up in segregated Rogers gave us a less-than-complete preparation for life, though we weren't conscious of that at the time. As any local would tell you with a sigh today, "That's just the way it was back then."

Despite this and other shortcomings, a kid could not help loving Rogers in that decade following World War II. It was just the right size, there was a seemingly endless supply of potential new friends and playmates, and there was a ton of things to do (not one of which required a laptop, a flat-screen TV, a cell phone, a Kindle, or an X-Box). We could roam freely and widely each day without our parents fearing for our safety, and we went to bed each night without locking the door. Hell, if you were fortunate to have a car you could park it downtown and leave your keys in it. And the only dope in town was that injected into patients at Rice Memorial Hospital. It might not have been a Golden Age for everybody, but it certainly looked like one to us.

3

710 North Eighth Street

From the time of our arrival in Rogers until I left for college in 1960 we lived at five different addresses, an average of one move every three years, as we zigged and zagged all over Rogers' neat little grid of streets. Without a doubt these peregrinations were Dad's ideas, and I can only speculate that he was mainly motivated by financial necessities: getting some extra cash by the sale of a house or finding the best rental terms. He was also, as I've suggested, generally an antsy, tightly-wrapped man, a person never at rest.

(Allow me here, parenthetically, to give you an example of his restlessness: One winter morning when it was too cold for Dad to work, he volunteered to give Patsy and Phyllis rides to their jobs—Patsy to the gas company office, Phyllis to the Rexall Corner Drugstore. When they took so long getting dressed and putting on their make-up, he got increasingly angry and threatened to leave without them, even though his only purpose in warming up the car was to take them to work. When his imposed deadline passed, he then actually *did* leave without them. That would show *them*, Goddammit! After driving around the block for ten minutes or so he cooled off, returned and eventually chauffeured them downtown.)

After the B Street stopover, we all moved into what I thought then to be a "great big" house at 710 North 8th Street in a semi-rural setting to the northwest of town. To tell the truth, it only seemed big to a toddler like me. It was little more than an oversized bungalow. It had a columned front porch that looked out on an unpaved road, and it sat on several acres of farmland bordered by a creek to the south and Olive Street to the north. (Dad sold four or five lots and built houses, with Bill and Bud pitching in, during the

44

years we lived there.) Eighth Street was a dirt and gravel road on which the occasional traffic produced prodigious clouds of dust, a nuisance that the thoughtful town fathers dealt with by sending a tanker truck around to spread used crankcase oil on it. What would the EPA have thought!

We had a farm, indeed, because in the years we lived there we had at one time or another and in different combinations, a cow, pigs, chickens, and a true vegetable garden located just to the north of a real barn, a barn just like on a real farm. I have little recollection of the cow but I do recall the taste of her milk after she had cropped some wild onions growing volunteer-like in our field to the south: not a good taste.

At first our new (at least to us) home had no indoor plumbing; neither did it have enough room for all of us. Dad and Momma slept in the front bedroom; Bill and Bud slept in the attic; and Patsy and Phyllis and their little brother slept in a back bedroom, not quite far enough from our loudly snoring Dad. We had also a living room, a dining room, and a small kitchen, of course. These rooms were heated by a centrally located "floor furnace" of a type I have not seen since; the gas-fired mechanism was located in the crawl space under the house and heat rose through a grate that you stepped on in winter with bare feet at your own risk. Indoor plumbing was installed as soon as it could be afforded (and Bill tells me I was recruited to crawl under the house to bring our plumber his needed tools) and a lean-to porch was also added on the back as a bedroom for my older brothers.

South of the house was a generously proportioned driveway/turnaround area for the automobiles that would be purchased as paying jobs and driver's licenses were acquired with the passing years. There also could be found a home-made basketball backboard on post for Bud, our most talented athlete and a star guard on the Mountaineer basketball teams of the late forties. This was where I played or fooled around with whatever mongrel dog happened to live with us at the time; and where my sisters played with me, dressing me up like a baby, or a girl, and wheeling me around in a wicker buggy, as several old photographs document. In a way, I was "adopted" by my two big sisters. (Fig. 14)

Fig. 14. Patsy, Aunt Ethel, Phyllis and me, c. 1946.

When I was about six this big dish-shaped driveway was on one especially memorable occasion the scene of a noteworthy boyhood adventure: one night our small, malodorous creek—fed as it was by the town's storm sewers—overflowed dramatically, flooded our fields to the south, and filled our driveway to a depth that reached the waist of my forty-inch height. I know because I thoroughly enjoyed wading around as I followed Dad and my brothers while they dealt with drowned cars and whatever could be salvaged in our barn. At the other extreme, those same fields at another time were covered with fire as Dad supervised the burning off of last summer's weeds; I can still see him, Bill, and Bud beating the flames with burlap bags as they performed this spring ritual, a practice still in favor in Midwest farming country. For example, while driving west across Kansas a couple of years back I came upon blackened fields on both sides of the interstate that resembled a post-apocalyptic scene out of Breughel: mile after mile of burned over acres with a line of low flames stretching to the horizon.

I loved our house on North Eighth Street, and in my memory, perhaps because I prefer this thought over the alternative, I love the life our family had there. We were all together—*close* together in that small house—and in my child's mind, all was right with the world. At the end of the forties Bill and Bud had graduated from high school but still lived at home, Patsy and Phyllis were still in school and were giving the difficult teenage years their best efforts, and I was in the second grade, an adorable looking boy if I do say so myself, a kid who would have looked right at home in an "Our Gang" movie. (Fig. 15)

Fig. 15. The author in a scratchy sweater, c. 1947.

And we had a pretty good life. Although for some years I preferred to believe that we were "poor" when I was growing up, I have in my "late afternoon" years arrived at a better understanding of what poverty really is, and I now know that we were far from being poor. Like most Americans we just didn't have much after we had satisfied our basic needs, like shelter, food, clothing, shoes, a car, gasoline, and the tools required to make a living. When I was a kid I was never hungry, cold for lack of a coat or a warm house, or deprived of anything I needed for school. In the 1950s virtually all transactions—home mortgages and car loans were the major exceptions— were on a cash basis, and you had to make that cash stretch to the next payday. Putting items "on account" was done with great reluctance and with a touch of shame about it; the days when huge credit card balances would become almost a basis of our consumer culture were far in the future, and unimaginable. You bought shoes—and as a kid I never had more that a pair at a time— school supplies, books, whatever, when you needed them; there were no luxuries. Even today I cannot completely relax and enjoy a big, cold glass of orange juice because when I was young orange juice was considered such an unimaginably expensive indulgence. "Can I really afford this stuff?" is the thought that still goes through my head. The only kind of O.J. we ever treated ourselves to came in a big can and was called "Donald Duck Orange Drink," or something like that; and it tasted a bit like battery acid. We never ate out; we never took a vacation; no one got a watch for Christmas, and whenever possible clothes were sewn at home and not bought off the rack. Gloves were unheard of; buy the kid a pair of gloves and he'd only lose them anyway. When we had snowball fights I covered my hands with socks; no sensation sends my mind more quickly to childhood than bitterly cold hands. And Dad, who worked outside in winter until the thermometer dipped below about twenty-eight degrees, never wore good gloves either. Instead, he championed "good jersey gloves," which cost about forty-nine cents a pair, as if they were the only kind anybody ever needed.

A luxury for us was an enormous bowl of mashed strawberries liberally dosed with sugar, and more than enough for the seven of us. A chicken dinner on Sundays (and *you* try dividing a chicken seven ways), accompanied by perhaps eleven side dishes, was a feast.

But almost everybody lived that life, or worse. I went to school with kids from the country who had no indoor plumbing at home, and our grade school classrooms smelled like the burrows of small, furry animals. I once got invited home for supper by the kids of the Creech family—no, not some characters out of Dickens although he might have invented the name—and, seated around the table with this enormous bunch, I dipped black beans out of pot with a teacup just like the others. (One of the Creech kids, incidentally, went on to have a successful career as an artist.) I also recall my family putting together a box of toys and other goodies to take to a family in straits even direr than those the Bassham family encountered. I particularly remember that because the box contained a drum that by rights should have been mine.

This is not to say that *everybody* was the same; this was still America, after all. Rogers had its "rich," the aforementioned car dealers, for example, and their crowd of insurance company people, small business owners, a lawyer or two, guys in construction or real estate, and in 1958, the executives who arrived with the transfer of the Daisy Air Rifle factory from Michigan to Rogers. But class distinctions, while real, were downplayed in keeping with the "good-ol'-boy" ethos of an Arkansas small town. To sell and to succeed you needed to like people and be liked, so getting on your "high horse" and putting on airs just wasn't done (there were exceptions to this rule, of course). Little of this mattered to us as boys in any case: my best friends were the sons of doctors (John Buckelew and Stuart Wilson), the boy whose dad owned the Chevrolet-Olds dealership (Chris Hackler), and the guy whose old man ran one of Rogers' drug stores (John Dacus).

And now this is the place at which I point out the obvious: I was a spoiled brat; I was a terror to live with, as my one remaining sister Phyllis can attest. On the way home from school or a movie downtown I would throw bits of gravel and perhaps larger stones at my furious sisters. I would moan, holler, or throw operatic hissy fits if I did not get what I wanted. Once my mother, before setting out on a major and rare shopping excursion to Fayetteville—allowing for a boy's inflation of geography this would have been the equivalent today of her traveling to Seattle—she made the mistake of asking nicely what I'd like for a present. Because I was already deeply into the military phase of my imaginative play life, digging "Jap Holes" and what-not, I said, naturally, an "army helmet." Well might you ask, where was an such a helmet to be found, in Fayetteville or anywhere else, by my mom in the early 1950s? When she returned hours later, not with a helmet but with one of those tacky, bronzed toy horses with a key chain hanging from its snout I was so disappointed I went crazy, yelling, screaming, all but frothing at the mouth. I pulled what a college roommate liked to call a "full foaming swivet." Oh, my poor, dear mother!

Another example of how awful I could be and often was: somehow I scared up enough money to buy a rubber tarantula spider, one of my more memorable purchases at Russell's Five and Dime. With this many-legged monster I experienced the most exquisite pleasure in terrorizing Phyllis, shoving it in her face or, when she sought safety in the locked bathroom, shaking its legs and feelers under the door and inspiring more screams and tears. In short order Dad tracked me down, snatched my spider, and threw it in the fields across the road. And, no, Dad did not stop to ask himself how this treatment might damage my self-esteem. But these are only the instances of boyish terrorism I can remember. What horrors has memory suppressed?

Left alone, which was often in those years before I started school and everyone but my mother was away, I was on surprisingly numerous occasions a danger to myself. Bill still laughs over my single attempt at childhood suicide. In an attempt to reenact a scene I'd no doubt witnessed in a Gene Autry movie, I decided one day to hang myself from a fruit tree in the side yard north of our house. I fashioned a noose, hung it around my neck, tied the rope to a low limb, and took the leap. Luckily I used an especially long rope, probably by design, so that my feet landed firmly on the ground. On another occasion, playing by myself and lost completely in a fantasy realm populated by monsters or Japs or Nazis, I was running around, flinging myself in all directions, and ran face-first into a barbed wire fence. The cuts on my upper and lower lips, whose scars have become more pronounced with the years, produced a lot of blood and necessitated a quick trip to the doctor's office.

Then there was the time I was playing in my sandbox and came upon the idea of making a catapult out of a board and a brick. I then covered one end of the board with sand and threw a brick down on the other, raised end. A good bit of the shower of sand thrown up landed in my eyes, and mom and I were off to see the optometrist and the tortures of having the sand picked out, grain by grain.

There were more pleasant times at 710 North Eighth Street, of course, a lot of them; I only wish I could recall them all. I took a sweet and privileged delight in having my mother all to myself in those seemingly long hours when my brothers and sisters were at school. Then I would "help" her with household chores, not an onerous assignment since it only required that I tag along while she did the laundry on the back porch (a chore lightened by listening to "washboard weepers"—the "soaps"—on the radio), or hung out the wash, or baked a pie. I kept a wary eye on the wringer of our washing machine, having been warned numerous times to keep fingers and hands away from the scary rollers of the wringer, advice that led, naturally, to at least one painful experiment. I recall the puzzlement presented by "bluing," which came in a corked bottle and looked like an over-the-counter elixir of some sort. How could "bluing" make sheets whiter, I asked several dozen times.

And on the rare occasions of pie-making there was the luxurious anticipation of bowls to be licked and sticks of extra pie dough baked into delicious, golden-brown crusts just for me. When Momma ran short of things to keep me quiet and busy she'd set me to embroidering on scraps of cloth stretched between neat little wooden hoops. But pie crusts and needle-work were only stop-gap measures used to buy time. Inevitably I would grow bored and cranky and our warm companionship would deteriorate quickly. My behavior would elicit the usual empty threats that she would "go cut a switch" (translation: She would break a small branch off a tree and use it as an instrument of torture when applied to the back of my legs or butt.) If that warning didn't alter the situation she would escalate to the weapon she always held in reserve: "Wait 'til your daddy gets home."

Our house's attic, besides serving as Bill and Bud's bedroom, doubled also as our indoor playground. Here Dad installed a plywood platform to support the unexpected luxury of a Lionel electric train, given at least nominally to me on one of our Christmases celebrated at the house but immediately taken over by Bill and Bud. They just as quickly hit upon the idea of constructing hills of stacked paperbacks so that we could watch the little engine strain heroically up the incline and then hurtle down the other side as my brothers pushed the power to the max in hopes of causing dramatic derailments. I don't recall whether or not "my" electric train made it through that winter; my memories are stalled on those crashes.

Speaking of my big brothers, I must say that although I got to know them over the decades (Bud died in 2000), I have little recollection of interacting with them when I was a kid, probably because they were so much older than I, but also, I think, because I just couldn't relate to them. Bill and Bud were older enough to be essentially of another generation; they were already "grown-ups." They were rough and rowdy with me, banging me with pillows or scaring me in the dark. Bill adored guns and was a dedicated fisherman, Bud was a fine athlete, and all of that was way out of my league. On a visit to Uncle Fred's one summer my brothers amused themselves by taking me out onto White River in a flat-bottomed boat and throwing me, a non-swimmer, overboard. A picture of sunlight dappled on the river's surface above me and bubbles playing upward is still lodged in my head and can be summoned at will. Almost immediately one of them jumped in to hoist me above the surface, at which point it became plain to see that the water was only three or four feet deep. Not that that mattered: I was terrified by the experience. Several years later, at perhaps age twelve, I finally learned a technique of staying afloat and inching my way forward in water that might be called a semblance of swimming, but even today I never feel completely comfortable in water.

Not that my big brothers harassed me all the time. As the oldest, Bill was frequently assigned to look after me, and when I was eight or so Bud, hoping to turn my attention to baseball, laboriously carved a bat out of a hunk of four by four lumber (maybe we were poor after all—couldn't afford a bat?). One day Dad told Bill to take me downtown to get "my ears lowered" –a haircut— at the four-chair barbershop near the Rogers Theater. "But don't let Henry Babcock (a made-up name) cut his hair," Dad said. "Babcock can't cut hair worth shit." When Bill and I got to the barber's the place was full. When it was my turn I sat in the big chair and asked the barber, "Is your name Mr. Babcock?" "No, why do you ask," the man said. "Because Henry Babcock can't cut hair worth shit," I explained, whereupon the shop erupted in laughter.

My older brothers had energy to burn off and often did so with other forms of boisterous fooling around that was sometimes too much for our shared living space. A pillow fight in the dining room one evening resulted in a broken window and winter breezes filling the house. For some reason Dad, pushed over his limits, came after *me* with his belt and I caught hell; perhaps Bill and Bud had gotten too big to spank.

My big brothers were athletic and outdoorsy and they were always ready to tease me, unlike Patsy and Phyllis who played "nice" and counted me as one of their own. What with embroidery, sharing a room with my sisters, and an aversion to alpha-male breast-beating in my background one would be justified in thinking I was well on my way to a career as a sissy. I will eventually get around to my own loud, athletic, and boisterous youth, but it is worthwhile pointing out here that to this day I am more comfortable in the company of women than with the relentlessly competitive men of my generation.

Then, as now, spending time alone was no hardship; far from feeling lonely, I reveled in hours spent amusing myself. I was in heaven when I came upon a treasure-trove of magazines, great stacks of them left in the attic by the house's former tenants. My favorite by far in those piles was *Life*, the great picture record of world events and American popular culture and a staple in most homes from its beginnings in 1936 until it lost the battle to television in 1972, after which it faded away as a monthly, then as a newspaper supplement. In its heyday, *Life* had a circulation of 13.5 million copies a week, and inspired a host of imitations, like *Look*, for example, but it never had an equal. The magazine's chief attraction to Americans, and to this little American specifically, was the brilliance of its photojournalism, fascinating layouts of photos by the world's best, including Alfred Eisenstaedt, Margaret Bourke-White, and Robert Capa, not that these names would have meant anything to me then. Frequently the pictures would appear as photo-essays illustrating a theme like "A Country Doctor," one of Life's classic articles, or, on the lighter side, in a weekly feature titled "*Life* Goes to a…" whatever: a debutante ball, a fraternity panty raid, a birthday party on the summit of Pike's Peak, perhaps. The great attraction to a five- or six-year-old was that reading wasn't required. And *Life*, while specializing in photographs, also took fine art seriously, as if its publishers thought Americans should know a little something about the Old Masters. Thus there were issues devoted especially to Michelangelo's Sistine Ceiling frescoes and to his later painting of the Last Judgment, and, while I was simultaneously shocked, embarrassed, and intrigued by the artist's depictions of penises, bare breasts, and naked butts, I was also truly in awe of, and even a little frightened by such marvels of painting. (Bare breasts could also be found if one had enough time to leaf through a shelf of someone's *National Geographic*). The one special edition of *Life* I wish I hadn't come upon was the issue that featured Jan van Eyck's Ghent Altarpiece with its eerie portrait of God Himself wearing a golden crown and staring out relentlessly at me, just me and no one else. I remember that I could only look at that frightening image for only a couple of seconds at a time before burying it deeply back in the pile. Did such early attraction to visual drama and entertainment, of both light and profound imagery, prefigure a later dedication to a life spent with art? Who knows?

I do know that cultural life at home was otherwise rather limited; no, drastically limited. We took the *Saturday Evening Post* like almost everyone else in America, of course. No home was complete without it. The magazine served, among other functions, to help Americans learn to live, or to aspire to live, enjoyable middle-class lives. When I did a book on Robert Riggs I had occasion to look at hundreds of issues of the magazine in my search for his illustrations. Nothing sends one's thoughts speeding back in time like the *Saturday Evening Post*, with its incomparable covers by Norman Rockwell, its serialized stories, illustrated usually by the top artists in the field, and its weekly features like "The Perfect Squelch" (funny anecdotes of the pompous getting their come-uppance), its "Where Are You" puzzles (details of U.S. highway maps), and its *Hazel* cartoons.

We also listened to the radio regularly with Dad the self-appointed dictator of the dial. And no one enjoyed *Fibber McGee and Molly, Amos and Andy,* and *Duffy's Tavern* more than he did. I can still see him red-faced and laughing until tears streamed down his cheeks. We also could tune in to the *Grand Ol' O'pry* broadcast from Nashville every Saturday night. Today radio on the A.M. bands features little more than evangelists, awful music, and right-wing political talking heads, but in the late forties and early fifties before the coming of television it was by far the most popular entertainment medium. J. Ronald Oakley points out in his book, *God's Country: America in the Fifties,* that there were 108 shows in 1950 that had been on the radio for at least twenty years. Radio had advantages not equaled by television. You could do something else while listening—iron, cook, or knit, for example— without having to look at it; you could be in another room, too. But mostly you could let your imagination fill in the pictures suggested by the program's narrative, helped along, of course, by expertly rendered sound effects. A running bit on *Fibber McGee* was the prolonged sounds of falling, crashing objects that always ensued when Fibber opened his overstuffed closet. Suspense thrillers on the radio—*Inner Sanctum* was the best—were much scarier than they would have been on television. And, finally, who can forget the rousing *F.B.I. in Peace and War,* brought to us by Lava Soap, featuring the doomsday voice of J. Edgar Hoover and the show's thumping theme music: "L-A-V-A. dum-te-dum, dum-te, dum-te, DUM," stolen from Prokofiev's march from *The Love of Three Oranges?*

The same console that housed the radio also featured a 78 RPM phonograph on which Bill and Bud played their handful of Hank Williams records ("Lovesick Blues," "Cold, Cold Heart," "Jambalaya"). I hated those hillbilly songs then, but I love Hank Williams today. We had one "classical" recording, Chopin's *Heroic Polannaise,* which Momma loved to play, probably because of its noble and uplifting sound, notwithstanding the rasping passage of the needle as it crossed the big record. Later she told me that while she loved the classics it made her sad to listen to that melancholy music. "It makes me think of all in life I won't be able to have," she said. Interestingly even Dad seemed drawn to serious music: Phyllis recalls his listening quietly and pensively to broadcasts of Toscanini's *NBC Symphony Orchestra*, for example.

Our time on our little farm on North Eighth street was the last we would spend as a family together. Bill married and began his independent life in 1950, Bud left for college about that same time and only occasionally came home for short stays before both he and Bill entered the Army at the beginning of the Korean War. By 1951 Dad had begun to grow restless, perhaps because of financial difficulties, perhaps because he wanted to move up to a nicer house, and was casting about for a new home for his family. I had finished my first three grades at Central Ward Elementary School and had settled in there. But before the next school year began we had moved to a house on the far north end of North Third Street, taking Bill's war bride, Betty, with us. The Bassham family was soon to add more in-laws and several babies; experience assorted ups and downs; see me go through the whiplash of puberty, and know good times and bad, altogether what Zorba the Greek called "the full catastrophe," as we all entered that marvelous and memorable decade of the '50s.

4

CHURCH AND STATE, FUN AND GAMES

OH, TO BE A BOY of eight at the beginning of the fifties! I was convinced we were living in high style, in a huge house on a little farm on the edge of town, far out enough, indeed, to seem that we were country folk. Dad was getting the steady work he had sought when he and Uncle Fred moved their families north to Rogers at the end of the war, and we seemed to be prospering, as so many Americans were in those first wonderful years of peace. America was on top of the world, and this grand idea filtered down to us all. I had two big brothers who tolerated me, teased, tormented, and rough-housed me, and two older sisters who adored me, in part perhaps because they could use me as their surrogate baby when they dressed me up to play house and rolled me around the yard in their wicker buggy. We began to add automobiles to our big driveway as Bill and Bud graduated from high school and went to work to earn their own money—how in the devil had we managed without one before?—and all was well with the world in that happy, short-lived moment when all the kids were at home and life's more complicated times lay before us all. I would say the world was our oyster but for the fact that in 1950 none of us had ever seen an oyster, and a hundred thousand other meat-and-potatoes Razorback fans would have thrown up in unison at the very notion of a raw bar.

I was a third grader, taking the bus right in front of our house to Central Ward Grade School, where I was intent on fulfilling my ambition to please my teachers and amuse my classmates, two talents I was to cultivate until I reached, finally, the end of my education at thirty-one, the age at which I earned my doctorate. "Central Ward," as everybody called it, was a one-story, red-brick, Georgian-looking affair with wings reaching outward from a core that contained the auditorium, lunchroom, and principal's office. (Fig. 16) It is now long gone, and not even a ghost remains today of its pleasant, stylish self that stood between Walnut and Poplar streets on the ample grounds where we played and grew up. The building had dark hallways with well-polished, creaky floors and classrooms appointed with the obligatory American flags and framed prints of the unfinished Gilbert Stuart portrait of Washington. I imagined the unpainted canvas at the bottom to be clouds, above which George spied on our behavior from Heaven. All could see it was an elementary school by the paper pumpkins and turkeys in our windows in the fall, followed by snowflakes and valentines in the weeks that followed.

Fig. 16. Central Ward Elementary School.
Courtesy of the Rogers Historical Museum, Rogers, Arkansas

Our teachers began each day's session by directing us to stand and recite the Pledge of Allegiance and then, strange now to remember, calling on each of us little darlings to recite one verse from the Bible, a requirement that the slackers among us satisfied by mumbling the briefest of texts: "Jesus wept." No context, no analysis, nothing, just that enigmatic "Jesus wept." The show-offs, of course, would do the whole John 3; 16 thing and then beam disgustingly while receiving teacher's smile as their reward. (Were there no Jews, Muslims, Buddhists, or atheists, among us to object? Not in Arkansas in the fifties.) Also, oddly, our beloved teachers, without exception women, would ask us in the days following the holidays to detail the presents we had gotten for Christmas, and, at Valentine's Day, tell the rest of the class how many cards we had each received. Apparently no one had as yet heard of self-esteem, class consciousness, or the gaps existing between the rich and the poor, the winners and the losers. The homely and the unpopular were left to suffer in silence while the rest got a sense of being on top in the grand scheme of things; we were already American consumers and snobs in training. For example, another index of one's place in the great chain of being was the size of one's Crayola box and the number and variety of colors inside. It followed that possessing "periwinkle" placed one at the pinnacle of society.

I did all right in the popularity department, despite my stick-figure physique and my pop-bottle-thick glasses (see below). But I had a cute, babyish face, and was unfailing in my delivery of entertainment to my classmates. Following the success of the terrifying film, *The Thing*, I was called upon time and time again to portray the movie's monster from outer space by stalking from the coat closet, stiff-legged and heavy-armed, to be met with the shrieks of my fellow fourth-graders. Additional evidence of my high standing was my election as "Valentine King" (Shirley Kennan was the Queen) in the sixth grade, a distinction that moved the development of my ego along nicely. The occasion was marked by a little in-class ceremony at which I was given a large and elaborately wrapped package by our teacher, Mrs. Cogdale. And how I glowed with anticipation: surely it *must* be a football, or a baseball glove, or the ultimate gift, a Nazi helmet! But no. Ripping off the pretty bow, ribbon, and box-lid revealed none of the above but rather an incredibly cheesy, fake-bronze figurine of a horse, an almost exact replica of the equally disappointing piece of junk masquerading as a present Momma had earlier brought back from a shopping trip to Fed'vil. Oh, the effort it required to keep that smile frozen on my face while I turned red with anger and the colossal let-down. But it was a valuable life lesson. Never again would I anticipate or pre-vision the contents of a wrapped present, a lesson that has served me well, since I have received some honeys in my time on earth.

I learned in elementary school all we were expected to gain: how to play nicely with others (most of the time); how to "behave" in class; to add a column of figures, and to subtract or multiply numbers; to locate Arkansas on a map; to tell the difference between a plant and an animal, and most important of all, to grasp the structure and make-up of the English sentence. In the sixth grade our teacher pounded correct grammar into our skulls so effectively that its rules and regulations have held sway over me for a lifetime, and have taken on the character of laws that, if broken, expose one as a language criminal. We began to diagram sentences on the blackboard and to learn the inviolate identities of prepositions, adverbs, and adjectives, and the majestic distinction between the nominative and the objective cases. We drilled verb tenses endlessly and came to believe that "swim, swam, swum" was as universally true as "2 + 2= 4." This training, I will admit, has made me into a language snob as well as a self-appointed grammar cop, who, when I hear a newscaster say, "Obama shrunk the budget." I shout at the television screen, "*Shrank*, you idiot!"

Central Ward and most of the country's other grade schools went about their business in the early fifties aided little by technology. Blackboards and chalk got a vigorous workout, and above our blackboards printed examples of the Palmer Method of penmanship proclaimed the unquestioned ideal of correct writing we were to emulate, no questions asked. (And ultimately wasted on me, since I've preferred to print since junior high.) Another classroom visual aid was provided by a board covered with felt onto which paper cut-out figures and numbers somehow adhered and could be moved about by our teachers or us little ones to illustrate a story; I was more interested in the board than the stories: how did it work? On special occasions we were marched to the auditorium where, joined by other home rooms (though I don't think we then called them that), we sat restlessly through a 16mm. film dealing usually with some patriotic subject intended to instill in us the belief that our country was tops in the world. (What is it they say about the Catholics? "Get them by the time they're eight and you've got them for life ") As I try to recall these images of true Americanism I see huge dams being built, lines of combines at work in fields of waving grain, fighter planes lifting off from Navy carriers, the Capitol in Washington, the flag being raised atop Mount Suribachi, and such like icons, accompanied by the rousing words of the narrator and stirring music. But I also recall how we laughed together in the film's first seconds, when the production company's logo rolled on the screen: "Urpie Educational Films." "Urp," you see, was one of our many words for vomiting.

I'm sympathetic to Garrison Keillor's expressed irritation at the rickety education we kids received in the charge of some of our teachers (I believe our state did not require a college degree to enter the classroom in those years), when we got a steady dose of half-truths, misinformation, garbled history, and downright lies. (Take a look at the fascinating book, *Lies My Teacher Taught*

Me by James J. Loewen). Keillor recalls being taught to say "Mo-jave (with a hard j as in jaws) Desert and he's still mad about it. I recall one of my teachers telling us how proud we should be to live in Arkansas with its marvelous scenery and its rich, unlimited natural resources. Why, alone among the states it gave America its only supply of industrial diamonds, for example. To illustrate how self-reliant we were as Arkansawyers, she asserted, a wall could be built around our borders and we would do just fine, thank you, without the aid of the rest of the world. "Jeez, *really?*" we'd think, duly impressed. But, much as the rest of the country might wish Arkansas thus walled off, especially during the administration of our infamous Governor Orval Faubus (could that actually have been his *real* name?), that would have meant giving up bananas, coffee, and pineapples among only the luxuries, and penicillin and the Salk vaccine among the essentials. We were also assured that the United States had won World War II almost single-handedly—true enough in the Pacific theatre—but told nothing of the Soviet Union's predominant role in defeating Hitler's armies on the Eastern Front, where Germany suffered three-fourths of its war casualties. Naturally, the less said about Russia during the Cold War fifties the better.

In the 1950s there was no doubt in our minds that we were the "good guys." For virtually the entire decade we even had the ultimate "good guy," Dwight Eisenhower, in the White House, and, even though we thought of him then as an old man who played a lot of golf and had enormous difficulty with the English language, he was a true hero who had led the Allies to victory in Europe in the great, just war to defeat Nazism. We believed our country was in those days, well, just about perfect. Everyone has seen the psychological perception test where you are presented an image of a fountain on a pedestal or perhaps an urn set against a black field. But, aha, look again, and you see not the fountain but two human profiles, in black, facing one another. And, try with all your might, you cannot see both simultaneously; it's either one of the other. So it is with how we view our country, and as I write today, roughly a third of the country's people hold an exclusively proud, positive, and patriotic love of country while another third believes our national policy to be deeply flawed, driven by selfish or malevolent motives, and ultimately a menace to the rest of the world. The one side views our history as a triumph of courage, determination, idealism, and a desire to improve the lot of humanity, while the other finds ample evidence of sin: the enslavement of blacks, the genocide of native peoples, the relegation of women to second-class citizenship, and massive corruption in high places. The two sides (especially in Texas!) argue passionately over how our history should be taught.

Our elementary schools never struggled over these issues in the 1950s. We boys and girls were blank slates ready and eager to be written upon. Our teachers and books presented American history as a grand pageant whose scenario had been composed by God and whose cast was made up of noble and handsome statesmen, soldiers, and pioneers, all of whom bore a striking resemblance to the heroic figures in the illustrations of N.C. Wyeth. I was an expert of sorts on our country's early history, by the way, because I played Nathan Hale ("I regret that I have but one life to give for my country...") in an assembly program. My favorite text book in my twelve years of public schooling was our fourth-grade history, "Wagon Wheels West," or some such title, which told the story of the "winning" of the West as a kind of outdoor pageant in which one of the settlers' biggest problems was how to make soap out of lard and ashes.

But one issue we did struggle with then was the polio scare that gripped the country in the early part of the decade, a time when the disease did its worst damage in America. In 1952, some 58,000 cases were reported, the overwhelming majority of which were children. Fear of poliomyelitis was exceeded only by the terror of the atomic bomb. Although its most well-known victim was Franklin D. Roosevelt, the illness came to be called also "infantile paralysis" from the time it was believed to strike only small children and toddlers. Parents kept their children close to home, especially in the summers, when polio was said to do its worst, and away from movie theaters, swimming pools, and any other places where kids loved to gather. In his novel *Nemesis,* Philip Roth recalled the rules laid down by parents when a polio epidemic struck Newark at the beginning of World War II:

> We were warned not to use public toilets or public drinking fountains or to swig a drink out of someone else's soda pop or to get a chill or to play with strangers or to borrow books from the public library or to talk on a public pay phone or to buy food from a street vendor or to eat until we had cleaned our hands thoroughly with soap and water.

In Rogers, the only case of polio we heard about, and it might have only been a suspected one, involved the younger brother of one of my classmates, and this news caused my mother to forbid me from playing with my friend for the rest of the summer break. At the Victory Theater, where I was thought to be immune from the disease, I suppose, each feature was preceded by a 2-3-minute film produced by the March of Dimes foundation, begun by President Roosevelt to fund research on polio, and the film exposed our shocked eyes to scenes of children in "iron lungs" and other kids, resembling the young Forrest Gump, in cumbersome steel braces or in wheelchairs while in the background we heard the stirring song, "You'll Never Walk Alone." Immediately following this pitch an usher passed up the aisle to take donations.

But this couldn't happen to us, could it? And it didn't: by 1955, thank God, Dr. Jonas Salk, a medical researcher at the University of Pittsburgh, had developed an effective vaccine against polio. Vaccinations were begun immediately, and at Central Ward, we were marched one home room at a time, to the cafeteria, a short walk that to each of us was like the proverbial "dead man walking" on his way to the electric chair. If you'd asked at the time, many among us might have opted for a case of infantile paralysis over the shot we were about to face. Arriving at the nurse's station, our worst fears were confirmed: the syringe seemed as big as a turkey baster, the needle thick as a soda straw. It hurt like bloody hell, but it worked, and we never had to get another shot. A couple of years later, another vaccine, developed by a Dr. Albert Sabin, could be administered orally, and, with that we were finished with that ordeal.

Another great fear that hovered over my childhood like a dark cloud was the threat of a nuclear attack or an invasion of the U.S. by our adversaries of the period, China and the Soviet Union. It was only a matter of time, it seemed, before we would be involved in yet another world war and perhaps this time even wiped out by hydrogen bombs. The 1950s began with war, and a fear of even more horrible conflagrations on the horizon pervaded the decade.

I was eight when the Korean War began and felt a pall descend on our home when Bill was drafted and Bud's reserve unit was called up. I remember Momma became so fearful that her boys would be killed –and more than 36,000 American soldiers did die in that war—that she became ill and took to her bed on numerous occasions. The "conflict" or "police action" as it was euphemistically called ended before my brothers saw any action (Bill was shipped off to Germany and Bud never left the States) but the Cold War persisted after an armistice was agreed on in Korea in 1952. For the rest of the decade and beyond the country seemed obsessed by the Communist menace and the threat of nuclear annihilation while we youngsters, if we tuned in at all, could never quite grasp the significance of the case against Julius and Ethel Rosenberg, or the purpose of Senate hearings, or why a "missile gap" was a bad thing, or who was responsible for "losing China," or the need to prevent more "dominoes" from falling. All these concerns and more filtered down to us because they seemed to be all politicians talked about. (My wife Carlyn recalls the day in her Catholic grade school when news arrived that Joseph Stalin had died and the classroom erupted in cheers led by the nuns. But did she and her fellow third-graders even know who Stalin was?)

And if we were pretty sure that no enemy bombers or rockets could reach our shores—hadn't American always been safe from enemy attack?—we had a pretty good idea of the devastating power of atomic and hydrogen bombs. We'd seen newsreel film of atomic weapons tests in the Pacific as well as footage of trees uprooted and of houses even miles from "ground zero" being blown to bits during tests on land. We'd been horrified by photographs of the aftermath of our attacks on Hiroshima and Nagasaki and the awful scarring of Japanese survivors. Popular magazines like *Life* pictured everyday families stocking their backyard bomb shelters with water and provisions in preparation for the seemingly inevitable day of nuclear attack.

At Central Ward our teachers led us through drills that would supposedly brace us against the shock of near misses. Obediently we put our heads down and covered them with our hands and arms. Or did we get *under* our desks? In either position, we were no doubt assured, our chances of coming through nuclear holocaust unscathed were increased.

We congratulated ourselves that other, more important cities would surely take priority over tiny Rogers in the minds of Soviet strategists, and that they'd not waste a bomb on us. What did Rogers have that Russians would want to bomb in the first place? The Speas apple vinegar plant? Still we worried. Hollywood kept us jittery with movies like *Five,* a post-apocalyptic, science fiction film about the five survivors of a nuclear war that wipes out the rest of the human race, and *On the Beach,* in which a few people left after a nuclear war gather in Australia and count the days before atomic fallout reaches their shores and kills them too. And on Saturday matinees we could thrill to movies in which our armed forces fought gigantic freaks of nature—huge ants in *Them,* a Godzilla-like monster in *The Beast from 20,000 Fathoms,* and, every shy boy's nightmare, a giant female in *The Attack of the 50 Foot Woman*—all of these horrors the result of mutations caused by atomic radiation.

But perhaps we needn't have worried so much. A colleague of mine, Robert Clawson, who spent much of his career as a specialist on the Soviet Union, told me a story of one of his visits to Moscow, when his dinner companion one evening was a Russian engineer who worked in a Soviet missile factory in the 1950s. When my friend told the old Cold Warrior how his grade school classes were led through safety drills to prepare them for nuclear attack, the Russian smiled and said, "In the unlikely event that a rocket built in my factory made it off the launch pad, there was little chance that it would hit anything it was aimed at in the United States." Better I should have heard this anecdote in the sixth grade!

But fear of polio or the threat of Communist aggression could never have trumped the sheer joy of being a kid. I simply loved school, especially our daily dose of music, where we all pitched in together to sing "Arkansas Traveler" and danced—with girls!—the Kentucky Reel, over and over and over. I also looked forward each day to lunch, and its opportunities for loud socializing. Our cafeteria meals cost our parents perhaps fifteen cents, and featured those neat little half-pint bottles of (whole) milk and, my favorite, chunks of government-subsidized canned beef, of a sort I now imagine to have been left over from World War II, perhaps because the war had ended before it could be shipped to the Soviet Union. Cholesterol didn't exist in the 1950s. We boys also used the occasion to show how we could swallow those slimy slivers of canned peaches without chewing them first.

After lunch we were all commanded to rest by putting our arms and heads on our desks, as if in this sitting crouch we could be expected to nap. I suspect it was all a con job to make us shut up and give our poor teachers some respite from our endless prattle, whining, and ceaseless adoration. Another ploy in our teachers' arsenals to calm us down was to coax us to play the "Quiet Game," which was no fun at all as a game: the first kid to make a peep was declared "out." Soon enough we came to think, "So what?" Only third graders whose chief desire in life was to be loved by his teacher could fall for that one.

Nothing could compete with the ecstasy of recess, rationed to fifteen-minute, two-a-day sessions with our teachers' supervision limited only to breaking up fights, comforting hurt feelings, or bandaging wounded knees. Boys became addicted to the fad of pitching marbles, and the best at this game could accumulate impressive stockpiles of winnings (stored in socks) until the school soon banned this youthful form of gambling. (Family oral history has it that Bud was held back one grade in elementary school because of his marble habit in the 1930s.) Girls hung together in twos and threes to gossip or vote on the cutest boy while we little guys played army or cowboys and Indians with rocks found on the playground standing in for our gold. How dirty we must have been and how we must have stunk when we returned to our desks! As we moved up through the years we were introduced to "Red Rover," a rough game that required a few kids in between two lines of classmates to capture those who tried running the gauntlet to the other side. This required those in the middle to grasp hands, perhaps boy's to girl's, another baby step in the socializing process, but, at ages eight to twelve there was not much risk then that any sexual electricity would pass through those little fingers.

On rare occasions, things could get rough on the playground. One morning I got into an argument with a classmate, who was the kind of quiet, geeky, awkward, non-athletic but very decent kid who would go on in later life to invent, say, the computer, and, thinking him an easy conquest to chalk up and add to my list of exploits, I challenged him to a fight. As I squared off, this nerdy kid assaulted me with both arms and fists flailing like the moving parts of a whirl-a-gig and scored enough hits to my head to make me rethink the whole affair. I was clearly and completely beaten. But this, my first and only fight, became a teaching moment for me, to wit, never form an opinion about a person's abilities until after you've seen them in action.

Although I did all right in school, I probably did better after I acquired my first set of eyeglasses—and they were *all* made of glass in those days—when I reached the fifth grade. I can still vividly remember the day that Momma walked me the several blocks to the optometrist to have my vision tested and my eyes dilated; afterwards she had to hold me by the hand and lead me, blinded by sunlight, back home. When those first glasses were fitted, suddenly, to my utter amazement, I could see birds, tree limbs, *twigs* even! You mean to tell all this time the teacher had been writing stuff on the blackboard? It was a life-changing transformation, all thanks to the town's Lions Club who then pursued its campaign to have every kid's vision tested at school. The down side was, of course, that glasses broke, as mine did regularly and expensively, while also branding me with the label of "four eyes" and making it difficult thereafter for me to carry on a normally active, athletic boyhood.

One of my elementary school achievements came when I learned that I'd been selected to serve as a crossing guard during my sixth-grade year; surely the rest of life could only go downhill from that point. I got to wear a bright white Sam Brown belt with shiny brass badge and to wield a little red flag. Ah, the power, the glory! My station was at a Poplar Street crossing, and the indignity I could muster whenever a driver failed to stop, or even to slow down, at my command! Combining my experiences as one of the school's safety officers with my emerging talents as an artist, I entered a poster contest on the theme of (what else?) school safety and won one of the top prizes, a distinction I can prove with a photo taken of the winners in all age groups in which I am on display as perhaps the dorkiest kids in the community. (Fig. 17) With my winning entry I was awarded a "scholarship" for a stay at the exclusive "Joyzell" summer camp located a few miles northeast of town on the road to Monte Ne. But when the time arrived to pack up and head off for my week of co-ed horseback riding, swimming, archery, and who knows what, I got cold feet and didn't go. I'd just returned to Rogers after a week at Presbyterian youth camp in Conway, Arkansas, where I'd suffered mightily from homesickness, and was not eager for another bout of the same.

School was okay but the summer "vacations," as we were wont to call summer breaks (we Basshams never went on vacations), were wonderful, and to my child's imagination, virtually endless. When we are young, time and distance are attenuated: summers last forever and a trip out of town seems never to end, especially if a kid is prone to carsickness, as I was. At the same time, the heat of an Arkansas summer—and in the fifties it reached 111 degrees one day—matters little or not at all to a boy. I could stay out in the sun all day, and often did, as I ranged about my circumscribed little world, to the south as far as the new water tower on West Maple. This territory included the toxic creek that formed the southern boundary of the Bassham's vast—to me—landholdings, a desultory, fragrant stream that trickled in dry spells and overflowed generously when heavy rains fell. Below the nearby Eighth Street bridge I'd build my canals and dams in the gravel and watch water bugs skate along on the surface. My sisters tormented me with tales of the trolls who lived beneath that bridge.

Fig. 17. Winners of the school safety poster contest. The author is the boy with glasses in the back row.

To the north lay "Rogers Heights," a newly emerged little housing development, where one of my first playmates lived. My memory whispers to me that he was named Don Wade. But this may be misinformation, since another Don Wade taught Classics at Kent State while I was there. Don (the first one) was notable for the set of exotic parents he lived with, a distinctly non-Arkansas pair who furnished their home with bamboo furniture and drapes featuring a lush tropical pattern, and who stocked and maintained a real fishpond in their back yard. Such a theatrical style could only have been affected by people from California or Hawaii or some other unimaginably distant, half-mythical realm. Together we'd frequent the railroad tracks near his house in search of chunks of quartz, "diamonds" to us, and with other neighborhood kids play army in the open fields that today have been turned into industrial parks. I was heart-broken when my friend and his family picked up and moved away, goldfish and all, soon after Don and I had hit it off.

My other dear friend lived near us on Olive Street in a house built by Dad and my brothers. She was Nancy Smith, my first girlfriend, a cute, slender, self-dramatizing little thing whose father was a businessman and, as such, he and his were thought to be a class above us artisan Basshams. Nancy and I roamed the fields and woods in our neighborhood together; for a time we were inseparable. On one "play-date," (though we would have laughed at the term then) we re-enacted, again and again, that threadbare old movie cliché, the re-union of two lovers, perhaps a war bride and a returning veteran, following a long separation. Thus we spaced ourselves apart, there in that Arkansas meadow, and then ran towards one another to embrace and kiss "passionately," my first experiences with the act, passionate or not.

I think of her occasionally, as her name and those of other ghosts from the past waft up to the surface of consciousness. Did she marry? Of course, but was she happy? Did she have children? Were they great successes, or disappointments? Etc., etc. An important part of our fantasies about Heaven, should there be one, is that we will all meet again, as that gospel song promises us, hug, and have all of eternity to catch up. That would be one colossal class reunion, and, like such affairs, it could be either great fun or a disaster. (But are disasters even permitted in Heaven?) We all have a personal history in which dozens and dozens of friends, lovers, acquaintances dropped into our lives, then dropped out again, and each of us will have asked the same question, "I wonder what ever happened to...?" But how interested, really, would we be? Wouldn't all those stories be more or less the same? We wouldn't need or want eternity to hear those life histories; we'd be looking at our watches and eyeing the door after thirty minutes.

We cannot, however, leave the Smiths—our social betters, remember—without relating a story that involves them:

My dad, for mysterious reasons known only to him, a secret, alas, he took to the grave, called our local newspaper the "Bloat." I can't begin to figure why he did this. He was not the type to say something like, "This paper is literally bloated with unnecessary, irrelevant news items." He just invariably called it the "Bloat," much in the same casual spirit he referred enigmatically, for example, to all soft drinks as "Cokes," all conifers as "loblolly pines," and all types of hay grown for fodder as "lespedeza." Perhaps he simply liked the sound of the words, especially one of his own invention, like "The Bloat." In any event, one day after he returned home from work to find that no *Rogers Daily News* had been delivered that day, he said to me, "Ben Lloyd, run over to the Smiths and ask them if we can have their 'Bloat' if they're finished with it." So I did what I was told. Nancy's father answered the door and I asked politely, "Could we please have your 'Bloat'?" To which Mr. Smith said, "Our what?" "Your 'Bloat'." "What's a 'Bloat'?" And so forth. Well, at last I made the intent of my mission a bit clearer and was able to return back home with the Smith's "Bloat." But I was mightily and unnecessarily embarrassed in the process—at the home of the prominent Smiths!— and, as you can see, have never forgotten it.

One of my boyhood acquaintances, a grown-up in his case, has stayed in my thoughts long after the rest of that cast of hundreds has faded from memory. He was Heston Juhre, a scion of one of Rogers' prominent families who lived along the Walnut Street strip of mansions. One of Heston's ancestors, Charles, owned a block of buildings downtown in the early years of the century in which he operated a butcher shop.

Around 1950 a small cube of a building was moved to the corner of Olive and Eighth streets, plunked down there, and soon our semi-rural area had its own little grocery store, with Heston as its proprietor and sole employee. For the next several years Heston, then in his early forties (he was born in 1909 and died in 1981) could be found there behind the counter, reading a paperback, listening to his radio, and selling pop, chewing gum, cigarettes, or a loaf of bread to the handful of customers who dropped in, letting the screen door, with its "Holsum Bread" logo printed on it, slam behind them. I was one of his more frequent visitors both as a customer—"Ben Lloyd, run over to Heston's and, get us a quart of milk."— and as a bored kid who just wanted to talk, or more to the point, to ask a lot of questions while pulling on a tall bottle of RC (Royal Crown Cola) or a Nehi orange or a cold Grapette. Heston, a distinguished-looking, handsome, heavy-set man, was invariably polite, happy to see me, and ready to put down his book and talk as long as I wanted to stay. We became buddies of a strange sort, and, at one point, co-conspirators.

One afternoon I stole a quarter from Bud's cigar-box stash of change and called on Heston to buy a pack of Camels. (Why Camels and not Luckies or Chesterfields? Because Camels were Uncle Fred's occasional, "store-bought" brand and he had made up stories for me many times, with the package as visual aid, of the adventures of the camel and his friends among Egypt's pyramids. So it was my favorite brand, too.) Heston arched his eyebrows and wondered aloud who among the stainless members of the Bassham household might be a Camel smoker. I probably said something like "Phyllis. No, Patsy, I mean."(Both of my sisters being in their early teens at the time.) "Well, okay," Heston probably replied, and pushed the pack across the counter. I then ran to our barn, and there, surrounded by straw, hay, and countless other flammables, lit up my first smoke. My head spun, grew strangely heavy, and fell between my knees; the other nineteen Camels never tempted me after that, and the barn was spared.

In the years since I have wondered from time to time about Heston. Where had he come from and why he was whiling away his life in that dinky little convenience store? In short, *who in the hell was he?* In the absence of hard evidence I have since those years made up my own narrative of his origins, history of employment, and the circumstances surrounding his exile to a tiny grocery on Olive Street. In one scenario he was an undercover F.B.I. agent. In another he left Rogers, vowing never to return to that Podunk town, for some big city up North like New York, where he had failed in business, or suffered a disappointing marriage and an expensive divorce, and gotten himself into some scandalous trouble. Vanquished, he'd returned to his home town with his tail between his legs. "What to do with Heston?" the family had perhaps asked themselves. "He can't just sit around the house smoking all day long. I know, we'll set him up in a little grocery store. That'll keep him busy and get him out of our hair, at least during the day." So it might have been. But regardless of the nature of his past, checkered or not, Heston sat day after day, Buddha-like, in his little store with a dignity, with even an aura of gravitas about him that stood in sharp contrast to the modesty of his surroundings. "I may own a money-losing, half-assed business," he seemed to be saying, "but I'm still *somebody.*"

The last time I saw Heston was at one of the Presbyterian church's Family Night Suppers, where he dined with family members who had apparently made it a project to interest him in church. Heston didn't look all that happy to be there. He had dressed up for the occasion and looked good, if a bit uncomfortable, in white shirt, jacket, and tie. With his jowly face and salt-and-pepper hair he bore a striking resemblance to today's Supreme Court Justice Anthony Scalia. He was a gentle, soft-spoken man who took a friendly interest in me so I count him among my first memorable male role-models, whether Heston was a loser or not. Dear Heston, are you up there in Presbyterian heaven? If so, please accept this little nod of thanks from a fellow Presby. It was good to know you.

5

⎯⎯➤◆⬥⎯⎯

A PRESBYTERIAN INTERLUDE

WHAT THE DEVIL IS *PRESBYTERIANISM* anyway? I went through all those Sunday school lessons, took the obligatory classes with our pastor before my baptism, and listened (kind of) to all his sermons, but I don't think I ever really knew what distinguished our church from that of the Methodists, Baptists, the United Church of Christ, or the other Protestant denominations in town. Turns out the church is named for the way in which it is *governed* and organized, Presbyters being elders of the church. Seems a lame way to name a whole denomination, doesn't it?

Presbyterians believed in *predestination*, which holds that because God is omniscient He knows everything that has happened and *will* happen, so everything is cut-and-dried from the get-go; according to Calvin, the sect's founder, you may be "saved" or among the "elect," or not. Only God, who knows the future, is privy to that information. How un-American is that? Why, we practically invented free will and self-reliance, didn't we? No wonder today the Presbyterian Church is drying up and dying away while those non-denominational super-churches, with sing-along verses on huge video screens and choirs backed up by Fender bass guitars, and with preachers telling their congregations that Jesus wants them to be rich, are filling their pews. None of that negative stuff for them.

If Presbyterians are known for anything, it is perhaps for the extremes of their blandness; the church is almost radical in its moderation. This trait was noted more than a century ago by the church's best-known literary figure, albeit one who never attended services if he could avoid them. He was Mark Twain, who was raised a Presbyterian in Hannibal, Missouri, and retained a sentimental fondness for his church into his old age. He said: "You never see any of us Presbyterians getting into a sweat about religion and trying to massacre the neighbors."

So will I join Heston, John Knox, and other Presbyterians in heaven? As the Presbys say, literally, God knows. I certainly worked on my credentials and qualifications for entry when I was a teenager, for unlike Heston, I was not a reluctant churchgoer, far from it. I got the Christian fever and kept warm with it until I departed for college at eighteen, at which point it simply started to go away, like the flu. But at one point I was ready to answer the call to the ministry and become Reverend Bassham, my only hesitation being the dread of having to prepare a sermon to deliver before a crowd of hard-eyed elders once a week, fifty-two weeks a year (not knowing then that in the future I would deliver eight or nine Art History sermons each week). I had been attending church since my toddler days in Mountainburg when Dad and Momma would drag me, squirming and whining, to that little church clad in the ugly brown stone of the region that still stands on Highway 71. I remember crawling and twisting about under the pews among the worshippers' legs and shoes. Perhaps I was bored or maybe I was trying to flee from that shouting, red-faced pastor up front who threatened all of us with the eternal fires of hell if we stole, lied, took the Lord's name in vain, or broke, or even *thought* about breaking any of the commandments. After hearing about "unforgiveable sin" I became obsessed with the notion. Never having been given a clear definition of what that sin might be, I worried long and hard, especially in bed at night after the lights were out, whether I might have inadvertently committed one. If so, there was no road back; it was all over for little Ben Lloyd. Fears such as these took, for I developed a conscience, and, like Huck Finn, but for different transgressions (like stealing that quarter from Bud), I was tormented by that inner referee throughout childhood, and still am. I believed for many years quite sincerely that if I said "goddamn" or "for God's sake" that I could be struck down by lightning. (I wonder: Did boys growing up in ancient Greece or Stone Age Britain have consciences? If so, how did they develop?)

As a kid in my early teens I did not wrestle with questions concerning the existence of God. I *knew* there was a God, because I had seen Him, or at least a picture of Him. When I was about 14, Patsy brought home a photograph and a fascinating, and to me even terrifying story about it. A week or so earlier she had been out driving around one evening with two or three of her friends, and they had all joined in a heated discussion about whether or not there was really a God. Suddenly one of the girls said sarcastically, "Okay, if there is a God I'll take a picture of Him," and she stuck her camera out the window, pointed it upward, and snapped the shutter. When the girl later picked up the developed pictures, she was shocked to find among them an image that appeared to be just a jumble of clouds until, pop, she saw a picture of God, or perhaps Jesus, with long hair and beard and dressed in a white robe! And when Patsy sprang it on me, I could see God too! In the early 1950s I had not yet become acquainted with such pictorial miracles—a Madonna and Child seen on the side of a rusty oil drum, a rutabaga shaped like the Baby Jesus—so this photograph floored me: I was afraid to look at it but at the same time could not *not* look at it.

So I had been branded a Presbyterian by the time we reached Rogers and with time I became utterly sure that God was up there looking down on me. But if church "took" with me, why did my parents lose interest in the church in our new home up north? My guess is that they felt that the congregation that met in that little domed cube on Walnut and Fourth Street, unlike their Mountainburg brethren to the south, was in a league above them socially. In dress and in speech, they perhaps felt out of place there. For the Presbyterian congregation, along with the Methodists, and to a lesser extent the Baptists, had the classiest buildings (red brick) and attracted the "quality" of Rogers' townspeople, the people who wore suits and their best dresses and hats to church in those years.

I suffered some shame throughout my teens because Momma and Dad never showed up there, except perhaps on the day I was baptized at age twelve or thirteen, so I doubled down on my piety to make up for their absence. I attended Sunday school faithfully, along with David Stiegler, Joe Moore (whose father was our high school principal), George Stare, N.L. Hailey, Jr., John Buckelew, Martha Wesley, and many other kids I was growing up with. (Fig. 18) I sang in the choir and looked forward each Sunday evening to the meetings of our youth group, the Westminster Fellowship. I also showed up faithfully at the aforementioned Family Night Suppers, albeit without family in tow. On those occasions my awareness at being the only Bassham in attendance was compounded by the fierce embarrassment I felt over the poor contribution I brought to the evening's buffet table, a dish my mother invariably slapped together at the last minute that consisted of equal parts cottage cheese and canned "fruit cocktail," a concoction that seemed at the time to say only one thing: "I can't cook, I'm not coming, and I don't give a damn what you think about my culinary skills!" Now I realize what she was really saying was: "I'm tired. I don't feel good. I've been cooking for a husband and five kids for twenty-five years who never expressed appreciation or love for what I was doing, and this is the best you're gonna get."

Fig. 18. My Sunday school class, c. 1953. Back row (left to right): unidentified, George Stare, Jerry Cavaneau. Front row: Joe Moore, David Stiegler, the author, N.L. Hailey Jr.

Left to myself, all this enthusiasm for Presbyterian affairs and the spell of Christianity under which I fell would not have come to pass without some special catalytic agent. My family (with the exception of Phyllis, when work allowed) was not made up of churchgoers, and my mother was never vocal in urging me towards the faith, unless it was with her gentle, but for the most part unspoken wish that I be a good boy. There was not a lot of reading of the scriptures in our domicile, and we never said grace before meals. The person who made it all happen and to whom I owe much for whatever success in life I've enjoyed since our meeting was Robert Moser, who became the minister of our church in 1954. Bob and his wife, Doris, were young (both were born in 1929) attractive, fresh, unconventional, and full of enthusiasm, in sharp contrast to the customary brand of stiff and tightly wound southern pastors who could be easily mistaken for undertakers. I believe the Rogers church was their first appointment. Unable to have children of their own (they would adopt two sons and a daughter after they left our church at the end of the decade), the couple simply adored young people and took every opportunity, indeed, *invented* countless opportunities to spend "quality" time with us. In a way, we were sort of adopted by them. (Fig. 19) They swept into Rogers from their home town of Camp Hill, Pennsylvania, near Harrisburg (therefore stamped with the stigma of Yankees before they'd had an opportunity to say "hello") and took our staid old church by storm.

Fig. 19. Bible Class. Seated: Rev. Robert Moser, Beth Ann Lair, June Rowland. In foreground: the author, Jerry Patterson. Courtesy of Mrs. Doris Moser.

So unconventional was Bob in virtually everything, from his Northern accent, his bubbling-over personality, and his devotion to romping with us kids (which was regarded by some church elders as inappropriate) to his outspoken championing of the national church's dedication to social justice that he, while he generally came to be well-liked, made many in our flock uneasy. So, what else is new? Exists there a Presbyterian, Baptist, Methodist, Lutheran or whatever church where there isn't someone who doesn't like the minister, or his/her spouse, or perhaps the minister's kids. And if you don't like the way things are going at your present church, you can pick up and move to another, or start your own church. We're not called Protestants for nothing, after all.

But Bob was all seriousness when he turned to his job in the pulpit. He worked hard on his sermons throughout the week and delivered them eloquently on Sunday morning. A graduate of Union Theological Seminary in Chicago, Bob had ministered to the city's impoverished South Side, and had been called a "do-gooder," "nigger-lover," and "Christer" for his efforts. He believed passionately in the need for the Presbyterian Church to serve as an instrument of social and racial justice, and when he voiced these views in the sanctuary he disturbed some peoples' comfort zones. Our congregation was dominated by senior citizens who, above all, simply wanted to be congratulated for showing up in their "Sunday best," but Bob insisted instead on talking to us about race and poverty. I still recall vividly one old biddy squirming in her seat during one of Bob's sermons, her eyes flashing, and making stage-whispered comments in her husband's ear that were clearly meant for all to hear.

The lovely, demure, and self-effacing Doris, a young woman in her mid-twenties who might have stepped out of a canvas by one of the Dutch Masters, was a perfect match, and foil, for her boisterous and funny husband. Her husband called her "Doe." Bob was a big man with a handsome face topped off with a thinning pompadour that eventually faded away to baldness. And, still in his mid- to late twenties, he was already what we then euphemistically referred to as heavy-set: the dinner table was both his passion and his problem. His physique resembled nothing so much as a pear, or perhaps a bowling pin. Once taken out to dinner by an elderly couple after church, Bob consumed a T-bone steak and baked potato with enormous relish. Finished before the others he announced, "That was so good I believe I could eat another." "Why don't you?" his host replied. So Bob did.

Yet, as is so often the case with big people, Bob moved with ease, quickness, and grace, especially on the vacant lots where we played touch football. And by "we" I mean fellow Presbyterians boys like John Buckelew, Joe Moore, Jerry Patterson, and others whose names have unfortunately faded, along with neighborhood kids drawn to our games by our shouting and laughing. Bob invariably appointed himself quarterback for both teams and, calling all the plays, flipped his left-handed passes. Occasionally, with no receivers open, he would choose to do a quarterback-keeper, and I can still see him running with legs a-blur while his upper body remained stiffly upright. At those times, his rear end resembled—as Bob himself described another kid's posterior in motion—"two Indians wrestling under a blanket."

He also from time to time served as peacekeeper on the field and as a referee of our overheated emotions, especially when it came to reining in my own volatile temper. In the heat of the game I would become so incensed by an opponent's remarks or smug expression that I would turn red with anger and, on the verge of tears, express a rage that bordered on hysteria. The perception of unfairness or slights, real or imagined, sent me around the bend, a problem of mine that I've wrestled with for a lifetime. Bob, still part boy himself, was simply wonderful with us during our mid-teens: patient, loving, and interested not just in the present state of our souls but also in the futures that lay in front of us. With his love of good music, his belief in the blessings of humor, his gift for bright, sparkling conversation, and his embrace of what William Dean Howells called the "smiling aspects of life," he was an indispensable role model for me. It's hard not to get sentimental about those Saturday afternoons when we'd gather at the Moser manse next door to our church to rake leaves while Bob's vinyl recordings of the Glenn Miller orchestra played in the background. Or the Halloween party that Bob and Doris dreamed up one year that involved turning the church basement into a haunted house and scaring the pee out of us by placing a brick on the organ's keys upstairs then turning off its power, thereby producing a terrifying chord that died off like a protracted moan.

Our church basement was alive with us school-kids in those years. Although I remember not one iota of this, I have it on the best authority— Joan Bender—that girls and boys from the Methodist and First Christian churches joined us Presbyterians there for pre-school breakfasts, at which Chris Hackler is said to have made scrambled eggs "stirring with his whole body." What purpose these gatherings had, beyond the obvious one of having fun, I can't say, though Joan has reminded me that when the Daisy Company moved to Rogers in the mid-fifties each of our little conclave was assigned as a contact person to reach out to the kids of recently arrived company executives, with a view to recruiting them for our churches. Perhaps this is the way that Martha Wesley came into our church.

Without children of his own to tend at home, Bob was ready for anything. He took us to Oklahoma City for a church conference, sleeping on cots with us in another church basement, then scoring tickets for us all for a University of Oklahoma football game in Norman during the glory years of the Sooners under Bud Wilkinson. (We saw an Oklahoma victory during the school's 47-game winning streak.) On another occasion he drove us to a Stan Kenton orchestra concert in Tulsa, a one-day, 250-mile round-trip over two-lane county roads in those days. He and Doris took me and a friend to a concert or a play at the University of Arkansas in Fayetteville and then to dinner afterwards, a rare moment indeed for a kid who'd never gone out to dinner before. Bob was one of the counselors when I attended church camp one summer in Conway, Arkansas, and later he encouraged me to serve as a counselor myself at a camp in Oklahoma.

Bob Moser became a combination of surrogate big brother and father figure for me during those difficult years when every teenager wants to see his parents disappear into the ether. But more than that, Bob exemplified in ways difficult to explain that life was potentially full of *possibilities*, that one could have a life that was full and different, lived beyond the conventions of small-town Arkansas. Near this charismatic man, one felt a sense of living larger. I think he saw something in me and tried his best to nurture it. Falling under his spell was a transformative experience for me. Every kid needs a Bob Moser to come along in his life at the right moment, and dear Bob did that not just for me but also for generations of young people at his next churches in Tulsa and Wichita, Kansas. In photos of us kids with Bob there is no mistaking how much I adored him. According to Doris, now 83, Bob was a boy to the last. A terror as well as a delight at the bridge table, another of his passions, he could carry on two conversations, crack jokes, and humble his opponents simultaneously. And then one day, beset by the coronary disease that plagued his later life, he collapsed while walking in a mall in Tulsa and died instantly at the age of sixty-seven.

Bob and Doris left Rogers in 1959 to take up a new post in Tulsa close to the University of Tulsa, where, mainly because they were there, I started college. The minister who replaced Bob in Rogers was a tweedy, professorial type who actually talked vaguely of leaving the church to pursue an interest in Shakespeare; compared to Bob, his successor was, not to put it too unkindly, underwhelming. My interest in church, where concerns seemed more focused on how to maintain our aging building than on the Four Gospels, waned slowly and then evaporated. Will that faith return? We'll have to see.

6

"Tilt the Table This Way"

In this boy's life, the closest I ever came to one of those golden, Norman Rockwell moments occurred on the evenings when, walking home late from basketball practice or from our workouts during track season, I would approach our house in the gathering darkness and I would know by the light shining through the condensed steam on the kitchen windows that Momma was at work on our supper, and that simple but filling "comfort food," and as much of it as I wanted to eat, would soon be on the table, and that the family, or at least as many of the original seven that remained at home, would gather there in something approximating a state of happiness.

I knew they would be waiting for me, but not for very long: Dad, who knocked off work at five sharp every workday, wanted his supper on the table as soon as he got home and had had his shower and read a bit of the afternoon paper. And since after supper came the news broadcast on television, this evening ritual had to unfold along a strict timeline.

If Dad was in an expansive mood at those times, and, having spent the day in the company of sweaty men, wish to seek the company of women, he might grace the kitchen with his presence. There he would hover around the stove and make good-humored but nonetheless unwelcome comments and suggestions about the evening meal's preparation, perhaps taking an unrequested part by adding to the pot of green beans a dollop of bacon grease we always kept handy in a coffee can near the stove. (This lifelong culinary custom underwent a major shift in the late sixties when Dad entered his prolonged Cheez Whiz period, during which all but the most closely supervised pots on the stove might be in danger of being dosed with generous portions of this viscous, cheese-like, or at least orange, product.) His visits to the women's territory were not popular with my mother who, in addition to his unwanted "help," had to endure the baby talk from his lips that passed for the only endearments he seemed to be capable of. His pet names for Momma ranged from "Droopy drawers" to "purty sang" (translation: pretty thing). And this sweet talk was frequently punctuated by gentle slaps to the cook's behind. But hover he would, and in our kitchen he made himself a hovering nuisance.

And so to the table. And every night, as soon as all the dishes had been brought to the table, instead of grace Dad would say, "Tilt the table this way!"

Not too many years later when I went to graduate school in Wisconsin, I lived with a family that practiced a similarly rigid evening routine. Dinner was served promptly at six o'clock to coincide with the broadcast of the local news, and we ate not at the table but from TV trays arrayed around the living room facing the television set. The lady of the house always brought us plates with judiciously measured portions of three items for our nourishment, a vegetable, a "starch" (potato or rice), and a meat dish. A small salad on a separate plate might round out the menu. And that was it! And you didn't get any more! No seconds! I couldn't complain, however; I was paying a pittance to this family for room and board. Besides, these meager offerings might well reflect some sophisticated, "northern" usage that I was hesitant to raise questions about, since it might well reveal my rustic, unmannered roots.

And in Madison, a sophisticated, university town, the evening meal was always "dinner." But in Rogers "dinner" in the Southern language is lunch everywhere else. And just as we say that the English drive on the wrong side of the road, good Arkansawyers huff at Yankees calling supper "dinner."

In Rogers in the fifties we didn't eat fancy but we ate *big*. Our supper table might feature meat, vegetable, and "starch" (although no one would have called it that), but that was only the beginning. There might not always be a meat offering on weeknights, but there were usually eight or nine other dishes to choose from. Depending on the time of year we might have fried okra and fried squash, both having been coated with corn meal and cooked in Crisco a half-inch deep in the pan. There would always be mashed or fried potatoes and plenty of them. (I ask: In what possible or desirable circumstance could you have too much in the way of potatoes of any kind?) Green beans or navy beans, black-eyed peas, pickled beets, radishes, and canned corn or corn-on-the-cob were always on the table, as were white bread—Dad called it "lightnin' bread"—or corn bread. Every night leftovers were hauled out for another go. If we had salad it was made from iceberg lettuce; if there was cheese it was Velveeta (cheddar was too sharp for our palates and Swiss cheese tasted like medicine). And the drink of choice with the Basshams and throughout the former Confederate states, was, in the spring and summers, iced tea, heavily laced with sugar, of course. As a sop to foreigners from the rest of the planet, Southerners will today politely ask if you want your iced tea "sweet or unsweet," but if you indicate the latter they will know deep within that there is something not quite right about you.

Vegetables now stylish—broccoli, cauliflower, and Brussels sprouts—never made an appearance on our table; to paraphrase Mark Twain on Wagner's operas ("better than they sound") such exotic stuff was better than it tasted.

On Sundays, holidays or any other special occasions we would have meat of some kind, usually fried chicken, but also beef or pork roast, pork "steak," or ham. Expensive cuts, like T-bones, however, were never in the picture; I can't in any case imagine Dad wearing an apron and grilling steaks outside. Besides, there were no grills in Arkansas then. And an Arkansas family like ours with a .22 rifle in the house might from time to time taste the exotic flavor of squirrel, or perhaps a rabbit bagged in a trap of Dad's own design and construction. Don't turn up your noses if you haven't tried it.

When we lived on North Eighth Street we had for many years a vegetable, or "kitchen" garden, where we grew fresh food for our table in season and the produce from which—tomatoes, green beans, corn, and so forth—Momma would "put up," or can for the winters ahead. (She used a pressure cooker for this, a massive affair I thought of as a steaming bomb on the verge of going off.) We seemed always to have enjoyed an abundance of berries, which were probably very cheap then at roadside stands or could be picked in the wild by Momma and her daughters, or with her sisters, my aunts, who on their infrequent visits to Rogers could turn berry-picking near the White River into a pleasant outing. Fresh vegetables, fruit, and berries, it has to be pointed out, were foods we ate and enjoyed at those times of the year when they came to market, unlike today's berries flown up year-round from Chile, or our supermarkets' tomatoes force-grown in greenhouses 24/7 during all months of the calendar and, in Garrison's Keillor's characterization, look great but taste as if they had been "strip-mined somewhere down in Texas." Tomatoes, like corn-on-the-cob, ripened and came to the table in August and September, period.

We kept a milk cow for several years when I was little— too little, in fact to master the art of milking her. The milk we drank unpasteurized and "whole," and country people like my folks called it "sweet" milk to distinguish it from buttermilk. Phyllis tells me that it took months for her to get used to the taste of "store-bought" milk. (Dad, who lived to age 99, had no fear of cholesterol, if indeed he knew it existed, and drank "sweet" milk throughout his life; he turned up his nose at skim milk, which he called "blue john") And briefly we kept pigs, or at least one pig about which I retain an especially vivid memory. We also kept chickens on and off through the years. We certainly ate a lot of them, and Momma got the job of killing them, not with an ax but with a quick snap of the neck.

A chicken dinner, incidentally, always posed a major, if not contentious, mathematical problem for a family of seven inasmuch as a chicken carcass is composed of six cuts, not counting the neck and the back, and those six cuts, even taking individuals' tastes into account, lie along a descending scale of desirability. Did Momma or Dad take the Solomonic option and cut the breasts in halves or thirds? Wouldn't have occurred to them, and Momma usually took the neck.

Our food, then, was simple and plentiful. When times were lean because there was no building project underway or because the jobsite had been shut down by prolonged periods of bad weather, we would have to cut back on groceries. At those times, and there weren't many such, fried bologna (pronounced "baloney," naturally) might be substituted for chicken, pork, or beef. And God created Spam for American families going through hard times. I recall one day in the fifties when our kitchen cabinet yielded only a can of corned beef hash for our supper, but whether that was because Dad was out of work or because someone just hadn't gone shopping I can't say. On the whole we weren't that "bad off," as the expression goes. We knew no luxuries, there was no discretionary spending, but we probably enjoyed a higher standard of living that most families in Rogers and the surrounding countryside. Like most other folks in that time and place, we would have been insulted at the very mention of the word welfare.

We never went to restaurants; spending money to sit down and be waited on was just out of the question. Apropos of this, my friend Mary Beth Harper, who grew up in Grand Island, Nebraska, recalls that her dad, an optometrist, would occasionally take the family out for breakfast, but when she and her siblings attempted to order orange juice, always for some reason priced at restaurants as if it were a luxury item, perhaps, indeed, as if those four-ounce glasses of OJ represented the last surviving specimens of the liquid on earth, he'd cut them off by announcing: "No, we can have that *at home!*"

Not a lot of experimentation went on in the kitchen even in the best of times; in fact we would all probably have rebelled at any changes in our diet of favorites. Ethnic food, if we'd known such a thing existed, would not have interested us. Like the father played so wonderfully by Paul Dooley in the 1979 film *Breaking Away*, our own Dad would have blocked any attempt to bring "ini" food—as in panini, spaghettini, or rotini, or even zucchini—into our home. That was the "dago" stuff Dean Martin sang about in "That's Amore." When the son of an aunt living in Tulsa dropped by one day and told us in passing about his idea of going into business with a friend to market frozen "pizza pie," we all nodded our heads but thought silently and unanimously that the guy had lost his mind. And no Hungarian goulash, no chow mein, no enchiladas, either, thank you very much.

As soon as each evening's cuisine had been dispatched—and we were not a family to linger at the table to discuss the bond market or the latest Book-of-the-Month selection—Dad would return to his favorite chair to finish off "The Bloat" and would issue this command: "Boy, go read' up those dishes now." This meant I was to carry all the dinner plates and silverware to the sink where Momma and my sisters would then wash and dry them and generally put the kitchen to rest. Dad's labors were done for the day and it was time for the "woman's work" to resume. In the years I was growing up—and doubtless in many, many households today—the line between "men's work" and "women's work" was a sharply drawn and sacrosanct one. The kitchen, indeed, the home, was the wife's realm—Dad's forays to the stove there notwithstanding—and the outside world, the "real" and more important world, where hard work was exchanged for wages, was the domain of the husband, the breadwinner.

(Decades later, when Dad and his second wife came to Kent in the 1980s for an extended visit—at least it seemed an extended one to us— my bride, having had her fill of my step-mother's advice on how to prepare meals, to raise children, and generally make her husband happier, made her escape one evening right after dinner to seek relief and solace at the nearby home of a friend. While Carlyn was out, I gave our very young daughters a noisy bath, put them to bed, and sang them their favorite bedtime song, "These Foolish Things," then returned to the kitchen to wash that evening's pots and pans. With a cool eye on my work at the sink Dad raised his eyebrows and intoned: "Well, boy [I was about 40 then], it seems your work just starts when you get home.")

But back to food—snacks, more particularly. Speaking just for myself, few food combinations in my boyhood could beat mustard sandwiches, unless of course I might decide on a given day to work up a Miracle Whip sandwich, by far my preference over mayonnaise. Or I might follow Momma's lead: take a tall glass, crumble up day-old cornbread in it, pour a generous dose of buttermilk into it up to the brim, and garnish with coarse-ground pepper. Mmm-mm!

And there was junk food, always in style, and always in mass quantities. In the soda pop food group (Dad called pop, especially the brightly colored kind, "belly wash") you had a nice range of "cola" selections: Coke, of course, but also Pepsi, and a now nearly extinct brand, called "R.C." for "Royal Crown Cola," the latter very much the poor cousin to the first two but with a distinctive taste and a shameful load of sugar. Coke, always called "Coke' Cola" in our parts when I was a youngster, invariably came in a six-ounce bottle and cost a nickel—5 cents!—from a machine as heavy as a bank safe and from which it descended the chute and landed with a satisfying "clunk." Oh lordy, a cold Coke on a steamy summer day: so cold, so sweet, and with that marvelous carbonated wallop followed by a powerful burn on the tongue and the throat—almost sinful. It couldn't be good for the body, but was balm to the soul. In his memoir of growing up in Georgia, *An Hour Before Daylight*, Jimmy Carter recalls that his Daddy and his friends called Cokes "dopes," because they were dead sure that the drink's secret formula contained a dose of cocaine. Maybe so, since cocaine was readily available at drugstores early in the twentieth century and was incorporated into many over-the-counter remedies and popular consumer goods. But probably the only high you got from Cokes was the sugar rush that arrived a few minutes after you'd downed one.

While we're still at the Coke machine I'm reminded of a little gambling ritual we'd sometimes go through to determine who'd treat the others to their pop habit. In the fifties Coke bottles had the name of a town embossed on their bottoms which presumably referred to the location of the bottling plant it had come from, though surely the bottles were used many times and were interchangeable from one plant to another. If your bottle "originated" in the closest town—or was it the town farthest away?—you had to pay for everyone's drink. Yes, life in a small Arkansas town could be exciting at times. (As an Arkansas Razorback fan who formerly embraced the myth that students at Texas A & M were the dumbest in the old Southwest Conference, I can't resist the urge to pass along this awful joke: What does it say on the bottom of a Texas Aggie Coke bottle? "Open other end.")

Sometimes we'd get a small bag of Planter's peanuts and pour them into our Cokes and enjoy sweet, bubbly, salty, and crunchy all at the same time. Try it sometime and discover what you've been missing out on all these years! Peanuts could also find a place in our diets through the good offices of "Goober Wheels," a hard disk of peanuts embedded in a sweet and crunchy brickle-like candy, the whole affair about three inches in diameter— alas, another of the good life's amenities no longer available. We'd also chow down on Paydays, another source of our minimum daily peanut requirements, Milky Ways, Snickers, Mars Bars, etc., and wash them down with enormous bottles of Nehi, the bargain basement soda pop option in which you got perhaps three teaspoons of sugar per bottle, and more fun than Coke and Pepsi because of Nehi's garish colors and preposterous artificial flavors of strawberry, orange, and, as sister Patsy would put it, "I don't know what-all!" Then there was Grapette, a drink developed by Arkansas' own Benjamin Tyndle Fooks in 1939. (He couldn't, after all, call his drink "Fooks," could he?) Grapette was purple in hue and vaguely grape-like in flavor, or rather a flavor we agreed to think grape-like just as we do when we stick a piece of "grape" hard candy in our mouths.

I would be remiss if I did not at least mention another gustatory masterpiece that, I'm pleased to report, is still available in selected outlets or can easily be concocted at home: the famous "Frito Pie," that greasy, salty, and oh-so-satisfying combination of the brand name corn chips and chili con carne. We bought them at Rife's, located across the street from school, and the dish came in the original paper bag that had been simply torn across one side and filled with chili. One bite and you were that much closer to Mexico!

The quite amazing fact is that we'd eat and drink all this junk and not get fat. Indeed, few kids, fewer than the fingers on one hand, of the friends I grew up with were fat, largely because we were all constantly in motion, usually outdoors, during recess at school, during phys. ed. classes at school, or at organized sports, or in summers spent outside from right after breakfast until long after dark in the evenings. Fat kids were a race of long-suffering, abused, and marginalized oddities, never chosen when sides were made up for softball or touch-football games, but picked on mercilessly by the rest of us for being soft "mama's" kids. But back to the Bassham family kitchen.

Momma was no Julia Child and didn't aspire to be; she didn't in fact get any special kick out of cooking. Cook for six hungry people and yourself seven days a week, fifty-two weeks a year, and the novelty sort of goes out of the thing. She had her specialties, however: chicken and dumplings, for example, with the chicken falling-off-the-bone tender; a macaroni and cheese made from scratch (our only concession to the cuisine of "diversity"), and, most vivid in memory, her pineapple upside-down cake. Roasts, however, emerged from the oven a dark grey mass that defied chewing or even cutting.

As far as Dad was concerned, he liked just about anything, as long as it was fried. He would have argued with the great black pitcher, Satchel Paige, who advised against fried foods because they "angered the blood." Dad wasn't fazed by indigestion; "Tums," taken in quantity, took care of that. Dad's palate was responsive above all to what author Tony Horwitz (*Confederates in the Attic*) dubs the "six major food groups of the South: sugar, salt, butter, eggs, cream, and bacon grease." (Actually, if you substitute duck fat for bacon grease, those sound like Julia Child's favorite ingredients!) Dad's undiscriminating tastes extended also to the "whitener" he liked to put in his coffee each morning, a perfectly disgusting liquid known as Pet Evaporated Milk. When I worked with Dad, we'd eat breakfast together and he'd make toast in a little toaster oven that did not "ding" and go off; you had to take out the tray yourself at that point where bread became toast. Invariably, he'd burn the toast, but would head off criticism by saying, "That's *just* the way I like it." He apparently had a long history at this, because when Bud went off to college in 1949, Patsy assured him that the family would send him weekly supplies of Dad's burned toast.

The only doubts I entertained concerning my mother's culinary skills slipped into my mind in about the fourth grade when I came across a recipe for making graham crackers in one of our school texts, probably one dealing with some aspect of hygiene. It occurred to me that the ideal mother who *truly* cared about the healthy upbringing of a child would be one who baked graham crackers, and I probably brought up my uneasiness on this matter with Momma and urged her to get busy on it. No doubt she had a laugh about this and said something about how it would be a much simpler solution to just go to the grocery store and buy a box. In short, she baked no graham crackers; she did not rise to the occasion. Only many years later did I learn that graham crackers were the brainchild of Dr. Sylvester Graham, a Presbyterian minister no less, who recommended his invention as a health food regimen to suppress "carnal urges," specifically as a preventative of the adverse effects of masturbation. Rev. Graham, bless his heart, believed that the consumption of bland foods—and is there anything blander than graham crackers? Or Presbyterians, for that matter?—would curb one's sexual appetite. I probably just thought that a steady diet of home-baked graham crackers would make me stronger and smarter. I didn't have any carnal urges or sexual appetites in the fourth grade; those came later and have not abated. Now, as I write this, I am seventy, and I haven't eaten graham crackers for sixty years. But I adore a big bowl of five-alarm *chili con carne*!

7

THE DEAR RELATIVES

I GO ON ABOUT FOOD not because I'm hungry as I write this but because meals are the occasion—indeed often the reason— that people get together, drop their guards a bit, and have fun, whether at the family dinner table or on special holidays, when we travel to see relatives or they arrive on our doorstep.

I remember going to Mountainburg to see Dad's brother Harry and his family, and to Tulsa to see Momma's sister Florence, or having them come to visit us and to sharing a meal. At those times, preparing the food and eating it together everyone was on their best behavior and enjoyed one another's company for a few hours before the "Now, y'all come see us!" farewells. For our family as well as for our aunts, uncles, and cousins, who also did not take vacations, these get-togethers were highlights of the years.

Sometimes we went on picnics. We have dozens of photographs scattered among family albums of outings when fifteen or more of us would drive to a designated spot—perhaps on the White River or Sugar Creek north of town— and spread our bounty (including the indispensable watermelon) in the shade on a cool gravel bar. Or there were the times we made the more adventurous car trip north of the state line to Roaring River State Park in Missouri, the site of a fish hatchery, where waterfalls and great pools filled with shimmering baby trout provided a blessedly cool escape from summer's blazing heat. And Uncle Fred and Aunt Ethel's wonderful place on the east side of the White River was a favorite weekend destination—certainly my childhood's favorite place to go. We never went to restaurants; spending money to sit down and be waited on was just out of the question.

Who came to these outdoor gatherings depends upon what era of the Bassham family saga you're talking about. In the late forties, around the time Bill and Bud graduated from high school and when cousins Dave and Marshall were still close to home, there would have been us seven and Uncle Fred's family of four. Mom's cousin Bill Blevins, a mechanic and sometime chicken farmer who lived briefly near Pea Ridge, would also have put in an appearance. But in the fifties, as the guys left home to perform their military service or to attend college, our numbers shrank for a season or two before rebounding as my siblings and cousins got married and added husbands or wives, then babies, to our growing family.

We were closest to Dad's brother and Momma's sister, Fred and Ethel, with whom we shared countless social visits. They had all known each other since childhood—remember that Dad dated Ethel before marrying her younger sister—and the four remained close their entire lives. Before television, the couples would get together at our place for supper and to listen to the broadcasts of the Grand Ol' Opry on Saturday nights. In the late fifties, the Sunday evening television programs—*Maverick* or *The Ed Sullivan Show* — became the centerpieces of these gatherings.

One of Aunt Ethel and Uncle Fred's visits stands out from the rest: the autumn day they arrived to help slaughter and then render one of our pigs. The spectacle is forever etched in my memory. First the innocent animal, who had been fed generously with table slops, baby-talked to, and humored along on his path to the executioner for months, was coaxed to the fence, where Fred dispatched him with one shot from his deer rifle, then cut his throat to bring forth an astonishing amount of blood. Next the pig, now just meat, was doused again and again with boiling water from a big barrel over a roaring fire and his coarse hair scrubbed away. Then the carcass was hoisted aloft by the hind feet on a pole structure so that the cutting could begin. Next Dad made a long incision through the beast's belly from crotch to neck and opened up the carcass to reveal the glazed pinks, reds, and purples of organs and intestines, which, with only a little additional cutting and urging came tumbling out into a tub. (For how artists have been fascinated by the raw brutality and color of this subject, see the paintings of Rembrandt and Chaim Soutine.) I recall someone remarking that much care must be taken at this point to avoid puncturing the gall bladder and the tainting of the meat that doing so would lead to. Finally, the men divided the animal's remains into halves, quarters, hams, ribs, etc. Perhaps my Uncle Harry, who owned a grocery and general store in Mountainburg and was an experienced butcher, was there to contribute his expertise. Back in the kitchen, Momma, my sisters, and visiting aunts were at work at the meat grinder, dividing the bounty into parcels to be meted out or packaged for storage at the town's big freezer-locker on Arkansas Street.

We'd visit Fred and Ethel's on weekends when we'd make the 20-mile, dusty drive on the punishing Prairie Creek road, then over the creaky, iron, antique bridge that spanned the White River to Wild Turkey Ridge, where Uncle Fred and his sons had built the family's picturesque and comfortable log cabin. I spent a weekend there as a boy while the house was going up and slept on a cot in a temporary summer house rather, I imagine, like the army barracks Uncle Fred had worked on with Dad during the early years of World War II. Built of wide pine boards and with a tar paper roof, its walls from waist up were just screen wire to keep out the bugs. We had kerosene lamps for light and an outhouse a few steps away for our "necessities." I was in heaven.

Aunt Ethel doted on me and liked to brag that I was her "baby." "Why, that Ben Lloyd," she'd croon in her country accent, "he just bags me and bags me to come stay at the river."

One reason I liked Fred and Ethel so much was that they carried about them a trace of the exotic and the adventurous. They had spent time in the West, that great, remote land of romance somewhere out way past Tulsa in the years after the war when they lived in Manitou Springs, Colorado, and Fred had supported them by finding work as a carpenter. Uncle Fred had more than a little of the wanderlust in him and gave every evidence that he worked just enough to make a living, to earn enough to allow him to go fishing whenever possible and to go deer hunting in the fall. He seemed content to retreat to his piney woods cabin, where he could exhale from the pressures of life and be his own master. (Fig. 20) He had a taciturn, and sometimes somewhat grim, character, as if were harboring some grudge or anger. He didn't suffer fools. But then he could change to a sunnier side and chuckle about some absurdity or another and be quite pleasant to be around. Uncle Fred had a thin and angular body, unlike Dad, who tended, though physically strong, to put on weight in his later years. With his big ears, his long arms and lanky legs and with knobs and bumps distributed somewhat arbitrarily throughout his frame, Dad's younger brother would have made a ready subject for the homespun art of Thomas Hart Benton. He possessed a natural "country" handsomeness, rather like the forties actor John Ireland. When I think of Uncle Fred I see him trudging slowly up the hill after an afternoon of fishing in White River, carrying his rod and reel and minnow bucket, and breathing with a great effort, the result of his lifelong addiction to hand-rolled cigarettes loaded with Prince Albert tobacco. I saw him last at Rogers' Rice Memorial Hospital, where he was being treated for the emphysema that would ultimately kill him. There he gave me one of his winning smiles and paid me this generous compliment: "Ben Lloyd, you've become a pretty good looking man." And "pretty good" in the South is high praise, indeed.

Fig. 20. Fred Bassham, late 1940s.

When in one of his sunnier moods Uncle Fred delighted in telling me one or another of the naughty jokes in his rather limited repertoire. He would haul out the same one year after year, not remembering, or perhaps not caring, that he'd told it dozens of times before. I'd sit through the retelling, nodding at the appropriate moments, and laugh dutifully at the punch line. The joke went like this:

Uncle Fred: "Have you ever heard of the Milermore bird?"

Me: "No, never."

Uncle Fred: "Well, the Milermore bird is a bird that can fly really high, thousands of feet high. Then he dives for the earth, head first, going really fast. And when its beak hits the ground he farts, and you can hear that fart for a mile or more."

Me: "Ha, ha, ha."

Uncle Fred had created in his country domain a cleverly contrived little settlement that is still vivid in my memory. The centerpiece of his cabin was a generously proportioned fireplace, which he fed firewood cut from his own back yard. The living room was a dark, masculine "man-cave" with hardly a trace of Aunt Ethel's feminine influence to be found in it. On his big, log front porch he could smoke his hand-rolled cigarettes and read his hunting and fishing magazines. A short walk to the southeast lay the spring that supplied the family's water. There Fred had constructed a small dam to form a reservoir from which an electric pump piped water up to the house. Past the spring were the steps he'd cut into the sloping hillside, a kind of stairway, lined with giant sycamore and cottonwood trees, that took you down to the river. And at the river's edge, chained to trees to prevent their escape in rising waters, were the long, flat-bottomed boats Uncle Fred had built and used for years to take him to his "trot lines" or on his nighttime frog gigging forays.

One week a group of my friends and I descended on this quiet place to go swimming and to do a little aimless paddling about in one of these boats. Before we climbed the hill to leave we neglected to chain and lock up the boat we'd used. (As Babar describes the whales that deposited and then left him and his family on a far-off island, we, too, were "thoughtless, giddy creatures.") That night as I was climbing into bed, I heard rain begin to beat on our roof and I remembered, "Oh, shit! I forgot to tie up that boat!" Surely enough, over night the river rose and washed the boat downstream. Fortunately it did not drift far; Uncle Fred found it caught up in some brush and was able to rescue it. But I don't recall ever again having the nerve to ask to use one of his boats.

Aunt Ethel, to put it mildly, was a piece of work. What a pair she and Dad would have made if dating had led to matrimony! She fancied that she possessed a touch of glamour, of star quality, about her. If there was a beauty among the Young sisters, it was Ethel. (Fig. 21) She had a mane of long, black hair that served as the chief source of her vanity. Momma liked to say that "a woman's hair is her crowning glory," and so it was with Aunt Ethel's. She delighted in piling the full, dark mop high on her head, in the manner of Gene Tierney or Linda Darnell, two dark-haired stars of the post-war years. Ethel also had a crafty, arty side to her personality that set her apart from the rest of the family: she was always busy making some knick-knack or goo gaw, whether crocheted pot-holders or little plaster animals (bison or kitty-cats, usually) that she'd cast in rubber molds bought in kits from Russell's Five-and-Dime and then paint in imaginatively conceived colors. One day she announced her ambition to buy a portable typewriter and begin a series of mystery stories like those "misters' at the Victor'" (translation: mystery movies at the Victory Theater). But, alas, she never quite got around to it.

Fig. 21. Ethel Bassham, c. 1950.

Her version of the English language was remarkable. Whenever Aunt Ethel was shown or told something that was beyond her ken, her favorite expression, one I have adopted in her honor, was "I can't tell *nothin'* about it." For her, things weren't just big, they were "e-norm-YOU-us." She had great fun calling people on the phone and asking if they "had Prince Albert in a can," and then with impeccable timing announcing, "You better let him out, 'cause he cain't breathe in there!" She was also creative in coining new and hilarious colloquial expressions. My all-time favorite was her way of asking if I needed to go to the bathroom before we began a long car trip: "Ben Lloyd, do you need to make big *grunty*?" Oh, Aunt Ethel, that silver-tongued phrasemaker! She could have been a big hit on Madison Avenue.

I dearly loved my Aunt Ethel and she loved me. When I stayed with her and Fred she'd put out a smorgasbord of all my favorites—macaroni and cheese, corn on the cob, mashed potatoes, sliced tomatoes, fried catfish—and take delight in how I'd swoon over her cooking.

She'd also spoil me by allowing me do just about anything I wanted. I'd pore over her sons' precious old collection of *Big Little* books, those small, thick, hard-covered comic books with the little pictures in the upper corner of the right-hand page that became a movie if you flipped the pages with your thumb just so.

(Phyllis remembers how she also loved those *Big Little* books, so much so that Aunt Ethel promised her that if Dad built a little bookshelf to house them that she'd make her a gift of them. Well, Dad made the bookshelf and Phyllis told Ethel that all was set to receive them, to which Aunt Ethel replied, "Why, honey, I cain't give you them books. They belong to my *boys!*")

Aunt Ethel would let me plug away at cans on a stump with Dave's old lever-action .22 and shoot off firecrackers until she must have been driven to distraction. And when I left her keeping, I would always "bag" to be allowed to come back again.

As she aged Aunt Ethel became a confirmed and vocal hypochondriac and announced to any- and everyone that "strokes and heart attacks" were bringing her "low." That she would outlive Fred and all her sisters was an irony that would have been lost on her in her lifetime.

The last time I saw my Aunt Ethel was on a hot summer day in the late 1990s when Dad and I drove into the country to a small farm where her son Dave kept a few head of cattle and a "manufactured home" that served as his mother's last dwelling. The temperature inside, the heat stoked up by the little building's metal sides and thinly insulated roof, must have been close to 100 degrees. Aunt Ethel, probably then nearing 80, but still the perfect hostess, busied herself by dispensing iced tea and carrying about a roll of paper towels from which she'd tear off sheets we used to soak up perspiration.

Fred and Ethel were our closest and dearest relatives, but we would also be graced from time to time by visits from Momma's sister Florence, a tall, slim, dignified woman, and her odd husband, P.V. Palone, who would drive over from Tulsa in their long, bulbous Nash Rambler. Uncle P.V.'s initials were not short for Paul Virgil or Peter Vanderlyn; he was just "P.V." A short, dark-skinned man, he resembled one of those Italian immigrants who got off the boat at Ellis Island at the dawn of the century and was captured on film by Jacob Riis. Indeed, "Palone" would appear to be an Italian name. Built on the order of a fireplug, he made one half of a peculiar pairing of opposites alongside his upright, rail-thin wife. (Fig. 22) How those two got together and got married still boggles the mind.

Uncle P.V. worked as a mechanic or pipefitter or something at one of Tulsa's oil refineries and I recall that he made much of the ever-present dangers of his job. "You might get blowed up today or some other day but you sure as hell will get blowed up one of these days," he'd say at every visit. He also liked to tease me about how he was "a real" Indian, and then dance a little jig and go "woo, woo, woo" with his hand at his mouth in a fashion made popular by Hollywood. Come over to Tulsa—"the oil capital of the world," he'd boast—and he'd show me some more "wild" Indians, he promised.

Fig. 22. Florence and P.V. Palone on a visit to Rogers, c. 1955.

As I grew older I began to doubt that Uncle P.V. was a genuine, Oklahoma Indian, but recently I searched on line for the name Palone and found a host of people with that name, many of them located in Oklahoma towns known to have concentrations of Native Americans. So maybe he was not kidding me after all.

On one of their visits Uncle P.V. and Aunt Florence surprised and delighted me with perhaps the most outstanding present I have ever received: a perfectly wonderful toy airplane terminal stamped out of thin metal with details printed on its surface in the manner of those cheap, made-in-Japan products of the immediate post-war years. It came with planes, gasoline trucks, and baggage wagons, and the terminal had a control tower as well as hangars for my planes. This little set made for hours of imaginative takeoffs and landings with sound effects provided by the terminal's proud owner and manager. I wish I still had it! But, if it wasn't later melted down as scrap metal it is probably rusting away in some deep, geologic stratum of a landfill somewhere in Arkansas.

As I progressed through junior high and high school I paid less and less attention to my aging aunts and uncles; they became just old people in the background. Beset by one illness or another, Aunt Florence and Uncle P.V. ceased making the long day trips to Rogers over the largely country back roads we had to negotiate in those days. On one of their last visits, it became clear to everyone but me that P.V. was slipping quickly into dementia. Aunt Florence had suspected her husband's unhappy turn for the worst when she accompanied him on a fishing trip on Grand Lake near Tulsa. They went out in bad weather in a small boat with a small engine and when a storm came up their boat was nearly swamped in rough water. Momma's sister said she'd never been so terrified and so close to death in her life. On one of their visits to Rogers, I clearly recall Momma taking me into a bedroom, closing the door, and, perhaps in response to my queries concerning my "wild Indian" uncle's strange behavior, announcing in a dramatic stage whisper, "Your Uncle P.V. is losing his *mi-i-i-i-nd*!" When treatment of P.V.'s mental decline—whatever in the 1950s that might have amounted to—did little good, I believe he was institutionalized. And Aunt Florence passed away towards the end of the sixties. So Aunt Ethel, who, to hear her tell it, was always on the verge of meeting her Maker, turned out to be the hardiest of the Young sisters, a group that for the most part, was not blessed with the genetic makeup, or luck, for long lives.

There was one other of Momma's sisters, a pretty one named Esther, who lived in Tulsa. When I last saw her during the winter of 1967 she was married to a certain Mr. Rind, another wonderful Dickensian name. This fellow—not Esther's first husband—was the manager of a drive-in theater, and he hired me one summer to sell tickets during the 1964 run of the comedy *It's a Mad, Mad, Mad, Mad World*. My job was to stand near the ticket booth, scan the incoming car's interiors in order to count the number of paying passengers, and multiply the cost of admission—$1.75, say—by that number. (Tough job. Quick, what's six times $1.75?) The hardest part was actually watching, or trying *not* to watch, the movie, since I had to stick around the lot doing other odd chores until we closed up near midnight and I could hitch a ride back to our new Tulsa home that Momma and Dad had moved to when I was in college. Not particularly funny at first viewing, this awful film, with an all-star cast of big names hamming it up for two-plus hours, started making me nauseous at the fiftieth viewing.

Another set of aunts and uncles was Harry and Lois, the pair that seldom came to us at any of our Rogers addresses because they were so busy with their business and so plugged into their little community of Mountainburg that we had to go to them. Harry was Dad's youngest brother, and his wife Lois (Fig. 23) was the petite, smart, and attractive daughter of Nobel James Brogdon, little Mountainburg's lone law officer, and his wife, Ada Frances, who owned and presided at a café at the foot of the hill where the Basshams lived. On visits to Mountainburg I'd sometimes hang out at the Brogdon restaurant and occasionally see Constable Brogdon there, decked out in Western garb and enjoying a big steak, which he'd always liberally douse with Louisiana hot sauce. He was one of the little burg's prominent citizens and he impressed me as one of the most colorful characters I'd ever encountered.

Fig. 23. Lois and Harry Bassham, c. 1945.

Harry was the proprietor of a grocery/general store set smack in the center of town along the major north-south highway between Fort Smith and Rogers. (As the years went by friends passing through would see his store's sign and later ask me, "Are you related to the owner of Bassham's Grocery?") He sold a wide array of goods—meat, cattle feed, bib overalls, groceries, Coke' Cola—to a mainly rural clientele. He spent most of his adult life in that store and worked hard. When I'd visit there as a kid he was all business and was seldom in a joshing mood. My Dad was a good-looking man but Harry, in his younger days, was downright, matinee-idol handsome. Family stories have it that he played bass fiddle and sang in a country band in his youth, a story hard to credit inasmuch as it's nearly impossible to imagine any of the Bassham brothers ready and willing to perform musically. Furthermore, Harry, like Dad and Uncle Fred, or my brother Bud, for that matter, appeared to have two moods, dour or upbeat, with little gradation of expressed feeling or thought in between. What if Harry's "upbeat" didn't show up the night the band had a "gig"?

Lois was (and in her nineties now, still is) one of nature's —-she would give all the credit to the Lord—great successes: articulate, wise, insightful, good-looking, loyal, and loving. During her long life, she has been a little bright sun shining down on many lives, including my own. As the daughter of two of Mountainburg's most well-known people, she, along with Harry, became a "pillar of the community" in her own right, particularly in the Presbyterian church, and also in their schools. She was always trying something new, branching out to help support the family and, if it doesn't sound too corny, to *do* good. For a time she ran a beauty parlor in a small addition Harry built onto their home up on the hill above the store, a place I avoided because of its pungent, if not toxic, chemical fumes.

When I visited to spend a week or so with their sons James Harry and Terry, Aunt Lois would treat me like one of her own boys and welcome me for long stays. I'd arrive on a Greyhound or Arkoma bus after what seemed an interminable journey south over the Boston Mountains—today only about 48 miles and less than an hour's drive over the new interstate highway.

The old route wound its way up hill and down dale through picturesque mountain country punctuated by ratty little tourist traps like a rock "museum" you could visit for a quarter or a depressing "zoo," where you could see mangy raccoons, woebegone coyotes, or foxes in chicken-wire cages, or get a glimpse of an ancient rattlesnake. Prominent among the highway's other attractions was a restaurant and metal observation tower atop Mount Gaynor, where for perhaps another quarter you could take a thousand stairs to the top and view this corner of northwest Arkansas for a hundred miles or more. (Fig. 24) Once, when I was around six or seven and on our way to Mountainburg I whined and begged to climb to the top of that damned tower so persistently and annoyingly that at last Dad relented. Taking me firmly by the hand he led me up the first few flights of stairs before I began to be terrified—the onset of my acrophobia!—and began crying and pleading just as hard to stop. But, no, goddammit! I had begged to climb to the top and that's what we were going to do. Dad had not yet read Dr. Spock's *Baby and Child Care*, so he was showing me who was boss by dragging me ever upward despite (or because of) my relentless bawling.

Fig. 24. Mount Gaynor Observation Tower

On most of my visits to Mountainburg homesickness would always set in and make my visits shorter than we'd planned. During one of my stays there word reached us that Dad had collapsed at work and had been hospitalized with "fluid on the heart." Miles from Rogers and homesick already I broke down and sobbed like a baby. "Oh, Daddy's going to die," I moaned, falling into the arms of my saintly Aunt Lois. I was on the first bus home the next morning. No one could know then that Dad would live to be 99. (Dad said once that if he'd known he was going to live so long he wouldn't have worried so much about dying when he was in his fifties. Wonderful, wonderful reasoning from the Ozark School of Philosophy!)

James Harry, a year older and much more gifted athletically than his four-eyed cousin, was a bit intimidating to be around on these Mountainburg visits, though I did enjoy our outings together, including camping out on the steep hillsides above their home and cooling off in a picture-perfect swimming hole at the Silver Bridge. In his teens he emerged as a star baseball player and a tough runner on his high school's six-man football team.

Later James Harry and I were students at the University of Arkansas at the same time, but by then we were in very different worlds, I the arty one and he in Business Administration, and never would the twain meet. We hardly even saw each other. During those years I began to get a sense at home that Dad and Momma might be comparing their somewhat unfocussed son with his country cousin James Harry, who during his college years appeared to be the straight arrow, all-American guy almost certainly headed for success. On one of my rare visits home from Fayetteville, my parents began in a stilted fashion to ask how— or, more to the point, what—I was doing "down't the university." I'll never forget how, while almost blushing, they revealed their embarrassment at hearing through some grapevine that I was hanging out with "that beatnik crowd." Well might they have wondered, for I often wondered what I was doing myself. But their faith in me never faltered, and Dad went into debt to pay for those college years and was very proud when I turned out to be an artist and a professor.

It says much about my Aunt Lois that she was a student at the university in the early sixties as well, after she'd closed the beauty parlor and set her sights on a bachelor's degree in education. In middle age, she became a non-traditional student, commuting over those same mountains to Fayetteville almost daily in order to earn a degree and work as a fully-credentialed teacher in Mountainburg schools. She and James Harry graduated together in 1963, and much was made of this happy mother-son moment in the local papers.

Today, at age 71, James Harry is still rather intimidating. After a distinguished career in the Air Force, where he served as navigator on B-52s, he made his way up the ladder to the rank of major general in the Air Force Reserves, was appointed adjutant general of the state of Tennessee, and served as head of his state's Emergency Management Agency. It's fair to say that no member of the Bassham family ever attained a more prominent position in public service than this cousin I used to play "army" with. His late brother Terry during those same years stayed home to take over the family business and make a success of that as he married and raised his own family in Mountainburg.

Further evidence of Aunt Lois's strength of character and her loving nature was how she cared for Harry, the great love of her life, during his final illness (he died of Parkinson's Disease). She asked if there was one thing he wanted to do before his death. "Yes," he replied, "I want to see Carlsbad Caverns." "Okay," she said. She then somehow got Harry comfortably situated in their car and then drove her husband the 1200-miles to southeast New Mexico and back all to insure that his last wish could be fulfilled.

And what of family closer to home, of brothers and sisters, of wooers and the wooed? Well, the family grew and grew; it went forth and multiplied its numbers. Bill married Betty Evans of nearby Springdale and they begat Shelly, Howard, and Stephen. After service in the Army during the Korean War, Bill worked at the Munsingwear plant before deciding to go into carpentry. In middle age, Bill and Betty divorced. Patsy, after working for a spell at the local gas company, got hitched to Joe Mathew, a brick mason, and they brought forth John, Linda Karen, Joe David, and Sarah. They lived in Rogers until the seventies when they moved to Colorado Springs. Phyllis, in a brief marriage right after high school to Bill Laughlin, gave birth to Philip. She toiled in a variety of jobs before settling on a long working life as a waitress at Lakeside Café as well as numerous restaurants in the Rogers area. Bud appeared on his way to lifelong bachelorhood until he met an attractive co-worker, Frieda, while both were employed by the DX Oil Company in Tulsa. They married, but, to make a long story short, it was a disaster. They were divorced within a year and Bud, who died at age 70 in 2000, pined for her the rest of his life.

Momma used to say: "You send your kids into the world and sometimes they bump into things, and come back and get patched up, and then you send them back out again." Finally, Momma, they have to patch themselves up on their own; or not.

Tolstoy begins *Anna Karinina* with this oft-quoted sentence: "All happy families resemble one another; each unhappy family is unhappy in its own way." But surely a family's life does not fall strictly into one camp or the other. A family's life together is a mixed bag of high and low moments: successes, pride in achievements, pain, love, disappointments, financial worry, jealousy, misunderstandings, grief, gains, losses.

Equally wise is the inane, threadbare cliche uttered by today's professional athlete: "It is what it is."

8

ASSORTED DIVERSIONS AND ATTEMPTS TO BE GOOD

WHEN I'M THOUSANDS OF FEET above fly-over land on a plane, say, from Chicago Midway to Albuquerque, a route I've taken many times, there comes that moment around dusk when, so bored that I'm ready to read the label on my seat cushion just for something to do, I turn off the overhead light, slide up the little window cover, and just peer down into the gathering darkness to see what is happening that evening in Iowa or Nebraska. Helped along at these times by one or two of those clever little bottles of chardonnay the stewardess is happy to supply, I am primed and ready to entertain Profound Thoughts, to chart and assess my life up to this point, perhaps even to lay noble plans for the future, or to just contemplate the Meaning of Life.

From my Olympian vantage point, an ass-numbing seat 35,000 feet in the air, I scan the quilt-patterned American heartland as it slides underneath our wings. One small town after another takes the scene, its grid of lighted streets, composed of gold and silver filaments of the greatest delicacy. The intersection of the two brightest lines are probably the main highways that cross at the sole stoplight downtown, before stretching outward to link this town with the next one, and then the next one. Those two or three rectangles of harsh white lights must be a stadium, perhaps with a game in progress, or the parking lot of a Wal-Mart. What's going on down there tonight? Are models and technical drawings being prepared for presentation to the U.S. Patent Office? Is the next Pulitzer Prize winning novel being written? Is a future president being born in the county hospital? Perhaps someone is translating Icelandic sagas into Mandarin?

Probably none of the above. Instead, people are doing what we busied ourselves with in small towns sixty years ago: trying to pass the time and fend off boredom with the resources at hand, only with more electronic, digital tools at their disposal. If they're not working the second shift at the plant or flipping burgers at Wendy's, they're at the computer, or on the phone, or eating, or driving around looking for something to do and someone to do it with, or watching the evening news or a DVD, or maybe making love—anything to stave off the creeping sense that maybe, just maybe, they might be stuck in this jerkwater town for the rest of their lives.

If you want to see some of these towns on the ground, leave Interstate 70 a few miles west of Salina, Kansas, and head southwest on US 56. You'll drive through town after town consisting almost entirely of a grain elevator, a filling station/grocery store, and—well, that's about it. (And before you take this route watch the 1955 movie, *Picnic*, starring William Holden and Kim Novak.) You can't help but wonder who lives in these tiny burgs and what they do to keep from going mad. (Incidentally—and coincidentally—on a drive across the Great Plains in 2001 I heard on the radio that the highest incidence of teenage suicide is found in North Dakota, a close relative in its bleakness to western Kansas.)

A friend and I made this trip across the beautiful landscape of Kansas on our way to Taos a few years back and stopped for the night, hungry and sick of the inside of our car, in Dodge City. At a Montana Joe steakhouse, we were waited on by a lovely girl of about twenty, and in an effort to be sociable and to work on our acts as affable and still charming, if aging, men of the world, we asked what the "young people" of Dodge City did for amusement. "Amusement?" she groaned, "Nothing! There is freaking [she used a stronger word] nothing to do-o-o-o here!" And this was the biggest town for a hundred miles in any and all directions— Dodge City, mythical home of Marshall Dillon and Miss Kitty! Our innocent question had moved this poor waitress to the point of tears. (But when it comes to boredom and that sinking feeling of *Oh-My-God, is this all there is?* size appears to have little to do with it. Kurt Vonnegut, who grew up in Indianapolis, once said that life there when he was a young man was the Indianapolis 500 followed by 364 days of miniature golf.)

A town's population and square footage certainly factor into the boredom equation but can be coped with— even triumphed over—if the kid who grows up there comes equipped with a creative imagination, a modicum of curiosity, a low threshold of satisfaction when it comes to entertainment, an insatiable hunger, and an innate ability to make friends. What keeps us interested and occupied varies with age. At seven a large cardboard box, maybe one that a new refrigerator had come in, can keep you occupied for days (like one of my daughter's favorite childhood toys being a "level" she made by filling a plastic Tic Tac box with water, leaving only a bubble to bobble along a straight side). But at seventeen you've outgrown the cardboard box and have moved on in your quest for adventure to members of the opposite sex.

So how did I keep busy and entertained back in little 1950s Rogers? What, outside of school and work, were our diversions and entertainments? Well, a lot of things. And were we ever bored, heartsick, and deep in the throes of existential angst? Did we sometimes, like the Dodge City waitress, despair at the knowledge of how small and limited our home town was? Yes, probably, although when you're a teenager, there are plenty of other matters to worry about before you get around to that. What's more likely is that you actually liked your little town; it's the people in Bentonville and Springdale who should be sorry that they live in such crummy places.

We had plenty to do. From ages eight to 11, fired by our vivid imaginations and inspired by war movies like *G.I. Joe* and *The Sands of Iwo Jima*, we played army in the open fields and woods in and around Rogers in the years right after the war. With Jimmy Garrett, Neal Bloomfield, and other boys now long forgotten I roamed the farmland around the Bloomfield's Osage Spring Trout Farm southwest of town. We'd equip ourselves with ammo belts, canteens, and caps acquired at army surplus stores and arm ourselves with rifles sawn and carved out of soft pine or, if our families could afford them, BB guns— unloaded, of course. Though that didn't preclude injury. One afternoon, in the basement of Jimmy Garrett's house, I took part in a "commando raid" on "Nazis" hiding there, and as I entered the furnace room, BB gun in hand, Jimmy's older brother sprang from behind a door with a loud shout and scared the bejesus out of me. Unfortunately for the older Garrett boy I had just seen *Invasion of the Mole People* at a Saturday matinee at the Victory Theater, and was still nursing a child's fulsome dread of the "moles" (midgets dressed in furry costumes) who had emerged from a well drilled to the center of the earth. Out flashed the barrel of my gun, as if self-propelled, and smash went the muzzle right into the guy's nose. He shrieked again, this time for real, and rushed upstairs to stop the bleeding.

As soldiers we dug "Jap holes" (fox holes), supplied machine gun chatter from our vocal cords, and threw dirt clods that hit the ground with satisfyingly lifelike shell bursts. At school we'd plan our strategies and draft classmates to form squads and platoons, though we didn't really know what either one was. I began a collection of military shoulder patches—the Seventh Cavalry Division, the Big Red One—which could be found in abundance and bought cheaply then, a collection, regrettably, that disappeared over time. Army was all we could think about. If we couldn't wait until weekends or summers to play soldiers, we'd content ourselves with fifteen minutes of battle during school recess. At Southside Elementary, which I attended for one year, we turned a pile of felled trees and brush near the playgrounds into a fort, digging in the dirt, piling up rocks, and returning to the classroom sweaty and begrimed with Arkansas' red clay.

When we tired of playing soldier we'd go on long, exhausting bike trips to Monte Ne or south towards Pea Ridge or down the steep hill to Lake Atalanta. I had one of those heavy fat-tire bikes that weighed about a hundred pounds. We couldn't have imagined that these cumbersome things would become sentimental decorations in sports bars a half-century later. It was great fun to coast down the long hills that plunged away from Rogers' plateau, handlebar streamers flying, but hell to try to regain altitude later in the day when, rubbery-legged, hot, and thirsty, I made my way back home. We envied the rich kids who sported the English bikes with the handbrakes and fancy gearshifts. How I lusted after one of those Raleighs! But I had to wait until graduate school and relative prosperity until I could acquire one. (Funny how the material goods one lacks early in life continue to haunt our acquisitive natures.) Even more fabulous were the motorbikes that came into vogue early in the fifties. When I lived on South Third around 1951 my closest buddy was Jimmy Garrett, who had one of those honeys, and one afternoon, after probably much pleading on my part, he let me take it out for a spin. Big mistake. Things went fine as I sped, terrified but happy, down South Fourth Street, but then the engine stalled on me and I didn't know how to bring it back to life. Jimmy's machine was great stuff under power but dead weight and unmanageable without it. When I tried my best to pump the pedals and power it home like a regular bike, standing up and giving it all I had, I'm afraid I kind of bent one of the handlebars upward, probably irreparably. But I managed to force the bar back a bit and then pushed the monster back to Jimmy, careful not to share the bad news with him. Sorry, Jimmy, but the statute of limitations has run out.

But aside from the delight and joy, what pain bicycles can bring to a kid! Beyond the encounters of youthful scrotums with that nuisance of a bar between the seat and the steering column, there are accidents ad infinitum awaiting the unwary. One Sunday after church, I was peddling the considerable distance home from our Presbyterian church to South Thirteenth Street when the right-leg cuff of my new, Sunday "slack-pants" became tangled up in the gears and chain of my bike, a sorry situation brought on by my earlier inexplicable decision to remove the chain guard. I couldn't for the life of me free myself from this awkward and embarrassing situation—the tangle was on the opposite side of where I stood— short of taking my pants off and stripping down to my Jockey shorts, and I wasn't about to do that. My bike and I were locked together, and the more I tried to get myself loose, the more I tore my one good pair of pants and the more of a frustrated, whimpering mess I became. Finally I gave myself over to my fate and simply walked and dragged the bike the rest of the way home with my pants leg still ensnared.

A prime destination for the kids of Rogers during the fifties was the Lakeside pool, the only public pool in the town then, and thus the sole alternative to seeking out a swimming hole along the White River or at Noel, Missouri, where my older siblings swam when they were teenagers. (Fig. 25) I'd swoop down the curving hill road on my bike to the little valley that contained our town's main recreational facilities: a roller-skating rink; a miniature golf course; asphalt tennis courts; a small fishing lake and boathouse, and the Lakeside Café and pool. Today the café and pool are closed, the rink serves as a meeting hall, and the entire ensemble of once popular gathering places gives every sign of having been made irrelevant by Rogers' recent rise to an affluence that has provided ample resources to build bigger and better public facilities. Lakeside was, however, once the place to go in summer, and I spent many days there, swimming, playing tennis, and working as a dishwasher and all-purpose gofer at Cactus Clark's restaurant.

Lake Atalanta
Rogers, Arkansas

Fig. 25. The Lakeside Pool, mid-1950s.
Courtesy of the Rogers Historical Museum, Rogers, Arkansas

I always approached the pool with some apprehension because I was then and still am a lousy swimmer, though I learned the secret of staying afloat and propelling myself through the water, employing a style resembling a shipwreck survivor's panicked retreat from a shark, on my own one summer when I was about twelve. I was also embarrassed to show up there in the required swimming suit because I was painfully, if not obsessively, aware of my skinny body, a physique that resembled that of a Soviet gulag prisoner on a two-month hunger strike. I was born in the wrong era: I would have been more comfortable in one of those laughable bathing costumes that were in style in the 1890s. But show up I did regularly, and coated in the Bassham family's home-formulated suntan lotion composed of baby oil and iodine (*what* were we thinking?), I'd linger at first mostly in the shallower end of the pool and, once I'd found the nerve, venture to the deeper end where the older, bolder, and louder teenagers hung out. The pool's deep end featured a thrilling slide and two diving boards, the higher of which provided opportunities for heart-stopping, cannon-ball drops to Lakeside's icy waters.

When I was twelve or thirteen I formulated a strategy to draw attention away from my stick-figure frame: bathing trunks that would break new ground in their unique, as-yet-untried material make-up. When I showed up one afternoon in the new trunks Momma had made me, a number of my acquaintances, cute girls included, noticed them right away and made no attempt to stifle their giggles. What was so funny? Did they know something I didn't? Perhaps they anticipated, as I did not, that once wet *terry cloth* well might absorb enough water to lower the pool level a good inch or more? And, yes, when I climbed the ladder out of the pool, my shorts weighed a good ten pounds and put great stress on the knotted drawstring Momma had installed in the waistband; it was all I could do to hold up the soggy mess my innovative new suit had become. Needless to say, I have not worn terry cloth trunks in a pool since.

Great summertime fun could also be had once a year at the Benton County Fair. We'd go over for an afternoon or evening of rides on the Ferris wheel, or the Tilt-a-Whirl, or some even more terrorizing contraptions. We'd stuff ourselves with cotton candy, corn dogs, and snow-cones and then maybe mosey down the midway and try our hands at a few of the rigged games, like the booths where you're given three punky baseballs to throw at bottles made of lead. Perhaps we'd pay a call, at a significantly higher entry fee, to see a "hootchie-kootchie" attraction or some God-awful freak of nature on display. I never got up the nerve to seek admission to the sexy shows going on behind those tent flaps, nor was I ever eager to pay precious money to look at sisters joined at the forehead or twenty-four-inch tall women. No, thank you. Not my cup of tea. Just the name of the show and the gruesome posters that advertised "The Petrified Man," whatever he or it could have been, was enough to rob me of sleep and torture my nights for weeks after the fair closed. What a peculiar fusion of the wholesome and the seedy fairs could be!

The circus also came to Rogers from time to time, though not the first rank of shows, like the Ringling Brothers, Barnum, and Bailey circus—the ultimate circus featured in *The Greatest Show on Earth*. It was usually some rag-tag outfit, more like the second-rate company so wonderfully portrayed in the film *Water for Elephants*, one that might have a couple of the big animals and acts performed under one big tent. For me and many other youngsters the tent, so big and inviting, was an attraction unto itself. As was that marvelous circus aroma, compounded of the smell of manure, human sweat, and the junk food sold at concession stands: seductive stuff to a twelve-year old. With the circus came that strange tribe of outsiders, rough, dark, and curiously exotic men and women, the roustabouts who rushed around to get the show ready, the animal trainers, acrobats, and musicians who barely glanced our way as they went about their business. How unsettlingly wonderful to see people so utterly different from the drab, respectable townspeople of our sleepy little burg. Burned brown by so much work outdoors, their skin branded with bizarre tattoos, speaking with strange, un-Southern accents suggestive of faraway places, their mouths missing more than a few teeth, these seedy people both fascinated and repelled us. Tattoos are now so ubiquitous in our culture (so much so that a beauty who might pass for Miss Mississippi doesn't try to hide the two-headed dragon emblazoned on her back), but they grate on my tender sensibilities because my generation grew up associating them only with carnies, sailors, and marines. The thought then seemed to be: you had to *earn* a tattoo by joining a distinctive club or profession.

Odd that some kids didn't like the circus; for these boys and girls the clowns looked like monsters out of their nightmares, and the frantic, loud spectacles of the big top were way too much stimulation, were too strange.

I remember other sundry attractions that passed through Rogers when I was a boy. Once a Negro baseball team played an afternoon game on the North Eighth street stadium field with a pick-up team of local guys, and that novel event drew a large crowd. And on those same grounds we could watch "Donkey" baseball games, one of western civilization's less notable achievements, in which batters, after hitting the ball, ride a donkey around the bases. On another week-end afternoon a troupe of stunt-car drivers arrived with their colorful, souped-up vehicles to put on a show that presumably would have featured daring leaps though space, driving on two wheels, etc., but the show never came to pass because not enough tickets were sold. I recall especially how angry these would-be daredevils were that the good people of our hick town didn't turn out for their show. I know all this because my brother Bud operated the concession stand at the stadium one summer and I tagged along to see such wonders of the world come to visit Rogers.

Rogers provided other amenities to keep us entertained and walking the straight-and-narrow during that decade when all of America seemed obsessed with an epidemic of "juvenile delinquency," a national concern reflected in (or perhaps exacerbated by) such B-movie hits of the early fifties as *Blackboard Jungle* and *The Wild Ones*, featuring Marlon Brando. How to keep the city's youth "off the streets" and onto the path to wholesomeness? Why, give them a place to act wholesome, that's how. I remember with some fondness the Masonic Youth Center downtown on Poplar Street, a combination headquarters for the town's Masons, an assembly hall for Boy Scouts and party center for high school kids. There the high schoolers who appeared to me, a junior high kid, to be so handsome, so mature, and so popular, the boys in their white sport coats and bow ties, the girls fitted out in dresses made voluminous by "petty coats, " would do their turns on the dance floor, jitter-bugging to records by Bill Haley and the Comets or slow dancing to the Platters' "Earth Angel" or Paul Anka's "Put Your Head on My Shoulder." The Masonic Youth Center's dance floor was always crowded in the fall after home football games; and on very special occasions, such as Homecoming or Valentine's Day, the place would take on a certain class when we'd dance to good renditions of Glenn Miller arrangements by the Charlie Gundlach Band, featuring his son, Maxie, Rogers' amazing clarinetist. (It was a strange decade of music indeed that opened with or the persistence of Big Band classics and closed with Gene Vincent's "Be-Bop-A-Lula.")

As time passed I attained sufficient confidence, and the requisite white sport coat, to be ready for my own appearances on that dance floor, where I, a self-taught dancer, would rock back and forth with a girl in my arms (someone I'd probably known since grade school), doing my best not to make a fool of myself and to not get too excited during the slow-dance numbers. The fast dances would always force me to make my apologies and a quick retreat to the sidelines; I just couldn't bring myself to try it. Years later I saw a bumper sticker that read, "Love Like You'll Never Be Hurt/ Dance Like Nobody's Looking." Good advice that I wish I'd heard when I was fifteen!

Not that I didn't try to overcome these inhibitions. I practiced jitter-bugging, but only in the seclusion of my bedroom, where I'd put on a 45 RPM record, maybe Jerry Lee Lewis singing "Whole Lotta Shakin' Goin' On," and go through the moves in front of my dresser mirror, contemplating, perhaps, the day when I could take this act public. (The scene in *Forrest Gump*, when a young Forrest, his legs heavy with braces, swings his knees and shoots his hips to all points of the compass to the guitar strumming of Elvis Presley, the Gump's overnight guest, sent me back in a flash to my own bedroom gyrations.) I can still sympathize with that Bassham kid's fears and insecurities that prompted such solitary, secret goings-on.

A quick snort of Old Crow or a couple of cans of Falstaff out in the parking lot before the prom might have loosened up me and my fellow wallflowers, but oddly enough by today's standards that would have been simply unthinkable during my early teenage years. Not only was drinking expensive and illegal, it was socially unacceptable, and would leave a serious and virtually indelible stain on one's reputation. If you were a jock, drinking meant you were also breaking training, a serious offense. If you drank you were a loser, period. You were bound for Skid Row. The people of Benton County were proud that their little corner of northwest Arkansas was dry. If you wanted a six-pack or a bottle you had to drive north to the Missouri line or south to Springdale. And woe to the drinker who was seen partaking in public. When I was in college I worked one summer in Rogers for a contractor on the design of a small ranch house, and he quietly instructed me to place a screen in the breezeway between the house and its garage so that "a man could drink a beer there in peace and privacy." Liquor stores in the south are still referred to as "package stores" because the evil brew comes in a brown paper bag intended to disguise its contents. Over the decades the good people of Rogers and Bentonville learned to have it both ways, as restaurants invited folks to join "clubs" to enable "members" to buy a drink. And today, liquor, wine, and beer are widely available, though you just can't buy booze in stores.

I suppose we lived by and with clearer distinctions between "good" and "bad" in the fifties. If you did something bad, you were supposed to suffer from guilt, the default setting of the teenager's consciousness. I reckon that guilt took up about 20% of a church-going Presbyterian boy's waking hours; it was simply a part of the price of being alive. Hell, most of us probably felt guilty about something even if we *hadn't* sinned. And there was no doubt among us that drinking was bad, a sin, so we did not drink. More honestly, we put off drinking to a later time. And when we did start drinking, first in a tentative, experimental way in the last moments of our high school years and then freely in college, and with a vengeance, as if to make up for lost time, we did so knowing in the back of our minds, that it was still, sort of, bad. That it was bad was, of course, part of the fun. Who wants to be a goody-two-shoes indefinitely? Drinking and handling alcohol was part of the rite of passage. Of course we knew that for some drinking could be a life wrecker, but that was always the fate of the other guy. The high school classmate who offered me my first drink of bourbon was a popular, funny, life-of-the-party, but essentially troubled kid who drank himself to death before the age of fifty.

And if alcohol possessed such an evil reputation, what do you imagine the good citizens of the fifties thought of those who smoked pot or crack, or dropped acid, or loaded their nostrils with cocaine, or injected heroin into their veins? Well, they didn't think anything about it, because there was no such thing as drugs in Rogers when I was a teenager. The only illicit substance I recall boys mentioning—and usually with a good deal of evil snickering accompanying the discussion—was "Spanish fly," a reputed aphrodisiac said to induce in girls a state of mindless sexual ecstasy in the back seat of your Chevrolet. But how you obtained this magic potion and what form it came in—pill, powder, a real fly?—was never made clear to any of us, so we boys, barely out of puberty and acne-beset as we were, had to depend on our pure animal magnetism to attract chicks.

Being good, avoiding sin, and living up to everyone's expectations was a calling I shared with almost all the kids I grew up with. But, as Huckleberry Finn knew better than anyone, such a routine could, and did, become deadly dull at times. It was then that the sirens' call to chuck it all and experience the seamier side of life became irresistible. There is a certain pleasure derived from testing the limits and doing the forbidden just to see what the experience *feels* like. I enjoyed from an early age, for example, running around with "rough" boys who liked to cuss, smoke cigarettes, spit, and say disgusting things about the opposite sex. Usually these were guys from the "other side of the tracks," working class kids—just as I was—but most decidedly of the type calculated to worry my mother. I accompanied these "hoods" over the years, first on foot as we roamed the north side of town, then on bicycles, and finally, most troubling of all, in cars, when we'd "bomb around," a favorite pastime in high school, just to see what was happening. The leader of one such group I hung out with, a boy who had driving privileges in his grandmother's huge Chrysler, was Lonnie Divitt (not his real name because if he's still alive he might send somebody to break my knees), a short, toothy, foul-mouthed little squirt who resembled nothing so much as the perfect movie cliché, the Dead End Kid. Or, if you know those over-the-top illustrations in *Mad* that began publication around 1952, you might think that Lonnie had served as inspiration, a model, for that magazine's artists. Lonnie had "loser" written all over him. He was a true outsider at school— puny, un-athletic, unattractive, un-everything from the perspective of polite society— but he talked brilliant trash, was funny, and was a kind of teenage pioneer on the frontiers of bad behavior. If you can recall your youthful moral instruction from Disney's *Pinocchio*, Lonnie could be imagined as Lampwick, the tough kid who despicably leads the puppet boy astray, much as Lonnie sought to lead me down the path to corruption.

One night, I recall with some embarrassment and residual guilt, our gang, in need of gasoline for Lonnie's huge sedan and unable to put together a dollar among us for three or four gallons, paid a call on the parking lot of a large construction firm and siphoned off enough from the tank of a truck to keep us going for the rest of the evening. I knew what we were doing was a crime, possibly a serious one; that's why my pulse rate must have reached 140 as we sped away unseen and why I worried for days afterward that I'd be found out, convicted, and sent to the reformatory. I was so frightened, in fact, that I never crossed that line into the dark side again. I had, however, discovered that I was capable of committing a felony.

It must have been after one of those late nights under Lonnie's spell that I slept until noon the next day and, arising at last, grumpy and deeply in a typical teenage funk, was startled to hear my mother ask, quietly and hesitantly, as if reluctant to bring up such a touchy topic, "Ben Lloyd, can I ask you something? Are you taking something— pills, maybe—with those boys you run around with, that make you sleep so long?"

Oh my dear Momma suspected that I had become a druggy! How I must have worried her. Her youngest, her baby was slipping from her and heading down to road to ruin. From Cub Scout to dope fiend in just five years! But drugs were not in the picture. It must have momentarily slipped her mind that teenagers are fully capable, without sedatives, of sleeping away half the day; in fact, I practiced the custom well into my twenties, and then observed the phenomenon first hand when my daughters took it up during their teens.

There were other troubling signs that I was going to the dogs, of course. I hung out frequently at the pool hall on Walnut near the Rogers Theater, for example, where I logged many hours in that foul-smelling, smoke-filled den and honed my skills in Eight Ball, Nine Ball, and Rotation, and, if I do say so myself, got to be a pretty good pool player. Patronized in the main by retired or out-of-work men dressed in khakis or bib overalls, the hall, a kind of working class men's club, offered nothing stronger that Coke' Cola or coffee and permitted no sinful behavior beyond spitting into coffee cans or smoking hand-rolled cigarettes. But it was no place for a clean-cut, decent boy like me and that's what I liked about the place. Besides, there are worse things than a skill at pocket pool to launch one's self into early manhood.

Even though the seamier side intrigued me, I was not a "bad kid," nor was I a "troubled teen." Didn't I go to Sunday school and worship services every Sunday and attend Westminster Fellowship on Sunday nights and Family Night Suppers at the church once a month, albeit unaccompanied by family? Wasn't I the teacher's pet at school? The skinny kid with glasses, always smiling, always talking, always ready to amuse, the kid who was comfortable around adults and eager to please, the youngster who would surely go far?

So naturally, I took every opportunity to pursue the pure life of the All-American boy, a veritable real-life embodiment of the kids on Norman Rockwell's *Saturday Evening Post* covers and in those heart-warming MGM movies of the thirties in which Mickey Rooney and his neighborhood pals put on a show in the final reel. I just wasn't very good at such endeavors.

I joined every club in sight, the Cub Scouts, the Boy Scouts, the DeMolays, every organization available and imaginable with the exception, I suppose, of 4-H and Future Farmers of America, for by the time I began my joining habit we were out of the dairy, pork, and poultry business (but if I'd had a calf or a goat I'm sure I'd have joined those clubs, too). By age eight, I had begun with enthusiasm my lifelong career as a serial joiner and a chronic resigner of clubs. Was it the uniforms of the Scouts or the colorful satin robes of the DeMolays, those future Masons of Rogers? The rituals and mumbo-jumbo, the high-minded pledges and oaths, the sense of order and purpose, the pleasure that came from pleasing sober adult authority figures? Or did I simply want to show I could be a regular kid and do what kids are supposed to do, like camping out, or undertaking wood-burning projects, leather crafting, airplane model construction, knot tying, or, in the last resort, helping elderly ladies cross streets? But the gap between imagining that I *should* be doing those things and then actually beginning to get satisfaction from doing them turned out to be enormous. Very often in life, one finds, I've learned, some things—like Katie Couric as a CBS anchorwoman—are better as *ideas* than as realities.

Rogers offered a generous variety of resources to assist a kid in finding, then walking, the straight and narrow path to good citizenship. I embarked on my quest for wholesomeness with the Cub Scouts, joining Stuart Wilson, whose mom served as our den mother, and other kids with names long lost to memory as we met once a week for, as the organization's website continues to state, "citizenship training, character development, and personal fitness." Odd, this last goal: When would we ever be more fit than at age eight, accustomed as we were to a boy's life of vigorous, unremitting motion? We must have looked adorable in our blue uniforms and short-billed caps, the whole ensemble embellished with patches indicating the den and pack as well as our progress, or "development," as we mastered first one skill, then another, and still another. Looking back, I feel that the Scout movement's emphasis on regimentation and loyalty to the group, the importance placed on belonging, underscored as it was by our quasi-military uniforms, was a bit overdone when applied to boys barely dry from the womb. And I think I resisted even then all those methods employed to instill in us the constant need to compete and to demonstrate our superiority by the number of merit badges on our shirts. Ironically, and unintentionally, my half-hearted commitment to Cub Scouts was manifest for all to see. I wore only half the regular uniform. Pants were an expensive option, it seemed, and I was a Cub only from the waist up.

But in time I moved on to Boy Scouts where, as a member in good standing for a couple of years, I learned conclusively that I was not cut out for such high-minded enterprises. I knew boys among my contemporaries and, across the arc of my life, read and heard about the sons of friends for whom Scouting was a sublime and formative experience, and who later went on to become successful attorneys, physicians, politicians, and so forth. A noteworthy example is that of Donald Rumsfeld for whom a summer as a counselor at Philmont, the wilderness ranch in northeastern New Mexico, where the cream of the Boy Scouts from across the country assemble for backpacking, rock climbing, and other adventures, set him on a path to becoming one of America's tough-guy winners. But all that camaraderie, that rough and rugged life of the outdoors, and that fascination with the mastering of knot-tying, semaphore, Indian lore, first aid, and on and on, held no appeal for me. One of the benefits of Boy Scout membership was an automatic subscription to *Boy's Life* magazine, a bewilderingly upbeat publication filled with uplifting stories, ideas for projects or new knots to tie, and news about astounding kids all across the country who had constructed a thirty-inch reflecting telescope in their basement or had climbed the Matterhorn during their summer vacation.

But the perfect, Platonic ideal of Scouting the magazine put forth only made me think how lackluster and inadequate my feeble efforts were, and would continue to be. Above all, there was always that sense of being behind the curve, of knowing immediately that the club was and would always be dominated by the super achievers who formed the exclusive inner circles of the organization and monopolized the praise and attention of the adults in charge. There was and would always be someone who'd gotten there first and was more Catholic than the pope. Those were the ones who made you feel you could be at the club meetings yet invisible at the same time. And is any publication more intimidating than the official *Boy Scout Handbook*, with its thousand projects just waiting to be undertaken, even though you don't particularly want to undertake them?

In his novel, *Solar*, Ian McEwan describes a British scientist's uneasiness at feeling in over his head as he joins a younger group on an Arctic outing: "This was a long-forgotten experience from his school days, not only being late but feeling ignorant and incompetent and wretched, with everyone else mysteriously in the know, as though in league against him." Granted McEwan's character is a son of a bitch who deserves every disappointment life throws in his way, but his sense of being out of the loop, of not being a full-fledged part of the group, captures my own bitter feelings of lingering at the margins back then.

Oh, my Boy Scout years! Painful to recall. I can't bring to mind one moment of the Boy Scout meetings, or merit badge projects undertaken, or oaths, pledges, and vows memorized—but, God, those camping trips, and the hell that was that week at Boy Scout camp!

One fall evening I joined my home town troop as we gathered with scouts from nearby towns for a Jamboree, a campout on the shores of Lake Fayetteville, a place about as rugged as most people's back yards. But "rugged" wasn't the issue. After we'd set up our army surplus pup tents, dug the little drainage ditches around the tent's drip lines as per the Scout manual instructions, had our hot dogs, beans, and s'mores, we settled in for the requisite period of whispering and giggling before lights out and the minor thrill of sleeping with only that thin canvas separating us from the cosmos. We'd all slept outside before but under quilts stretched over saw horses, and then close to home, where we could always go inside, and usually did, when the ground grew damp beneath us or we heard a night sound we didn't like.

That night near Fayetteville we were stuck there until the next day. Very soon the ground grew hard and cold and I couldn't climb into a North Face, feather-light sleeping bag good for 20 below zero or rest on my oh-so-technical self-inflating camp mattress. I tucked one blanket under me and one over me. But that just wasn't getting it done that night, even though the temperature was probably only in the forties. On the verge of whimpering, I emptied my duffle bag and snuggled into it, but soon I was just as cold— no, colder—than ever. So sleep was out of the question that night, and my mind was filled with nostalgia for my bed back home and with sympathetic thoughts for Washington's troops at Valley Forge. I didn't venture onto a camp ground again for another 40 years, when, with my newly forged motto— "It's never too late to have a happy boyhood"—I began pitching my tent all over the American West.

That week at Boy Scout camp nearly did me in. The gathering of Scouts from all over the state was situated in Devil's Den State Park south of Fayetteville, a hellhole that got its name not only because of its dramatic geological formations—deep ravines, bottomless crevasses, steep sandstone cliffs—but also probably because it provided the sinners among us with a foreshadowing of the eternity that awaited us after death. Fitted out with dormitories and dining halls built by the CCC back in the years of the Great Depression, Devil's Den that week challenged little boys like me with the whole magilla: stinging and biting insects, record-breaking heat, plants with thorns that oozed toxins that could bring on life-threatening dermatological catastrophes, inedible food, bullies intent on making life miserable for pre-pubescents, and adult counselors who appeared to be suffering from a astonishing variety of mental illnesses. Job would have felt quite at home there that week at Devil's Den.

The troop leader in our barracks ended each day with ghost stories after lights out, tales embellished with vivid dramatizations full of shrieks and moans that left a few of us youngsters missing our mommies. He also took a sadistic pleasure in telling us about the black widow spiders that built their nests in the latrines where we planted our boyish butts each day, and that thrived, he added, on a diet of human flesh. As for those latrines, who knew such odors existed in nature? You could find your way to the john in the dark of night just by following your nose. Little wonder that some boys locked up their bowels and didn't open them again until safely home in the family john with the door safely locked.

In those six days, I endured numerous indignities. One of my barracks mates bent a wire clothes hanger back and forth until the metal broke and then pressed the hot ends into my left arm as if illustrating how calves were branded in the Old West. The two scars are still there today. And then, while sharpening a hatchet in the manner laid down as law in the *Boy Scout Handbook*—two wooden pegs are driven into the ground and the hatchet blade held in place and tilted upward as illustrated—the blade slipped and I wound up carving an hors' d'oeuvres-sized chunk of meat out of the palm of my left hand. I wore an enormous gauze bandage on the wound for the rest of the week. But the ultimate madness came when the camp's adult supervisors, men who probably were pillars of their communities back home, sober, hard-working, church-going, grown-up men, in their wisdom cooked up a game, a competition, an ordeal, call it what you will, to conclude the week's misery. Designed to involve the camp's full contingent of Scouts, the game pitted three evenly numbered groups, the "Indians," the "Outlaws," and "Wells Fargo," against one another. "Wells Fargo" was to start at one end of the park and transport a bag of "gold" (oranges) to the other end. The task of the "Outlaws" and the "Indians" was to steal the "gold" from the good guys then keep it from one another as well as the "Wells Fargo" guys, and the Scouts of all groups were allowed to use *any means* necessary. Whichever group wound up with the most "gold" won. As might be imagined many of the boys at the end of the ordeal were wearing torn and bloody clothing, since some of the action had taken place in a wild berry patch—this was Devil's Den, after all—and a few of the guys even wound up in the infirmary. Even at age twelve I had the good sense to hang around the sidelines and watch, with morbid satisfaction, as the older boys tore at one another in an orgy of violence. At least in this activity, promoted as the culminating event of the week, I came through unscathed.

If, as has been suggested often, the Boy Scouts is an organization calculated to brace a lad for later military service by acquainting him with the pride of wearing a uniform, the subordination of self to the group, the necessity of following directions and respecting authority, and the learning of leadership skills, those lessons were lost on me. Indeed, such experiences as the ones I endured at Devil's Den that summer when I was about twelve confirmed in me that I was not cut out for the rugged life. I didn't like the great out-of-doors when I was a kid unless it was of the tamed, domestic, and cultivated variety. Anything approaching wilderness scared me, frankly, and "big boys" constantly on the lookout for sissies to terrify and intimidate found a ready target in me. As a Boy Scout my performance fell far short of being "only okay." I was a wash-out.

But I was not through with joining. My attitude was: "Sign me up, where's the membership roll, add my name, that's two S's, please, and when's the next meeting?"

And, perhaps to satisfy my need for associations of the tamer, more civilized, type, I turned next to a club with which I was to have even a briefer brush with membership, the DeMolays, or more formally, DeMolay International. This youth club, a kind of ideological child of the Masons, met at the Masonic Youth Center. Memory fails me when I try to recall who or what might have gotten me interested in a young people's group so little related to my background and my family interests or connections. No man in my family had links with the Masons or aspired to. But then, that might have been a part of the attraction: Ben Lloyd was just doing his own thing.

The DeMolays were yet another of those character building, young-leaders-of-America, better-angels-of-our-nature youth organizations of the day, but it did all others one better by possessing a multi-layered mystique, a kind of aura of quasi-religious, even cultish secrecy and sanctimonious hauteur that functioned as powerful mind candy for boys in their early-to-mid teens. Not just any old body could be ushered into its inner circles; you had to be deemed "special." Behind the door past which only the "select" could go, the DeMolays promised wonderful rituals and an inside track on lore denied to non-members.

Named for Jacques DeMolay, a fourteenth-century French knight who served in the last days of the Crusades as the last Grand Master of the Knights Templar, the organization stood for noble purposes and ideals; I just never learned what they were, and to this day I still have no idea what its deeper, underlying principles are. (What did it offer a kid that he couldn't get at church or in the Scouts, or at home?) At fifteen, I didn't ask these silly questions; I just wanted to be accepted for membership, initiated, and be in on all that arcane mumbo-jumbo. During my initiation I learned all about how Jacques DeMolay, in all ways an admirable character, had led a group that had loads of money and, moreover, was owed tremendous sums by Philip IV of France. Not surprisingly at all, Philip had DeMolay and his confreres arrested and tortured into submitting false confessions, after which they were burned at the stake. (As Mel Brooks, playing Louis XIV, notes in his film *History of the World, Part I*, "It's great to be da' king.") In a melodramatic reenactment of this tragedy during initiation ceremonies, one of the town's more colorful characters, James Andrew Duty, dressed in colorful satin robes and armor of a sort, brought DeMolay's martyrdom vividly to life as he writhed and screamed through his performance. Unfortunately, his sugary southern accent probably brought to mind Margaret Mitchell's Atlanta more than Philip's fourteenth-century Paris.

So, I wonder now, did DeMolays stand for anti-monarchism, as in democracy, or did the tale suggest that you've got to hold onto your funds no matter how many slivers are jammed under your fingernails?

I didn't last long in DeMolay International either. As with the Scouts, I simply stopped going. But no worries, Demolays everywhere. Your secrets—the handshakes, the passwords, the chants, the different modes of bowing—are safe with me: I can't remember a single one of them.

9

THE FAMILY WHEELS

EVERY AUTUMN THE BIG EVENT in Rogers was the Homecoming parade, and I saw them from all angles: as a spectator, as a clarinetist trying to play with the rest of the band and keep in step at the same time, and as a suited-up, carnation-wearing escort for a "Maid of Honor" in the Queen's court.

We are not talking Rose Bowl parade dimensions or glamour here. Our parades were modest affairs featuring the high school band and an assortment of floats reflecting a widely varying range of imagination, available resources, and effort on the parts of their creators. The Future Farmers of America contribution consisted of a tractor pulling a hay wagon with members of the group—mainly boys, of course—dressed as Mountaineers decked out in bib overalls, straw hats, and fake beards and holding rifles or pitchforks. The guys tried to stay in character for these brief performances but they usually managed to display an endearing self-consciousness at the novelty of being on display and the silliness of it all. The Boy Scouts marched and the Cub Scouts were herded along under the watchful eyes of den mothers. The Lions Club could always be depended on to take part, with their members throwing candy to the kids and trading greetings or insults with pals watching from the sidewalks.

An unvarying feature of every one of these parades was the sparkling array of brand new cars, often convertibles, loaned by the town's automobile dealers, both to show their support of our team and, for good business reasons, to give many of the townspeople their first glimpse of the next year's new models. Each car was driven by its new owner or by some representative of the dealership, or perhaps one of the dealers themselves—our small-town celebrities. Dressed in their finest, key personalities in that year's festivities waved at the crowd from the back seats or riding atop the folded-back ragtops and greeted those assembled along the parade route like royalty. The gleaming paint jobs and all that glittering chrome lent an aura of transcendent luxury to these fleeting moments.

So the Homecoming parade was like an auto show as much as anything else; it was the new model year's debut. In the fifties the big car companies changed the look of their products every year without fail, sometimes drastically, sometimes only a little, but always just enough to send the signal that if you had a '53 Buick it would look suddenly outdated and just a little tired next to the spanking new '54 Buick. "Dynamic obsolescence" one corporation big-wig called this not-so-subtle maneuver to encourage you to trade in the old one. And some guys (although no one any of us knew) would buy a new car every year just to show that they were living the American Dream. One reliable source records that, on average, Americans traded up every two years!

The release of new car models took place in the fall, not in the willy-nilly fashion of today, and was always a grand occasion to look forward to, especially among us guys in our teens, who would often pay calls to dealer showrooms, sit behind the steering wheels, smell the new car bouquet, and pester the salesmen for some "literature" on the new Ford Fairlane 500, say, or the Oldsmobile Super 88, or—my favorite car moniker— the DeSoto Firedome. We all had a fascination with cars that was in our DNA, implanted there not by nature but by the car companies and their clever advertisers. And while all red-blooded American guys love cars, Southern boys have got the fever *bad*. How else to explain the South's mad devotion to stock car racing—America's number one spectator sport— and its star drivers, all of whom talk as if they're from Macon, Georgia, even if they're from New Jersey... or Italy, for that matter.

And if you grew up in the fifties you were witness to, and perhaps even an actual driving participant in probably the greatest, or at least the most bizarre, if not grotesque, age of American automobile design. After 1950 cars became longer, lower, wider, and roomier, and they were weighted down with so much chrome and detailing and accessories that, as my sister Patsy might say, "it just made your eyes *tired.*" Inspired by the aerodynamic forms and futuristic symbolism of airplanes and the rocket ships of science fiction, designers began fitting out cars with tailfins, nose cones, turbine-shaped doo-dads, and sexy wrap-around windshields that to today's sensibility appear to suggest a culture gone mad. And when autos weren't symbols for the power and excitement of flight they might take on weirdly anthropomorphic imagery. Buicks, for example, had grilles with sets of chrome "teeth" that made them seem like road monsters in search of prey, and they also featured circular vents on the front fenders that made you imagine an engine inside more appropriate for a B-29 than an automobile. (Fig. 26)

Fig. 26. A 1951 Buick

And those cars were big! In the late fifties I went on a trip to summer church camp with N.L. Hailey, Jr., whose father owned the town's Ford-Mercury dealership, in his mother's 1958 Mercury hard-top "Turnpike Cruiser," and that car (which had a rear window that could be lowered and raised electronically) seemed as big as somebody's basement recreation room. For your interest, I add that this model also had "Twin-Jet" air intakes above the windshield, "Seat-o-Matic" adjustments to insure your driving comfort, and—always —chrome, chrome, and more chrome. And not just chrome but accessories so varied, so showy, so ridiculous!

Detroit gilded the lily to a fare-thee-well because they knew Americans would love it. More was not just better, it was necessary. Of course you could have a two or even three-tone paint job, with the colors divided by a lightning slash of trim extending the length of the car. You could have white-wall tires and hub-caps with chrome spokes. You could order "fender skirts" to cover the rear wheel wells, and, most sublime of all extras, the "Continental kit," which was an extension of the rear bumper with a kind of metal case for your spare tire, a classy allusion to the origin of the form in Ford's famous Lincoln Continental of the 1930s. As for safety features, forget about it! Those cost money and no one wanted them anyway. It didn't matter that Americans were being smashed into hamburger by the tens of thousands on our highways in the fifties. Seatbelts, padded dashboards, and head restraints atop seats were years away from becoming standard features in cars, and airbags would have prompted nothing but laughs from Detroit's power elite.

More was better than less for a public that had been scrimping and doing without through the Great Depression and then World War II, when Detroit made tanks, trucks, and planes instead of cars. Americans were ready to let 'er rip. We'd won the damned war and now we deserved some means of expressing prosperity!

And there were so many different cars for a prosperous country to choose from. Ford turned out its reliable old brand in a broad range of prices and also produced Mercurys and Lincolns; then, mid-decade, it introduced its thrilling new Thunderbird. General Motors sold Chevrolets, Pontiacs, Oldsmobiles, Buicks, and Cadillacs and called its line-up the GMC "ladder of success": As you and your family became increasingly "well-to-do" you could move up the line until you could finally express your "financial maturity" with a Caddie Eldorado. GM brought out the first Corvettes, their sports car, in 1953. Chrysler, the stodgiest of the companies, relied on the repeat customer loyalty of a more staid and conservative clientele to buy its Plymouths, Dodges, DeSotos, and top-of-the-line Chryslers, and it didn't join the finny jet age until later in the decade. In those days before European and Japanese brands became such aggressive competitors, there were also Packards, Hudsons, Studebakers, and Nashs on the American roads, perhaps in not quite the numbers sold by the Big Three but certainly outnumbering such long-departed and little-missed brands as Willys, Crosley, and Kaiser-Frazer. Most of the "little guys" faded away because they couldn't afford the yearly model changes that consumers demanded.

On the eve of this fabulous decade, my family, however eager we might have been to join in this automotive extravaganza, was very much on the outside looking in. We didn't own a car of any kind, no tailfins, no "Hydra-Matic Drive," nothing. Hard as it might be to imagine, the Basshams didn't have a car from the time Momma and Dad got married until my brother Bill bought his first one in 1948. Dad didn't even know how to drive. For more than twenty years he had depended on family and co-workers or buses to get to jobs, to travel on family visits, or to do whatever shopping had to be done. Uncle Fred, who'd appear in our driveway over the years in a series of big, black sedans familiar to fans of those gangster movies of the thirties, could always be depended on for a ride to work or to set out on a visit back to Mountainburg. Emergency trips were taken in cabs, and grocery stores routinely made deliveries in those days. If we wanted to go downtown to see a show at the Victory Theater, we'd just walk the two-mile round trip. We did a *lot* of walking back then, as did most people.

We simply couldn't afford a car until Bill and Bud graduated from high school (in '47 and '48 respectively) and went to work as carpenters/laborers/ gofers with Dad and began to supplement the family income while saving a little for themselves. And when enough cash could be set aside, they joined the car craze like gangbusters. Dad, though, was hesitant to get behind the wheel. And because he waited until he was almost fifty before learning to drive, he never quite lost his amateur status. Nor did he ever develop a love affair with cars, as Bill, Bud, and I did. He always said, until we grew tired of listening to it, that cars represented only one thing to him: "TRA-A-A-A-N-S-por-ta-shun!" This credo, which my brothers could ignore because they were older and ready to begin their independent lives, was to become a curse to me, still stuck as I was under the family roof but ready to embark on what I hoped would become my adventurous, exciting years of teenage romance—for which I'd need a car with some *style*, preferably one of those sexy numbers manufactured by Detroit's Big Three.

Alas, it was not to be. For the remainder of the fifties that I was a driver, I shared a car with Dad and those cars had to do double duty, hauling tools by day and wheeling around a testosterone-ladened teenager by night.

Of all the men in our family Bill was the most adept and enthusiastic of car traders; he seemed to have been born with the skill, and he began honing his art almost from the first time he got into the driver's seat. Car trading in our family became quite the "man's thing" and Bill refined the practice with the passing of years; oddly women, among the Basshams and in general, do not take much interest in the pastime and don't seem to "get it." And if you wanted to deal, of course, you had to deal with dealers, and Rogers had some colorful ones. There was "Newt" Hailey, who had the Ford-Mercury dealership on South Second Street, surely one of the handsomest and most architecturally adventurous buildings in town.(Fig. 27)

Fig. 27. The Hailey Ford Dealership, early 1950s.
Courtesy of the Rogers Historical Museum, Rogers, Arkansas

And there was also Charlie Decker, who sold Buicks and Pontiacs at his dealership at South Second and Poplar, as well as Tom McNeil, whose home was one of those eye-catching mansions on West Walnut and who owned the Chevrolet-Oldsmobile franchise on South Second across the street from the Victory Theater. For used cars—and for most people in town that was the default option—you went to Vol Blevins, who had a lot at the corner of New Hope Road and Highway 71 that seemed to grow with time into a used car empire. Rogers also had a Chrysler-Plymouth business on the north side of town, but there was no place where you could buy a Cadillac. I don't recall that anyone in Rogers drove a Caddie, but if you wanted one, you had to go shopping in Springdale or Fayetteville.

Of all these wheelers and dealers in Rogers the only one I got to know was Joe Bill Hackler, who moved with his family from Mountain Home, Arkansas, in the early part of the decade. He was a handsome and very likeable man. He had a sweet and musical way of talking that, combined with an irresistible southern personality, could and did charm everyone, an attribute that was the sine qua non of the car business. Joe Bill with his wife Eloise opened their home to me when I got to know his sons Chris and Tim; we were neighbors for a brief time after Dad moved us all to South Fourth Street when I was in junior high. The Hackler home became a popular meeting place for a circle that congregated around Chris, who was an all-around all-American boy, good looking like his mom and dad and gifted both athletically and academically. Stuart Wilson, John Buckelew, Steve Pelphrey, John Dacus, and I were constantly at the Hackler home. Chris and I became best friends and I was his best man when he married after graduating from Hendrix College.

Joe Bill, now in his nineties and living in Fayetteville, was a veteran of the air war in Europe and had spent time as a prisoner of war after his plane was shot down over Greece. It was said that he bailed out of his plane when it was in a near vertical dive; he and the tail-gunner were the only survivors of the crew. Taken along by their captors as the Germans fled Greece, Joe Bill and the other American were rescued by a party of Yugoslav partisan fighters and turned over to U.S. authorities.

After arriving in Rogers and taking over the Chevrolet-Oldsmobile dealership, Joe Bill prospered and became one of the prominent men in town; he was active in both his church and the community, serving on the draft board, among other duties. It's impossible to think of Rogers in the 1950s and not recall Joe Bill. It was said that he would trade for virtually anything and that anything didn't necessarily have to be a used car. A boat and trailer, a diamond ring, a lot to build on— you name it—he wouldn't turn up his nose if the thing had some value.

My brother Bill had started saving for a car right out of high school and had some money set aside when the especially harsh winter of 1948-49 shut down all construction and made it difficult for anybody to work from January to March (if the temperature went below 20 degrees in Rogers it was deemed too cold for outdoor work). Bill's little nest egg ended up going toward groceries to feed his family, not wheels. When at last he was in a position to leap into the market, Bill bought a used 1940 Ford and paid about $250 more for it than it had cost new ten years earlier, so sought after were cars during those first five years after the war. At last he owned the object of his desire, despite the fact that *he* didn't know how to drive either. Cousin David came to his rescue and taught him the fundamentals, first in our big driveway and then on country back roads. After securing his driver's license (a document we routinely kept not in our wallets but in a plastic sleeve secured to the steering column) Bill embarked on an energetic campaign of wheeling and dealing over the next couple of years, a pastime that he went on to indulge in over a long lifetime, as he traded the coupe for a pick-up, the pick-up for a sedan, then back to a pick-up, etc, etc. He ordered his first "brand new" car, a Plymouth, just before being drafted into the Army one year into the Korean War. Then before leaving home for basic training in Indiana, Bill traded his precious new coupe for a truck that Dad could use in his absence.

It was in this pick-up that Dad set out to master the art of driving. Phyllis remembers him driving slowly back and forth in front of the barn, going through the gears, learning the distinction between clutch and brake, stalling the engine, and trying not to lose his temper. Finally behind the wheel at age fifty, Dad did his best to retain his dignity, and though trees were nicked and ditches entered, he at last gained at least a rudimentary knowledge of the art and science of driving. Perfection, however, was never to come within his reach. For the next thirty years or so—he stopped driving around age 80—a car ride with him could be a bracing adventure. He might pass a car on the highway and miss an oncoming one by a scant few feet, causing his passengers to hold their collective breath or suppress what might be their final, agonized cries, and then smugly say, "It might as well have been nine *miles.*" No garage door jambs were ever quite safe from one of his dramatic arrivals home, and even the rear wall of the garage took the occasional hammering. And the inevitable bouts of "car trouble" could send his bad temper, never far beneath the surface of his conscious life, into hitherto unvisited territories of white-hot anger. Dad took all unexpected and undeserved forms of car trouble personally, as if the car were a sentient creature plotting his destruction. It didn't help that cars then, whether new or used, but especially the ones that we owned, were not very good. Engines stalled, overheated, or failed to start in the first place. They rusted. They rattled. Their clocks and radios were crappy. I do not recall a car clock in anyone's car that actually worked. Tires were not much better, and were always seemingly bent on spoiling a family outing or one of my dates. Unlike today's tires, which can last for nearly the lifetime of the vehicle, tires in the fifties, or at least the ones we could afford, had paper-thin walls and inner tubes that were not quite up to the challenge of our rocky, treacherous Arkansas roads.

(In the 1920's Arkansas government officials, in an admirable effort to bring our state into the twentieth century, sold bonds to finance a major campaign to pave the state's rocky gravel roads and to build new ones, all in an effort to promote trade and tourism. Then, Arkansas got caught by a triple whammy. The 1927 Mississippi flood covered much of the eastern part of the state, wiping out many of the new highways and destroying that year's cotton crop, a key source of the state's trade and revenue base. Then, two years later, the Great Depression followed by a drought that ruined still another year's cotton put our state's finances in the dumper, and Arkansas could not make its bond payments. At one point, the state's general fund in the thirties showed a balance of $4.62. It was not a total disaster, though— bondholders agreed to a restructuring of the debt and payments did resume, somehow. But no new highway bond issues were forthcoming from Little Rock until 1949, meaning that no new roads were paved for twenty years.)

Nor did our cars in those days get good gas mileage. Not that anyone seemed to care. Nobody talked about gas mileage or gas shortages or gas anything in the fifties. We produced all the oil we needed right here in America and of course there was an unlimited supply of it. Gas cost about a quarter a gallon; we were splurging when we'd pull into a filling station (nobody pumped their own) and say, "Give us a dollar's worth"

On balance automobiles were a greater source of worry than pleasure. Rare was the out-of-town trip that didn't get interrupted by one damned car or tire failure or another and sometimes a combination of both. Once, to cite a vivid example, Dad was returning from a construction project near Van Buren and, while traversing the uphill, hairpin curves of Highway 71 over the Boston Mountains, had the hood he had not fastened down quite securely come flapping up and bending back like a sail over the windshield. Somehow he managed to pull over and deal with the problem before plunging down the side of a mountain.

So what was a typical fifties automobile, the kind of car the Bassham family could afford to put in its driveway, likely to be? Put another way, what was it like to drive one of those beauties, one like say, the '52 Plymouth

"Cranbrook" that Bill bought sometime during the early sixties and was kind enough to let me borrow one summer? Putting it as nicely as I can, they were archaic.

Today we are pampered and spoiled by cars loaded with devices and amenities that were once luxuries but are now standard issue. We have power-everything: door locks, windows, brakes, steering. Loading us up with this stuff is symptomatic of a kind of automotive arms race from which no manufacturer can opt out. Besides, we have come to feel we deserve all these luxuries that have overnight become necessities.We shut trunk lids and rear van doors with the push of a button, and we can get information that we didn't know we needed—miles per gallon, miles to an empty tank, tire pressure—by glancing at our dashboard. You can even get "rain-sensing" windshields, as if you might not recognize rain if you saw it!

An inexpensive car in the fifties was unlikely to have power anything. (A few years back for fun I took an early VW Beatle for a spin and found that steering and braking required a surprisingly rigorous total-body workout. It was like being in one of those nightmares in which you push buttons, turn switches, and press hard on pedals and nothing works.) Nor did cars come equipped with directional turning lights. In temperate months you stuck your left arm out the window and signaled your intentions, or maybe you didn't and just kept the guy in back of you in the dark. Front and back seats in sedans were like loveseats, and often served as such. They were upholstered either in a soft, plushy covering resembling in both color and texture a mouses's fur, or in a sort of woven, slick "fabric"stuff that seemed to be composed of the same chemical compound from which linoleum is made.

Radios brought in only AM stations if they received anything at all, even if your car was equipped with an antenna as tall as a ship's mast (but handy for hanging a wet bathing suit on in summertime). Air conditioning might be fantasized about but was a rarity because of its cost. The conventional wisdom said that a moving car created its own breeze, a truism that applied in pleasant weather but lost considerable clout when it was 95 humid degrees outside. Absent in almost all cars was automatic transmission, so most of us learned to drive with three-speed manual transmission, and could lay down a handsome strip of rubber on the road by revving the engine then popping the clutch. I still feel, vaguely, that if you're not using manual transmission you're not really driving the car, you're just pointing it. And "straight shift" was not yet "four in the floor," because the gear shift handle was mounted on the steering column. And you wouldn't find a headlight dimmer switch opposite the gear shift, either; to dim the lights you pressed a little metal button on the floor with your left foot. With your right foot you operated the brake and the excelerator (no cruise control) which, for reasons lost to history, my siblings called the "foot-feet," an automotive term of their own invention.

And over time those dear old cars' interiors acquired a distinctive, evocative aroma, vaguely organic in character, that arose perhaps from the results of too much rain sweeping through open windows, or from carelessly consumed food, or from the osmotic action of fuels and lubricants adding their own bouquet, or simply from the contact of human bodies over the car's history. It was an odor rather like what one encounters in a seldom-visited attic at an elderly aunt's home. I actually kind of miss it.

I don't remember very much about our earliest cars, but I do recall fondly the two spiffy Studebakers we drove in the mid 1950s. The first was a '51 two-door coupe—the "Starlight Coupe," if you please— of a dull green hue and with a rocket-shaped front end and wrap-around rear windows that resembled the cockpit, in reverse, of a B-17 Flying Fortress. (Fig. 28) Strange is the word that best describes it. In short, it was an automobile that, like the early Saabs—another of my favorites!—was so profoundly ugly that only its designers and owners could love it. Not that Studebaker didn't turn out some stunning cars. In fact, Studebakers of that era still have a cult following, and deservedly so. That brand was truly innovative one in those days. That '51 still holds a place dear in my heart, for it was the car I learned to drive in— even if "driving" then meant putting it in "D," aiming the car in the appropriate direction, and stepping on the gas. Film critic Roger Ebert devotes an entire chapter in his memoir, *Life Itself,* to his love affair with Studebakers of the fifties. He recalls that all he knew about the Studebaker was "that kids joked about how they looked like they were going in both directions at once." He also points out that the 1953 Starliner was designed by the great Raymond Loewy and earned the distinction of being recognized as a work of art by the Museum of Modern Art. So there— my taste in automobiles validated!

Fig. 28. A 1951 Studebaker

About the time I was learning to drive that dashing, rocket-ship of a Studebaker I leaped into the brisk trade in automobiles myself. While working at the Rexall Drugs, my boss, Fred Applegate, hinted heavily that maybe, just maybe, he would be willing to let go of his very spiffy little 1930 Chevrolet coupe, a darling, deep blue number that he was often seen tooling around town in; indeed, it seemed at the time inseparable from the druggist's own somewhat antique look and style. (Fig. 29) My head swam when I thought of owning not just my first car but a cute, historic relic at that. Why, maybe it could be featured in a Homecoming parade. Did I care that its little engine rattled ominously, that its gearbox scrunched when I went from first to second, that the whole contraption failed to meet the safety codes, however ludicrously lax such guidelines were then, or that it, um, stank inside? A hundred times No. But Applegate wanted $50 for this prize, and this at a time I could not for the life of me imagine ever having as much as $50, and there were few prospects of acquiring it. When you have next to nothing, 50 bucks seems as unattainable as 5,000.

But I did have twenty-five dollars socked away in one of the town's savings and loan banks. So I appealed for help to my brother Bill, who was always game to haggle when it came to car-trading. Together we pooled our resources and soon owned half-shares in the town's only '30 Chevy. (The people at the savings and loan were not happy when I arrived one Monday morning to withdraw the $25 I'd deposited on the previous Friday.)

Fig. 29. A 1930 Chevrolet Coupe

But only a matter of weeks after we'd closed the deal that little coupe moaned, groaned and gave out an ominous death rattle, and refused thereafter to respond to any mechanic's efforts to revive it. Did Applegate know something about that wreck he'd sold us that we didn't? Somehow Bill succeeded in unloading the car onto the next gullible buyer who fell in love with it, though my 25 bucks were gone, gone, gone.

Our next Studey was a spiffy '55 two-toned (blue and white), four-door sedan that, by a hair, qualified as "cool" and worthy of use to squire around the girls I was beginning to date during my sophomore year. And it was that very sedate family car that I pushed to 90 miles an hour one summer night on the two-lane highway between Rogers and Bentonville just to see what 90 miles an hour felt like. Had I blown an engine or a tire that night, I would probably not be remembering now how stupid I was then. But that Studebaker was more exciting, really, not when it was moving but when it was parked, especially when I parked it strategically on a back road with one of the girls I was fortunate to be dating during my romantic high school years. (And I should point out that there were considerably more unpaved back roads then that you'll find around Rogers today.) In general, the American family car has served many purposes, and one of them has been to function as a portable parlor far out of earshot and view of prying parents. And since front seats were more like sitting room sofas they were much better suited to the intimate goings-on of us teenagers than today's bucket seats and cumbersome gear shifts and other interfering appointments that separate boy and girl today.

A couple of examples illustrate the key role of the automobile as I set out on my path to master the art of love:

One rainy Saturday night after a movie I drove my date (no names, please) to a lonely country road west of town where we pulled over to the side, parked, turned off the lights and, for the next half hour or so, "necked," a form of rather chaste love-making that went just so far and no further, because good church-going boys and girls didn't do "it." (Or, at least, we didn't.) After reaching that wordlessly agreed on point when it was time to leave and call it a night, I started the Studebaker, put it in "D," gave it some gas, and found that we were hopelessly stuck in the ditch. After several tries at back-and-forthing I gave up and, feeling both embarrassed and slightly panicked, got out of the car and walked to a nearby farmhouse whose lights we could see from about a half mile off. I thought I could call a friend to help. God forbid I should try to get my Dad out on a night like this. When I knocked on the farmhouse door, a middle-aged man answered. and I began to tell him of my plight and to ask him if I could use his phone, but I before I finished a sentence he turned away, saying, "Let me just get my coat." Outside, he headed for the barn and, over his shoulder, directed me back to the car and said he'd be there in a minute. Within five minutes our savior was driving up on his tractor. He hooked a chain to the front of our car and, presto, pulled us out of the ditch. I burbled over with thanks and offered him something for his trouble, which he declined. I asked him how he had diagnosed our situation so quickly. "Sonny," he said, "you may not believe me but I do this all the time in bad weather, winter or summer. You kids certainly must love the view from this road."

On another big date I asked Bill if I could use his car. Bill, who was working at the time at the big Munsingwear plant at the end of South Fourth Street, reluctantly went along with this idea but stipulated that I had to pick the car up at the plant and return it before he finished the second shift at 11:00 that night. That agreed on, I got the car, took my date –same girl— to a movie or a party, and then we both headed out in search of still another deserted country road for more smooching and up-to-a-point-but-no-further groping in the dark. When I brought the car back to the Munsingwear lot and went to meet Bill at his knitting machine to return the keys, he took one look at me and laughed. "Good God!" he said, "Get the hell out of here. Go look at your face!" My curiosity aroused (my second arousal that evening), I headed for the closest men's room to look in the mirror and saw that, "Good God!" indeed, the lower half of my face was completely covered with a red, glossy pigment that resembled nothing so much as a young lady's lipstick. Ah, youth! Where hast thou flown?

I had borrowed Bill's car because, not long before the night of the red lipstick incident, a colossal hammer blow had landed squarely on the crucial transportation segment of my teenage love life: Dad, without so much as a whisper to anyone of his plans, had one summer Saturday taken "my" beloved Studebaker downtown and returned in a brand-new, sickly green Ford pickup. I was furious. My mother was not happy either, but it was a done deal and Dad didn't give a damn what anyone thought of it. Since, by circumstances, we were limited to one vehicle it made perfectly good sense that that car should be a pickup truck that Dad could haul around the tools and materials necessary for his work, the work that paid the rent and put food on our table. But teenagers don't think that way. I couldn't and didn't want to see the big picture. I took it personally. How could he do this to *me*? Why, at the very least, hadn't he sat down with us to tell us of his plans the way Robert Young, the perfect dad on *Father Knows Best*, would have done, calmly explaining all the good reasons why a pickup in the building trade made so much more sense than a four-door Studebaker? Of course I can see the logic of his decision today, but it was the manner in which he sprang the thing on us that rankled: He was the head of the family, he was the Man, and real men didn't hold namby-pamby consultations with women and teen-age boys on such major decisions as buying a car. This event became the cause of an ugly stand-off between the two of us, and as my anger mounted Dad settled into a profound, sulking anger of his own. I recall one evening after for the hundredth time I'd registered my fury and frustration at what I considered his selfishness and his stubbornness, I ran out to the garage, picked up the first object that came to hand, and hurled it with all my strength at the hated truck.

Today, after having experienced many of the same adventures raising teen-agers of my own, I can grasp what should have been obvious to me then: that any Rogers girl who would have been interested in going out with me wouldn't have cared whether I drove a Studebaker sedan or a pickup truck.

(Granted they might have been swayed by a Corvette.) And, truth to tell, some good times were had in that pickup. One winter week-end, for example, after Rogers had been covered by a soggy snowfall that made for ideal, hard-packed snowballs, a bunch of us—John Buckelew, Chris Hackler, John Dacus, and I—loaded a supply of said missiles into the back of Dad's pick-up, drove around town, and let fly at acquaintances and perfect strangers equally.

And, yes, girlfriends saw the inside of that truck's cab. On another embarrassing occasion I ran out of gas one night and had to ask the girl to stay with the truck while I walked to the nearest gas station, where, to make matters worse, the attendant told me it was policy there to require some deposit to secure the use of the borrowed gas can. So back to the truck I went, where luckily I found one of Dad's electric Skil saws in the back, which I then lugged back to the filling station.

Do the girls involved in these little episodes remember them at all? Probably not, but I dearly hope so.

10

GLUED TO THE TUBE

HAVING JOINED, HOWEVER TARDILY AND modestly, the rest of the American motoring public, by about 1953 we Basshams were eager to make still another momentous leap into modernity: buying our first television set. Everybody my age or older can remember with the mild sense of gravity we associate with signal events in our lives the occasion when that first television appeared in our living room. For years we had heard of television in the abstract, then it was viewed wistfully through shop windows, or marveled at in the living rooms of the town's first privileged owners. If you knew someone whose parents actually had a set you'd beg to be invited over for a few minutes of envious gawking and gaping.

People still talk with amusement of how they became instantly popular in the neighborhood after their parents purchased their first set. Months before Dad made his big purchase, in fact, he had been a frequent guest on Friday nights at the home of a neighbor near South Thirteenth Street who had issued a standing invitation for Dad to come over to watch the *Friday Night Fights*, sponsored by Pabst Blue Ribbon Beer and Gillette, maker of razor blades ("To look sharp...!") Sometimes I would tag along, although I would not be offered a beer, since I was underage and hadn't yet developed a taste for the stuff; beer then tasted to me as if a 1943 zinc penny had dissolved in my mouth. But Dad would partake, and it may in fact have been on one of those occasions that he first expressed his fondness for beer, particularly when he drank one when he was "real hungry," as he put it. Of course he would have liked beer then! After all, a beer on an empty stomach gives you ever so much better a buzz.

But now there was no need to traipse over to a neighbor's on Friday nights. *We owned a TV!* We had arrived! And if buying a TV was a way of demonstrating that you'd arrived, then tens of thousands of Americans began arriving every day. Television sets sold like proverbial hotcakes throughout the 1950s, and by 1960 nearly everyone in the country had one, and many had two of the things. The medium was arguably the fastest and most culturally transforming technological development of all time, surely the hottest, must-have item before the mobile phone. Sales of sets made owners of appliance stores rich in a matter of months.

(One of my favorite stories about the early days of television is that of the film actor Victor Mature, the pudgy, sleepy-eyed matinee idol who seemed to appear in every biblical epic Hollywood cranked out in the early fifties. You can see him on TV around every Easter season when the networks dust off and air such inspiring oldies as *The Robe* and *Demetrius and the Gladiator.* Never fond of the movie business, Mature took early retirement from pictures to devote himself to golf, a game to which he was addicted. In order to support his habit Mature opened several electronic stores in the Los Angeles area and sold enough TV sets to become a rich man, or perhaps simply a richer man. And when he was rejected for membership in a country club because the club had a firm policy of excluding actors, Mature, to his everlasting credit, is said to have remarked, "Hell, I'm no actor, and I've got 62 movies to prove it.")

Dad probably bought our first television, a "Hollywood blond" console, that was more like a piece of furniture than an electric appliance, from his boss, Cedric Watson, the building contractor and co-owner of Rogers Radio and Electric downtown on Walnut Street. Cedric may have given Dad a deal, but probably not; the man was famously tight-fisted (one Christmas Dad's bonus from Cedric was a flashlight, *sans* batteries). And so, like most such expensive additions to our home—whether a car, a refrigerator, a new sofa—we bought it "on time." I don't recall whether our set was equipped with a 19- or a 21-inch screen, but I clearly remember that all we saw on that screen, at least at first, was what we then termed "snow." Reception was terrible. It was what one of my daughters wittily described recently, speaking of her own set, as "crap-definition" TV. Not only snow but the infuriating scrolling of the picture ever upward, separated by thick black lines that resembled film being slowly wound forward, drove us viewers, especially our excitable *pater familias,* batty. Television sets had a dial to deal with this problem, the "vertical hold" thingy. You have to love it: instead of eliminating this failing, they give you a dial to try to solve it yourself!

When you purchased a television you did so on a hope and a prayer: Will I be able to watch anything on the damned thing? With the set itself you had to buy all the other pricey and necessary accoutrements to go with it. At the outset that involved a stationary roof antenna, which would be pointed, we hoped, in the general direction of the town or city where the nearest broadcasting station was located. Our closest stations were in Tulsa, some 125 miles to the west; in Pittsburg, Kansas, KOAM-TV (for Oklahoma, Arkansas, and Missouri) more or less 80 miles to the northwest) and in Springfield, Missouri, about 100 miles to the northeast. A bit later, because we were greedy and wanted to be able to tune in to all these stations, Dad installed a new antenna equipped with a little electric motor with which you could turn the antenna to all points of the compass by using controls mounted in a little plastic box kept on top of the console. So, if we wanted to watch ABC instead of CBS, we'd hit the dial atop our set and —drone, drone, drone (you could hear the little motor at work on the roof)—bring the antenna around and the picture would coalesce in fuzzy black and white, kind of like an image called up in your head. And if the picture was lousy, or if it started its insane rolling over routine, there would be much "god-damning" of this mixed in with a lot of "son-of-a-bitching" of that, because somebody, somewhere had to be responsible for our television being so totally awful.

But when, miracle of miracles, the weather was just so and all the planets were perfectly aligned and our television set conjured up nothing but the sharpest picture of the most perfectly balanced contrast and horizontal stability, well…there wasn't much to watch. Just like television programming in 2011, when we have not three fuzzy channels but a thousand, all in crisp, high definition color. In fact, if the early fifties constituted the Golden Age of Television, what, one imagines, could a Zinc Age of Television or a Manganese Age have been like?

But no matter how awful the offerings were in *TV Guide*, the little program guide found on top of everyone's set, we watched the stuff anyway, because those black-and-white pictures flickering on the screens of our Zenith's, or Admirals, or RCA Victors were a little like watching water being turned into wine: It was miraculous. We watched just to see the pictures change, and we watched from sun-up to "signing off" time, when stations bade us farewell for that day's round of broadcasting at midnight or 1:00 a.m. by playing an ancient film of Old Glory waving to the tune of the *Star Spangled Banner* followed by a "test pattern" to which we were to adjust our pictures, much as the first-chair violinist tunes the rest of the orchestra. *And we watched that too!* In those Paleolithic days of television's beginnings the local stations as well as the national networks seemed to be saying, "That's enough television for one day. Now go to bed like the sensible, hard-working, salt-of-the-earth Americans that you are."

Our TV set needed the rest as well, for we kept it on ceaselessly not just because it was a marvel but also because it added another dimension to our hum-drum lives there in the middle of the Ozarks. It connected us to a faster, more interesting, funnier, more stylish, more sophisticated world somewhere vaguely over the horizon. We left it on just as we'd always left our radios on. And when we were in the same room, we couldn't *not* watch the thing. It blared and flickered throughout the day and was left on whether anyone was watching it or not; it remained a living presence no matter who might have something important to say or whether a guest might drop by. If Jesus Christ Himself had knocked at our door and asked if He might have a word with us for a few moments, Dad would have invited Him in, asked him to sit, then asked "Want some ice tea?" all the while continuing to watch Jackie Gleason at least until the commercial break, when at last he could give our Savior his attention.

With no remote control wand with which to surf through the channels or turn down the sound Dad would stay seated comfortably in his chair after a long day's work and use me as his remote. "Ben Lloyd, get *Jack Benny* on," he'd say. Then clunk, clunk, clunk the channel dial would go, and, if necessary, our little aerial motor would hum away to point us to Tulsa or wherever. And the moment the 10:00 local news program ended, he'd command, "Boy, turn it off and blow these lights out." It was time to go to bed, or it was time for *him* to go to bed. In our family Dad was regarded, and not always fondly, as a graduate of the Joseph Stalin School of Communications Control and Oversight.

I must have gotten my fill of TV during the decades between the 1950s and around 2000 because I rarely watch network programming today and cannot abide commercials, which I mute with the remote, an ingenious device that I, the son of my father, never willingly cede to another person. And a television set left on in an empty room sends me around the bend; it's not the waste of electricity that bothers me, it's that it drives me back to my boyhood when the idiot box so dominated the Bassham family living room.

It would be tedious beyond all measure of good taste to list everything we watched, because we watched everything. So here's a condensed laundry list by category, and in no particular order of preference or importance, accompanied by my random comments, and the whole lot of it much better in nostalgic hindsight that it was in the original viewing.

Sports.

Today, for a price, you can get about a dozen ESPN channels and even more networks that specialize in tennis, golf, Big Ten football, NASCAR racing, etc. But in TV's infancy there were only three networks and they didn't do much with sports programming. College football wasn't much of a presence on television then, and professional football didn't begin to get much coverage until the 1960s. Quaintly, the NFL and NBA opted not to broadcast a lot of games because both leagues feared that free television programming would hurt ticket sales at the gates. For baseball you watched the *Game of the Week*, though any game that didn't showcase our heroes, the St. Louis Cardinals, wasn't that big an attraction. Play-by-play man Dizzy Dean, the former Cardinals pitcher, who, with his sidekick Peewee Reese, once shortstop for the old Brooklyn Dodgers, made for irresistible entertainment. Dizzy had about an eighth grade education and his color commentary on games demonstrated week after week his merry, guileless fracturing of the English language. When runners were on base and the batter hit a foul ball into the stands Dizzy would say, "And the runners return to their respectable bases." A listener once scolded him for his repeated use of the word "ain't" because she felt it set a poor example for the country's youth. Dizzy replied: "A lot of people who don't say 'ain't' ain't eatin'."

Professional basketball games were televised but were not the mass entertainment spectacle of today. The games featured an enormous amount of fancy dribbling, passing, and long-range, two-handed "set shots" by a lot of white guys like Bob Cousy and Bill Sharman in short-shorts, and they were entertaining and edifying if you wanted, as I did, to learn how to make a hook shot from the top of the key. A minority in fifties pro basketball was a

Jewish guy named Dolph Schayes of the Syracuse Nationals. Blacks wouldn't begin to dominate the game for another couple of generations later. And TV didn't need slo-mo in those days since the action, typified by a big guy named George Mikan, the 6-foot 10-inch center of the Minneapolis Lakers, was *played* in slow motion.

Of course we watched professional wrestling— "rasslin'—which was a staple of television then as it is now (and just as dumb). The hours we spent in front of the tube watching showmen like Gorgeous George may well have caused permanent brain damage and are perhaps why I have such a rotten memory for names now. But wrestling worked on early TV because it was confined to a compact ring that could be taken in by one camera, not spread out over several acres like baseball and football games. The same was true of boxing, the truly classic sport of the fifties because it was the time when so many great prizefighters were at the top of their game. Floyd Patterson, Rocky Marciano, Ezzard Charles, Sugar Ray Robinson, Jersey Joe Walcott, Archie Moore on "free" TV! It was a brutal yet beautiful sport, perhaps the best thing on television.

Variety Shows.

A true dinosaur of television's Jurassic era, these hour-long mish-mashes of song, dance, stand-up comedy, juggling, dog acts, etc., hosted by pop singers like Nat "King" Cole and Perry Como, or other celebrities, were once watched nearly every night in living rooms across America. The most popular were Milton Berle's *NBC Texaco Star Theater* and the wacky *Your Show of Shows*, which featured Sid Caesar, Imogene Coca, Carl Reiner, and other comedians, with material by a team of writers that included Mel Brooks. These shows were essentially televised vaudeville, broadcast live and full of over-the-top skits, slapstick humor, and, in Uncle Miltie's case, outlandish costumes. Ernie Kovac's show was a hit among the guys in my circle, but was too strange for the Bassham household, so I rarely had the chance to watch his creative antics. Besides, if his show happened to be on opposite something like the *Lawrence Welk Show* there was no chance of my dialing it up.

One program we never missed on Sunday nights was *The Ed Sullivan Show*, a variety hour that enjoyed a very long run (1948-1971) largely because the host, a former newspaper gossip columnist, always offered up an imaginative smorgasbord of acts so extensive that there was bound to be something amusing for everyone. An aria by Metropolitan Opera star Lawrence Tibbett might be followed by the ventriloquist Señor Wences. And the stiff Ed Sullivan, who possessed no apparent gift of gab or personality, was unintentionally entertaining; he had all the charisma of a corpse bound up in a straight-jacket. Comedians savaged him with their impersonations. In addition to the show's rather surreal line-up—juggling followed by ballet followed by Elvis Presley—Sullivan's occasional ad libs were notorious. One night on a program in the middle of July, we watched as Sullivan became befuddled when he was faced with a minute of air-time to fill at the end of the hour. First he thanked the audience for coming, then he cautioned them to drive home carefully—from mid-town Manhattan, no less—after they'd left the theater. Then, probably in response to frantic hand signals from the show's director, he searched his mind and then came up with, "And, please, have a very, *very* Merry Christmas!"

Another of our favorite variety shows was the long-running *Hit Parade* (actually, *Your Hit Parade*, but we never called it that) which was sponsored by Lucky Strikes—in the days when tobacco companies advertised on TV—and ran every Saturday night for what seemed an eternity. This show featured the vocalists Snooky Lanson, Dorothy Collins, and Gisele MacKenzie singing that week's top pop tunes, and it always concluded with a rendition of that week's No. 1 hit on the "charts." It was fun to see what this sort of white bread, middlebrow cast would do with numbers made popular by such hotter stars as Buddy Holly ("That'll Be the Day") or Kaye Starr ("Wheel of Fortune"), or with the insane novelty numbers like "How Much Is That Doggy in the Window," (Patti Page) "Hot Diggity, Dog Diggity, Boom, What You Do to Me," (Perry Como, regrettably) and "Come On'a My House" (Rosemary Clooney). Around 1954 a ditty called "This Ol' House" (also by Rosemary Clooney) a nostalgic paean to the singer's homestead topped the charts for months and we all waited breathlessly each week to see how the *Hit Parade* people, after reaching the bottom of their bag of tricks, would stage and style its presentation yet again for what they probably hoped would the last time.

I suppose the hugely popular shows headlined by Jack Benny and Bob Hope could be called variety shows, too. Essentially televised versions of their long-running radio programs, their shows were also made up of comedy routines, songs, and skits. We were crazy about Jack Benny and his sidekicks, the butler and chauffeur Rochester, Irish tenor Dennis Day, Benny's real-life wife Mary Livingstone, band leader Phil Harris, and accent master Mel Blanc. Blanc's recurring character, Sy the Mexican, as well as the gravel-voiced Rochester would not see the light of day in our present-day politically correct world. Yet, I don't think there's a show on television today that's as funny and lovable as that one.

News and Documentaries.

The networks' daily reporting of news in the early years of television was minimal, and its presentation—always by a handsome, middle-aged "talking head" who had had at least a smidgen of journalistic experience in his background—could only be described as quaint, and very low-tech. National news reports were limited to fifteen minutes and that seemed like a long time when all you saw and heard was a guy reading from a script. Because videotape was long in coming, visuals were provided by still photographs and film, hence the old cliché "film at eleven." Douglas Edwards was the "newsman" on CBS (Walter Cronkite took over the duties in 1961) and John Cameron Swayze, armed with his persuasively convincing name, did the job for NBC. I am still amazed when I recall how, without a trace of embarrassment or irony, Swayze seamlessly segued from reporting the latest disasters or international incidences to doing the commercials, and doing them live. He simply stood up from his desk and walked to the requisite props located nearby on the set. Swayze amused us (and probably himself) with his ads for Timex watches, which he would subject to imaginatively conceived trials and abuses, once strapping a watch to the propeller of an outboard motor mounted on a glass tank and then giving the starter cord a yank. After five seconds or so he'd stop the engine, retrieve the watch and show us that, as he memorably put it, "Timex takes a licking and keeps on ticking!" Thus your watch would be okay if you happened to leave it on your motorboat's propeller.

By comparison, local news shows were rather amateurish productions. The anchors, weather forecasters, and sports reporters were regular guys who probably also sold ad time during a normal workday. A full head of hair and great looks were not required if you bore at least some resemblance to the members of the local Rotary club. Sets lacked the pizzazz of today's glossy and electrified ensembles. The news set for a local station I watched in Madison,

Wisconsin, around 1964, for example, was backed by a huge map of the state cut out of a sheet of plywood that was left unpainted so that the homely grain of the wood could shine forth.

In the fifties the news departments of the big three networks had sufficient clout and prestige to insist on independence from the entertainment sides of their companies, and they took themselves very seriously. This was especially true of CBS, whose chief personalities—Edward R. Murrow, Robert Trout, Charles Collinwood, Eric Sevareid and Walter Cronkite—possessed an aura of credibility and gravitas fairly earned as radio reporters during World War II in Europe. These craggy, balding, chain-smoking professionals had an authenticity all too lacking in today's telegenic, blow-dried, male news readers and former beauty queens.("Beauty queens" doesn't quite describe the women on Fox News, most of whom look as if they were hired for the day from an escort service.) I had little interest in Murrow's famous *See It Now* and *Person to Person* programs (celebrated in George Clooney's film *Good Night and Good Luck*), but I hung on Uncle Walter's every word for years from the time he hosted a hokey docudrama called *You Are There*, in which costumed actors recreated key moments in history while occasionally stepping aside to be "interviewed" by Cronkite.

There weren't many documentaries broadcast in the fifties but the best of what we did see (and it still holds up) was *Victory at Sea*, a multi-part, extensive history of the naval battles of WW II in both the Atlantic and Pacific theaters that aired on Sunday afternoons, a time slot that came to be known as the "cultural ghetto." The series was the ancestor of today's constant re-hashings of the war by the History Channel or, as some have dubbed it, the Hitler Channel. But *Victory at Sea* was in a class by itself, due largely to the stirring musical score by Richard Rodgers. But as a kid, it was the scratched, black-and-white footage of kamikaze attacks and U-boat sinkings that I found riveting.

Westerns.

Another casualty of America's constantly changing tastes and steady demands for the next new thing, westerns are not seen at all on the tube anymore. There were so many of them broadcast in the 1950s into the 1960s that the American public probably became sated and have not asked for any more.

The granddaddies of TV westerns, aside from the earliest silent movies, were *Hopalong Cassidy*, starring William Boyd, and *The Lone Ranger*, both of which I eagerly tuned in to see. *Gunsmoke*, a Saturday night must-see, was by far the most popular and stayed on the air for twenty years (1955-75). The long list of other westerns includes *Wagon Train*, featuring the veteran of John Ford films, Ward Bond, *Have Gun-Will Travel*, a highly stylized, "modern" western with Richard Boone, and *The Rifleman*, with former baseball and basketball star Chuck Connors. Our favorite western by far was *Maverick*, which aired on Sunday evenings and always attracted Uncle Fred and Aunt Ethel to our living room, the reception east of the White River not being up to our relatives' exacting standards for this important weekly event. The sly and ironic tone of this show, starring a very young James Garner and Roger Moore in his pre-James Bond days, was enjoyed enormously by Dad and his brother, whom I can still picture leaning back on our sofa, smoking one or more of his hand-rolled Prince Albert cigarettes ("Roll your own with thrifty 'A' and take a puff or two") and laughing at Maverick's uncanny knack for outwitting some black-hatted bad guy once again.

Game Shows.

There were two types of game shows: the serious, dramatic, suspenseful question-and-answer formats, wherein single or pairs of contestants attempted to win big bucks by answering increasingly difficult questions (*Twenty-One* and *The 64,000 Question*), and silly shows in which celebrity-studded panels would with witty asides (one hoped) and self-regarding, snobbish displays of sophistication, try to guess the identity or occupation of mystery guests (*Masquerade Party* and *What's My Line*). The first type of show ran for many years but ultimately lost favor when it was discovered that *Twenty-One* was rigged: Contestants were given the answers to questions in advance and told when to lose. The mystery guest shows had incredible staying power; *What's My Line* ran for seventeen years because, I suppose, we loved watching noted Manhattan publisher Bennett Cerf, actress and society somebody Arlene Francis, and columnist Dorothy Kilgallen be their darling, amusing selves.

You Bet Your Life didn't fit neatly into either game show category since it was essentially just a platform for Groucho Marx to interview guests and ask very easy questions. He delighted in making fun of a seemingly limitless string of unusual or eccentric contestants, and his bizarre sense of humor was made all the funnier by his straight man, the soberly intellectual George Fenneman.

Late Night Talk Shows.

After Dad pronounced the day's TV viewing to be at an end I would sneak back into the living room and turn on *The Tonight Show*, hosted by my favorite star of my teenage years, Steve Allen, and then, when Allen moved on to his own weekly variety show, by Jack Paar. Since the sixties most viewers have thought of *The Tonight Show* as the personal property of Johnny Carson (1962-92) and then Jay Leno, but in the mind of this seasoned viewer, a late night watcher by age 13, the show had its best days with Allen, and then Paar behind the desk. Steve Allen (Fig. 30) was that rare bird, a polymath— gifted jazz pianist, composer, actor, author, and raconteur—who communicated an inspiring sense of joy in everything he did. I can still hear (and experience again on You Tube) his high falsetto giggle. Clearly no one enjoyed his show as much as he did. His embrace of silliness found kindred spirits among me and the guys I ran around with. Unlike Carson, who talked over or interrupted almost all of his guests and did skits on a comedic par with Uncle Miltie's brand of vaudeville humor, Allen let people on his show shine their brightest. And he surrounded himself with talent, from those of his band leader, Skitch Henderson, to his regular bunch of very funny sidekicks Tom Posten (decades later on *Newhart*), Don Knotts (Barney Fife on *The Andy Griffith Show*), Louis Nye (on *Curb Your Enthusiasm* very late in his life with Larry David), Bill Dana (known for his very un-politically correct Mexican character Jóse Jimenez), Gabe Dell (one of the Bowery Boys as a child), and others. With these guys, each in a recurring character, Allen regularly conducted his "Man on the Street" interviews, a bit that we at school regularly tried to reproduce for our classmates the next day in school. Another of Allen's standard turns was to sit at the piano and ask audience members to shout out words at random then, without missing a beat, he'd make up both lyrics and music based on their suggestions. One I recall was the word "occupado," to which in a Latin rhythm Allen sang, "My plane's john was occupado so I returned to my seat." (Maybe you had to have been there?)

Fig. 30. Steve Allen

Jack Paar was a totally different character. He was not a comic, like Allen, Carson, or Leno, but a "humorist" who made snide and snarky comments on the passing scene in his whining, neurotic manner or went on endlessly about himself and his family, especially about his pudgy teenage daughter, a girl who bore a striking resemblance to her dad. He had a finely tuned sensibility that he showcased by hosting a bizarre stable of regular guests to act as foils for his more intellectual persona. Paar's bandleader, Jóse Melis, an army buddy from Cuba, also provided sharp contrast to Paar's cultivated, urbane presence. (It says much about Paar's cynical side that he enjoyed tremendously as we did Melis' role as spokesman in live ads for Real Lemon juice, a product that came out in his Hispanic accent as "Ril'limon.") Paar is perhaps mainly remembered for his dispute with NBC when the show's censors cut out a joke containing a reference to a "W.C." (for "water closet," a British term for toilet). In an emotional, signature gesture Paar walked off the show and stayed away for three weeks.

I thought Paar was fascinating. And so did he: how he loved to hear his own voice! There was always a sense of dramatic tension when he spoke. You never knew what preposterous observations he was going to offer up. At the same time you could be appalled, and entertained, by his obnoxious, ceaseless, self-centered prattle. His show was all about him, and you either loved him, as I did, or you thought he was the biggest jerk on television.

Dramatic Shows.

As with TV today, there were plenty of dramatic series about police: *Dragnet*, starring Jack ("just the facts, Ma'am") Webb, *The Untouchables* with Robert Stack as Eliot Ness, and *Highway Patrol*, with Broderick Crawford, an Oscar winner reduced to appearing in this cruddy series. And there was also a ton of courtroom dramas, first among which was *Perry Mason*, starring Raymond Burr. And then there was the FBI's tireless search for Communists, as in *I Led Three Lives*, featuring Richard Carlson. Crime has always paid on the tube, it seems. And we never failed to tune into *Alfred Hitchcock Presents* (on from 1955 to 1962) for thirty minutes of murder and mystery that featured quirky twists on conventional crime stories. Hitchcock appeared at the beginning of each episode to introduce the program in his plummy British butler's accent and to set the tongue-in-cheek tone for this witty show. I vividly remember the typically off-beat plot in which the wife clubs the husband to death with a frozen leg of lamb and then feeds it to the detectives who've come to investigate.

But if this period in TV's evolution may be called a golden age, that claim has to be based on a group of one-hour or 90-minute shows that offered televised dramatic productions written by accomplished talents like Paddy Chayefsky and Rod Serling and performed by top-billed actors or younger talents at the beginnings of their careers (Paul Newman and James Dean, for example). At one time there were no fewer than eleven such "theaters" such as *Studio One*, *Robert Montgomery Presents*, and *The United States Steel Hour* on the air each week. It is still mind-boggling to me that these shows were telecast live, with flubbed lines and camera miscues going out to America along with the fine writing and acting. Watching such dramatic teleplays could restore a smug feeling of superiority to those of us whose self-respect had been damaged by watching too much pro wrestling.

Situation Comedies.

Build a one-room, multi-level set representing a cozy family living room or apartment, people it with a typical white, American, upper-middle class family comprised of a working dad, a stay-at-home, aproned mom, and two adorable, verbose, and witty-beyond-their years kids and have them all resolve a problem or misunderstanding in the course of 25 or so minutes and wrap it up with a valuable lesson learned, a dispute disarmed, family harmony restored, and a moral to take to heart and you've got the formula for a successful situation comedy. A laugh track, which everyone knows is phony, nevertheless punctuates it all nicely. It also helps, of course, if you have either an established star or a dynamic, popular newcomer to anchor the whole thing. Think Lucille Ball (*I Love Lucy*), Danny Thomas (*Make Room for Daddy*), Robert Young (*Father Knows Best*) or those cute kids on *Leave It to Beaver*. Oddly, my favorite was *I Married Joan* whose mindless theme song I still like to sing in the shower ("I married *Jooooannnn*! What a girl, what a whirl, what a life…"). The show was a vehicle for Joan Davis, who, like Lucy, played a zany, scatter-brained housewife married to a successful businessman/executive who invariably came home (always dressed in a suit and carrying a briefcase, in contrast to the show's fans in Rogers) to deal in his ever-suffering, patient way with yet another of Joan's screw-ups. We watched the show religiously despite the contributions of Joan's co-star Jim Backus, then very probably the most obnoxious actor in America.

All of these shows, from football games to the news, variety shows and situation comedies, the whole panorama of schlock, was provided free of charge by the giant corporations as well as mom-and-pop businesses that only asked that we stay in our seats and watch their ads and maybe think about buying their products, please. And watch we did (Indeed, watch we still can, for many of the "spots" can still be accessed on YouTube, prompting inevitable amusement at their low level of technical sophistication with many of the advertisements performed live). And how those ads succeeded! I can *still* remember their pitches and jingles.

"Light up a Lucky. It's light-up time.
Be happy, Go Lucky. It's light-up time.
For the taste that you like
Light up a Lucky Strike.
Relax: It's li-i-i-g-h-t u-u-up time."

Advertisers could advertise anything they wanted to —whiskey, cigars, cigarettes, and all the rest of those unhealthy, now-forbidden products –and they could do so in any preposterous way they wanted to. Want to baldly assert that Camels are gentler on the "T-zone"—the mouth and throat? Go ahead, who's stopping you? How about "three out of four doctors recommend Chesterfields"? Make that claim, too. Tell people that smoking Luckies *during* a meal aids digestion and get away with it. The freedom that encouraged such nonsense seems astonishing, even exhilarating today. The laissez-faire environment of the fifties appears also to reflect the eat, drink, and be merry attitude of a period before by-pass surgery, chemotherapy, and the whole medical buying of time that prevails today, when, as Woody Allen put it, "death in America is considered optional." Fifties ads seemed to say, "Do what you want. You're going to die anyway."

Speaking now from my self-appointed position as a gray eminence who was there at the birth (or at least infancy) of the medium, I can say that it has been a sometime fun and even occasionally educational experience but, as a whole, a rather depressing waste of time. At the end of the day it's a little like that feeling of self-loathing that descends on you after you've eaten (and probably all the while watching the damned tube) an entire, family-sized bag of Cheetos. "Oh my God, *how* could I have done it?"

The tale is told many times, but is worth repeating: The chairman of the Federal Communications Commission in the early 1960s, Newton Minnow, famously called the offerings on network television during his tenure "a vast wasteland." Sure enough, the story goes, one avid TV fan wrote to ask what night and at what time *The Vast Wasteland* would be on.

11

⟫◆⟪

Sports and Balls of All Kinds

Early in a junior high football game, when I was a ninth grader masquerading as our team's center, an unlikely assignment given my height to weight ratio—six feet tall and perhaps 130 pounds—I prepare to snap the ball and carry out my carefully practiced blocking duty. As we are running a version of the classic single-wing offensive formation, my first job will be to pass the ball with a neat, firm spin between my outspread legs to my friend Chris Hackler, the tailback.

This action requires that I briefly see the world upside-down with my target Chris, a human fly, suspended by his feet from the grass. And then, "Ready, set, hut, hut, hut," and the play begins to unfold.

(But, time out for a completely necessary digression. Our high school football coach, Howard Sutton, a newly-arrived, twenty-something ex-Marine, a good-looking and good natured fellow who was more laid-back than your usual A-type coach, would look in on our junior high practices from time to time with a view to scoping out young talent in the pipeline that channeled them towards varsity careers. One day Coach Sutton turned a critical eye on my centering technique and offered this advice: "Ben, after you've snapped the ball, don't keep looking back through your legs to see if the ball got there all right or not. I know you're curious, but once you let go of the football, there's nothing more you can do about it; it's going to be a good snap or a lousy one. You've got to look up and start blocking immediately or that guy across the line will be all over you, or already past you." Good advice, but it was a habit hard to break, especially when I was called upon to sail the ball in a tight spiral to our punter, an occasion that seemed to come up frequently. But now back to the action...)

My assignment as an X in the play diagrammed dozens of times on the blackboard is to seek out and knock the crap out of the O, our opponents' linebacker, who is supposed to be waiting to be blocked just beyond their defensive line. I snap the football, take a couple of steps past the line of scrimmage, turn right, per my instructions, and there he is ripe for destruction. I throw my scrawny physique toward him in what I intend to be a picture-perfect cross-body block maneuver that in today's game, called a chop block, would probably draw a 15-yard penalty. But he is a bigger boy than me, by far; he's a ninth-grader who could play for the Wisconsin Badgers. My rib cage hits one of his well-padded thighs, a thigh, moreover, that resembles the trunk of a young, substantial oak tree, and I am down for the count, the wind knocked out of me, my right side in profound pain, my participation in that night's game at an end. My opponent, unharmed, trots off to join the ongoing play. As I'm helped from the field, gasping for oxygen, a thought bubbles up from my subconscious: Much as I might want to man up and be like the other tough boys at our school, perhaps contact sports are not for me.

In a varsity B team basketball game in nearby Bentonville, I'm at the free-throw line ready to shoot the first of two foul shots. Although I have made the varsity team as a sophomore I am mostly a benchwarmer and get to play only on those rare occasions when we have a commanding lead or are hopelessly behind. To give marginal players like me some action we are sometimes "loaned out" to the B team and allowed to play a couple of quarters in games that occur first on a game-night double-bill. B teams, it must be said, were usually stocked with kids who possessed more energy and enthusiasm than talent or alertness, so sprinkling the lineup with a few ringers wasn't such a bad idea—except, perhaps, on the evening I'm recalling. As I step up to the free-throw line I am very focused on peering ahead to judge the height and distance of the basket from me, for, you see, I'm trying to play that night without my glasses.

Acquired in grade school, my eyeglasses had opened up a new world to me and made me look oh-so-much smarter than I really was (and am), but they proved to be a profound and embarrassing handicap to mixing it up and playing aggressively and confidently on the basketball court. But as childhood hero of mine, George Mikan of the Minneapolis Lakers, a giant by the standards of the day at six feet ten inches, had played with his glasses taped to his face, why couldn't I? Because they fogged up, because they broke, and because they were expensive to replace. So that night I did my best to play without them.

After sizing up the range to the rim I launch my first shot, an anemic arc of an effort that falls perhaps three feet short of the rim and makes a dull thud as it lands. *A-I-R* b-a-l-l-l-l! I glance nervously at our bench. Although I can't see him distinctly, I can well imagine that little smile of amusement on Coach Sutton's lips, a signature expression with which he expressed his judgment of our ineptitude in particular and life's ridiculousness in general. The ref hands me the ball and, taking a deep breath and recalculating the physical laws that I had so egregiously gotten wrong in my first shot, I launch the second of my free throws. Luckily the game's outcome does not depend on me, I think, as this shot slams against the backboard about three feet above the basket and bounds back with surprising force.

Yet another year later it's the spring of my junior year and I am on the track team. (Although there is really no "team." There is no picture of us in the high school yearbook that year, so officially we didn't exist. But some of us did run track that year; otherwise I wouldn't have this miserable story to relate.)

We couldn't have a full track program because we didn't have a track; the dirt and gravel path that ran around the bleachers and goalposts at our football stadium and that served as our practice area was inadequate for hosting meets. In addition we had no facilities for field events such as shot put, discus, pole-vault, or long jump. So a few of just got together informally and trained after school under the eyes of a couple of coaches, and took part in meets held at area schools. I ran the 880-yard relay team with Paul Waldrip, Steve Pelphrey, and some other kid. And we were not bad. We won a few medals that spring, although I can't document that today: the medals, my varsity letters, and a basketball letter-sweater I once wore so proudly I left at home when I went off to college and they've all been lost in the shuffle of my family's life.

I loved track. For one thing track was a spring sport, and it felt terrific to be outdoors and running then. Unlike football, which was too rough for me, and basketball, where my ineptitude was all too obvious on display before stands full of people, track was something I could do without pressure. And

I was good at it. When I put on those hand-me-down leather track shoes with the real (and very sharp) metal spikes that the school provided, shoes that had probably been around since Bud ran track back in the late 1940s, I felt terrific, like a cartoon human blur with speed lines trailing behind me. Think Wile E. Coyote. If you've ever dreamed of running and in those dreams you've passed dogs, deer, or even speeding automobiles, you have a sense of what running felt like to me that spring.

Too bad, then, that I learned from Steve Pelphrey at our fiftieth class reunion that track was the ugly step-child of our high school athletic program and was so poorly regarded by students that every spring coaches practically had to beg kids to come out for the team. Apparently anyone who could stand erect and had a pulse stood a chance to compete in track. Thanks *so much*, Steve.

The only truly indelible memory I have of track that spring is this:

We are in Siloam Springs for a very important meet. (When I told this story at a party several years back one of my friends remarked—rather cruelly, I felt at the time—that he didn't know there was such a thing as a "very important" track meet. Well, *we* thought it was damned important.) For those unfamiliar with the format of a relay race: the race is run by a team of four in four segments, or "legs," of, in this case, 220 yards each. Each runner is responsible for carrying a baton and handing it off to the next runner. Just prior to the hand-off the runner poised to receive it takes off so that he is almost up to speed when the baton is passed. On this day I am running the third leg—the fastest runner on the team is assigned the final 220 yards—and am bunched with our opponents' third-leg runners on the track looking back for my approaching teammate. And, just as my guy rounds the bend with the baton, someone—may his soul roast in Hell forever—yells "Quick, everyone, get off the track!" And…we *do*. Or at least a couple of runners do. Unfortunately, I'm one of them.

Maddeningly, and inexplicably, there is no foul called, although an official stood right there at the scene of the crime, and no protest lodged by our coach, David Camfield, or anyone else. Whether the ploy was spontaneous or planned in advance we never learned. Clearly this was just another case of tough luck, kid. Imagine my ride home on the bus that day. I must surely have caught it from Camfield, who had a white-hot temper and hated to lose at anything.

At our next meet I took the opportunity to make up for my sins by blazing through my leg of the race, beating all the other schools' runners to the handoff, and *enabling* (it is my book, after all) our team to come in first. I still feel great about that day's performance.

My short career in sports had other little triumphs, too: a block that helped our quarterback race into the end-zone for a touchdown; a couple of last-second, Hail Mary jump shots that won *two* basketball games and the vaguely-recalled "Honorable Mention" award in basketball I received from the district, or the conference, or perhaps only at the family dinner table my sophomore year. Hell, even *making* the varsity basketball team that year was something to brag about.

These snapshots of my "only okay" athletic record may give a fuzzy, skewed picture of how I did in sports, but they illustrate my frustrating, lifelong, love-hate battle with things athletic, and the constant fear that my performance would reveal my mediocrity as an athlete for all to see.

Teddy Roosevelt's stirring words, "the credit belongs to the man who is actually in the arena" and "there is no effort without error or shortcoming," were not known to me in high school and probably wouldn't have been much encouragement in any case. A sensitive soul, I took my moments of looking bad in sports very hard. My teammate, Bob Ross, who made a career as a teacher in his old high school, tells the story of my kicking a bucket in anger after a football game one afternoon and crying out, "Dammit, I blew it and we lost again!" "But, Ben," Bob says he counseled me, "we didn't lose. It was a *tie!*" Obviously I couldn't even keep score.

I wanted, of course, to get tough and good at sports like all my friends. My brother Bud had been something of a star before his graduation from Rogers High, and had gone on to play on the freshman basketball team at Arkansas State Teacher's College in Conway before doing his military service, so his achievements were still fresh in my mind and a standard to measure myself by. But the eighth grade, at age 14, the first year I tried out for a team sport and the first year I was cut, was a bit early to start getting tough. Consoled by Bud, I cried like a baby.

After all, only months earlier I had been playing army with friends like Neal Bloomfield (brother of Clyde "Buddy" Bloomfield, Rogers High's most accomplished athlete of the 1950s), Jimmy Garrett, and others, fueled by still prodigious powers of imagination and our abilities to reproduce the sounds of machine guns, exploding grenades, and even our own accompanying musical soundtracks. There were no organized athletic activities available to us prior to junior high school; no Little League baseball or Pop Warner, "Pee Wee" football programs existed then, and the "mini" soccer craze lay far in the future. In the absence of such adult supervised regimentation and nervous moms and dads watching from the sidelines, we invented our own means of amusing ourselves. We were allowed to continue being kids.

But too quickly we had to grow up and, observing St. Paul's admonition, put aside childish things. The process was aided by the virtually overnight, inexplicable loss of those powers of invention and fantasy that allowed us kids to pose as Nazis or Japs or Indians on the playground. And is this connection I have an untested, unscientific, and admittedly bogus theory to explain how Nature makes it happen: As boys go through puberty, a scary transition a bit like getting old, but much more sexy, the testosterone pumped into their systems kills off the inventive imagination cells in the brain and stimulates hitherto dormant cells that demand a new focus on girls, territoriality, and masculine competitiveness. Seemingly overnight a boy begins to take a burning interest in such commonplaces as the hair on the nape of a girl's neck, or what a training bra can do inside a too-tight sweater. Thus childhood ends, to be replaced by a hairier, deeper-voiced, sweaty, and smelly guy culture, centered around, not our riotous army battles and games of Old Maid, but take-no-prisoners athletics and off-color conversations about female classmates.

I was and up to a point still am ambivalent about the society of guys, with its constant diet of dirty jokes, boasting at high volume, put downs, and non-stop competition, whether overt or subtle but never completely absent. Note in this connection how when a number of guys join together on an out-of-town trip, the composite group I.Q. seems to drop a few points as the group grows in size. Is this true of all the primates? Bonobos, chimpazees? Do our ape cousins get together, chatter loudly, punch each other on the shoulders, compare penis length?

Joining the junior high football team in the ninth grade enabled me to become one of the guys for the first time. We practiced on the grassy field of the school's stadium on North Eighth Street just a few blocks northwest of the high school, a spot now occupied by the town's post office. Practices began then, as now, in the moist, wilting heat of August with the rhythmic chug-chug of water sprinklers playing in the background. As the conventional wisdom of the day held that drinking water during practices made players sluggish and perhaps soft, we were denied water until the end of each day's practice— just another ploy to toughen the boys up. (When I read today of the deaths of football players at all levels from heat prostration during summer workouts, I can sympathize, and can't help but wonder what completely sane person would submit to, or order, such an ordeal.) The second practice was over we all ran to a huge oil drum that contained the coldest and most delicious water in Arkansas, and there, in an orgy of relief, plunged our faces in it and drank.

At the north end of the football field sat a concrete-block building that housed the stadium's restrooms, locker room, and showers that served both junior high and varsity teams. It was a kind of "black hole of Calcutta" among the Rogers High athletic facilities, dark and dank, and reeked of filthy uniforms, bacteria-laden shoulder pads, and cleated shoes passed down from prior generations of long-gone athletes as well as the cumulative odors of rancid socks, jockstraps, and sweatshirts. The place might have been a candidate for Superfund rehab after its demolition. Here we dressed before games, got ankles taped, our abrasions anointed with iodine, got our charley-horses rubbed with Atomic Balm (a salve that packed a terrific super heating action), showered noisily, and snapped each other's butts with towels.

And there we could learn *way* too much about each other. We had a lone toilet in the establishment and you did your business right out in full view of God and everybody else—no enclosure, no door. One day, memorably, one of the coaches took a leisurely BM while carrying on a conversation with several players dutifully attending him, just like LBJ having one of his advisers or speechwriters follow him into the john while he continued to gab away. Full frontal defecation, it might be termed.

In the locker room we also accumulated information on whose underwear was consistently the filthiest, and who possessed the most luxuriant number and variety of pimples. On that count, one upperclassman, whose broad, muscular back was a veritable garden of zits, was our clear front-runner; indeed, his back might well have been the original source of the acne pandemic that plagued us all.

Our junior high football coach was Charles Brooker, a fortyish, trimly built, debonair fellow who stayed at our school for only a couple of years but who in that short time made a strong impression on many of us. I liked him then and the passing of time has made me even fonder of him. The man had a certain *style*. He had a big head topped by a graying pompadour, a powerful jaw, wide shoulders that padded jackets made even wider, a trim waist, and legs rather too short for his stocky torso. In short, the build of a wrestler. (There's a picture of him in one of our yearbooks in which he's dressed for a student-faculty basketball game, a photo that suggests, if anything, that the man had, shall we say, a bit too much bodily hair.)

He spoke with a polished authority in clipped, nasal tones surely acquired in a northern city, perhaps Chicago or Detroit, and he smoked unfiltered cigarettes with a cool, negligent air right out of a *film noir*, B-grade mystery movie. We youngsters generally liked him but thought him slightly weird, as in *different*. And we were amused by the readiness with which he supplied information on virtually any topic imaginable. He was a true *Besserwisser*, an authority who simply knew more than you did about everything, though admittedly this was no great distinction when your audience is a bunch of ninth graders. Once he was driving us to a basketball game in his car when Chris Hackler and I began to try to sing "Dry Bones," (As in "Them bones, them bones, them *drrrrry* bones.") and failing that, started speculating on the origins of the song. Had an orthopedic surgeon written it, perhaps? Then Coach Brooker, overhearing our conversation, began to lecture, "Actually, boys, 'Dry Bones' is a part of that long tradition of..." All of us giggled. He knew all about "Dry Bones," too! After that we always referred to him as Coach Dry Bones.

Brooker and his wife, Ruth, who also taught at the high school, left us in 1959, just before my senior year. In Rogers, among people of my generation, rumors are still attached to the reportedly unusual circumstances surrounding their departure, rumors almost certainly too preposterous to be true and not printable here. I prefer to believe that the Brookers got a more appealing appointment elsewhere in a setting more suited to their talents and with colleagues and students who didn't brand them as odd because of their accents, origins, and fuller life experiences. The Brookers may have been Jewish, as their name suggests. And in Rogers, a two-stoplight town where the suspicious citizens thought someone from Bentonville, eight miles away, was the exotic Other, the Brookers surely must have felt out of place.

In the midst of this ballsy-guy athletic scene I learned that nature had unaccountably short-changed me. While almost everyone else seemed to fill out and develop muscles as if that were the natural order of things, my body grew taller but remained essentially a preliminary sketch of a physique, with its pipe-cleaner arms and legs and every rib on full display, like each bar in a vertical marimba. In the words of that old vaudeville routine, other guys' arms made my legs look like fingers. A skinny, be-spectacaled twerp since the fifth grade, I was saddled with a seemingly defenseless frame that made me in elementary school a ready target for bullies on the school bus and playground. My sisters Patsy and Phyllis looked out for me on the bus rides to school until they graduated, but after that I was on my own, and expecting sand to be kicked into my face at any moment.

I was particularly mortified on those occasions when I ventured to the Lakeside swimming pool during our blazing summers, my worst season, since conditions required that I wear short-sleeved shirts that seemed to shout, "Look, everybody, how bony and miserable my arms are!" One confrontation with a bully took place in the Lakeside pool locker room, where we changed into our bathing suits and put our clothes in large metal baskets. Famished after hours in the pool, I walked into the changing room with a 15 cent hotdog laden down with mustard, ketchup, and relish and a nearly sinful, drooling anticipation of my one indulgence of the afternoon. Suddenly some big jerk loomed over me and loudly announced, "Hey, kid, lemme have a bite of that," and then proceeded to snatch it from me and bury three-quarters of my dog in his pie-hole. "Thanks," he said, handing me back the split, butt-end of the bun, less the meat. (Professional and amateur Freudian psychoanalysts alike are requested to leave this anecdote alone.)

By the time I was fifteen I was already more than six feet tall and, even though I was seriously skinny, I could still run, pass, and shoot the basketball (dribbling was another story) after a fashion, so I began to think that I really could be a basketball player. Maybe I wasn't destined to be the star Bud had become in the late forties, but at least I could aspire to be a "fair-to-middlin" one, as we say in the Ozarks. Besides, there was a brisk market in high school basketball circles for kids who stood six feet or taller in those days, so at six two I appeared to have a bright future ahead of me. I played on the freshman team so when I went out for the varsity my sophomore year the coach, David

Camfield, who seemingly coached a bit of everything, already knew me a bit and picked me for the team. (Fig. 31)

Fig. 31. The 1958-59 Rogers High Varsity Basketball Team
(Left to right) Billy Joe Jones, Dale Deason, Ken Green, Cleve Branscum, Raymond Graham, Bob Maloney, Jerry Davis, Me, Steve Pelphrey, Steve Willis, Jimmy Gibson, Johnny Rumley, Coach David Camfield

Of course, I knew I could look forward to warming the bench while the juniors and seniors played the games and to going in only after we'd achieved that rare thing, a safe lead, or had given up any hope of catching up. For the rest of us second-stringers the dearest hope in our hearts was to chalk up enough quarters playing time to qualify for a letter at the end of the season.

I played a little that sophomore year as we hosted schools from the area in our own brand-spanking new Kirksey Gymnasium (named for a long-gone superintendent) where we were cheered on by the girls' Blue Demons corps, all decked out in blue and white, and crowds of townspeople that, strange to say, never included anyone from my own family. Not that I minded. Dad always protested that he was too tired at the end of a workday to show up at seven o'clock to cheer on his son, and I believed him, accepted that as a fact and moved on. Tired or not he would probably have felt out of place sitting in those bleachers and trying to display any enthusiasm, though he'd probably have been there before with Bud. Today, when parents feel they might be ruining their children's lives if they don't show up at every soccer match from the kid's age of six onward, moms and dads wouldn't dream of missing their kids' game. Not so in the fifties; parental attendance was not such a big deal.

Our team also got on the bus and hit the road, "visitors" at a delightful variety of venues both near and far: Bentonville, Springdale, Russellville, Huntsville, Harrison, Alma. We even once ventured north to West Plains, Missouri, where we suffered such culture shock from being out of our home state that we played in a kind of daze and took a terrific shellacking. We competed in gymnasiums big and small, some of which had facilities so different from our own comfy home arena that we could only smile and shake our heads; goals, for example, set nine feet above the floor or ten feet, six inches, rather than the regulation ten feet. Some gyms had backboards mounted on the gym's end walls with out-of-bounds areas that measured perhaps a foot deep, so that lay-ups had to be carefully choreographed lest we crash into the cinderblocks. A few gyms were so dimly lighted we seemed to be playing in a prolonged twilight.

We'd leave on those bus trips in the early afternoons and return late at night, worn out but happy and in prime towel-snapping humor if we'd won, or appropriately solemn and hang-dog if we'd lost. It didn't look good at all to goof off if you'd lost. Before the games we'd stop to chow down at a truck stop or mom-and-pop diner, where we were admonished to not make pigs of ourselves, an order we'd file away before proceeding to stuff ourselves.

Practices were held before school beginning at eight o'clock and would always conclude with wind sprints, dashes from one end of the court to the next, over and over, until I began to see stars before my eyes (cardio-vascular endurance was never one of my strong suits). One night in Van Buren I got so winded chasing from front court to back court then back again that in desperation I called time out rather than faint right there in front of everybody. Coach Camfield was not pleased at all with me: I'd called time out with only three seconds left in the quarter!

After morning practice we'd shower, dress and be ready for classes at nine. Then back to more practice when the school day ended at three. We had some great guys on the teams: Johnny Rumley; Steve Willis, a new Daisy kid from Michigan; Billy Jo Jones, who after graduation got a number of basketball scholarship offers; Steve Pelphrey, a transplant from California who was our school's best all-around athlete; Harold Rhoden, a terrific kid and quarterback of the unbeaten 1959 football team, and Cleve Branscum, our best player.

From the beginning my glasses were a problem, since one could never count on a basketball game being devoid of physical contact, and some of it quite nasty indeed. (This all happened years before some genius came up with contact lenses.) Once in a game against Siloam Springs, in fact, we were getting whipped by one of their players who sported a pair of the biggest and thickest spectacles we'd ever seen, and Coach Camfield told us to "get in his face" and perhaps maybe sorta see if we could dislodge his eyewear and put a crimp in his style. I never managed to achieve that level of play wearing my glasses, even though we tried a number of somewhat comical steps to deal with the problem. Playing without them clearly didn't work. Taping them on at the temples didn't solve anything because they could still get broken; having my frames plastered on so tightly just resulted in the lenses steaming up. After some considerable searching, the coach ordered me a leather-padded metal face guard that resembled the top half of a catcher's mask, a hideous and funny-looking contraption rather like the sort of thing you strap on the snout of a dog to keep him from biting defenseless children. You can imagine how ridiculous I felt wearing it. As I appeared on the court already like a patient in the last stages of *anorexia nervosa*, I did not need an additional feature to make me look like the school's geek-in-residence! We finally settled on eyeglasses made especially for sports, a pair with metal frames and thick, "unbreakable" glass. These were okay except that the little pads that rested on the bridge of my nose were made as delicately as Teddy Roosevelt's *pince-nez*, and every blow I took to the face bent them this way and that, hurting like the devil. As it happened the only truly safe place for me was on the bench.

From that vantage point I had ample opportunities to see our coach in action, and it was not a pretty sight. David Camfield was a young man, perhaps in his mid-twenties when he came to Rogers; essentially he was a kid right out of college. If memory serves, he had been a hot player himself and was also the son of a coach with a solid reputation, so the pressure on him to succeed must have been overwhelming. Rogers had had champion teams in the past and had an especially good team my senior year, when Cleveland Branscum, the best high school player I ever saw in action, came into his own. But the teams I played on were merely so-so, and it ate Coach Camfield's heart out. One night in Van Buren we were beaten by a score of something like 42-17; imagine scoring only seventeen lousy points in a basketball game! Camfield took mediocre play and big team losses like that hard and channeled his disappointment through a volcanic temper directed both at us and the referees. On the bench or pacing the sidelines he'd start steaming, turn red in the face, and begin harassing the refs. He seemed to take a perverse pleasure in acting out before the crowd and his players. More than once he'd roll basketballs onto the court to provoke the inevitable technical fouls and face-to-face yelling matches with the officials. It was a sad spectacle, and there was no assistant coach on our bench to rein him in.

Camfield was a true Jekyll and Hyde case: He could be a sweet and thoughtful man (he once paid a visit to our home to see me when I missed a week of practice with the flu) or a jerk, but nothing recognizable as human in between. On one occasion, when we were getting killed by our opponents' center, he beckoned me from the end of the bench and in his theatrical way said, "I want you to go in there and stop that guy!" It was like a scene out of a grade-B movie. I responded, as earnestly as the occasion seemed to demand, "I'll try, coach." "Try, nothing. You just keep sittin' there. I want somebody who'll do the job!"

Coach Camfield was a kindred spirit of Bobby Knight, and, like the Indiana coach (a near contemporary) he knew how to push all the buttons to prod, discomfit, and, often, hurt his players. He took pleasure in needling me and calling me, and by no means in an endearing way, "Benny Boy," a belittling nickname he knew I hated. As the promise I showed as a sophomore failed to meet his expectations, Camfield appeared to write me off as a bad bet and to treat me dismissively. But if I let him down, he in turn ruined basketball for me and to this day I cannot forgive him for it. Since then, whenever I've seen a coach, or a parent, vent his rage at a kid I think of the way Camfield abused the boys who tried their best to play for him, and I only wish for them what they deserve: to be sent to Devil's Island with the rest of their ilk far from where they can do high school athletes any harm.

When towards the end of the 1958-59 school year Camfield asked me, "Benny Boy, you coming out for basketball your senior year?" it was with a mix of pleasure and sadness that I replied, "No way."

Camfield didn't stay at Rogers High long after my class graduated. Around 1963 he left to take a coaching job in Texas and eventually wound up at a school near Amarillo, where he and his teams enjoyed a long run of success well into the 1970s. At my class's fiftieth reunion I heard that he had passed away. Perhaps it was time to reflect maturely on the past, to let bygones be bygones, to put to rest the unhappy memories of my dealings with a young man, then at the beginning of his career, who wanted so dearly to win and be successful, no matter what it took; in short, to find peace through forgiveness, to move on, to "get over it."

Nope! I don't *think* so.

12

---⟫•⟪---

A MUSICAL INTERLUDE

BY THE FALL OF MY sophomore year the prospect of scorching August practices and more collisions on the gridiron put an end to whatever thoughts I might have entertained, however halfheartedly, of a future in varsity football. Actually Mother Nature cast the deciding vote in that decision inasmuch as I weighed, at age sixteen, about 135 pounds and stood a bit over six feet in height. In addition, the sissy dwelling inside was ready to assert itself. By that time in any case I was poised for a navigational change in my career, swept away as I was by a new enthusiasm: playing in our high school band. So when Coach Sutton, using his nickname for me that he never took the trouble to explain, asked, "Now, Digger, are you coming out for football or have you decided to become a horn-tooter?" I had to own up, in a barely audible voice, "Horn-tooter, sir."

And what horn did I opt to toot? The English horn? Trombone? Fluegelhorn, maybe? Why, the clarinet, of course. And why the clarinet? Because I wanted to be like my hero, Maxie Gundlach, the coolest musician at Rogers High.

Maxie was the absolute opposite of those handsome, brawny, big-men-on-campus sorts who made all the girls swoon and got elected president of the senior class even if they were failing all their courses. He was the prototype of the shy guy who never got the girl, but he was a marvelous clarinetist who shone in regional and state musical competitions and who, with his dad, Charlie, a saxophonist, played Big Band arrangements at dances all over our area. (Fig. 32) By day, the Gundlachs ran a dry-cleaning business, and Maxie could often be seen making deliveries around town in his family's panel truck, but clearly they got more enjoyment out of their musical moonlighting. He was a musical prodigy, a whiz not only on the clarinet but also on drums, piano, flute, trumpet, trombone, and saxes of all shapes and sizes. After concentrating on the clarinet from junior high, Maxie got so good that during his senior year he was selected to sit in for one or two numbers with the Marine Corps' traveling concert band, the gold standard of perfection for such rousing ensembles all across the country. This was a high honor, indeed, and one that our high school band was bused to Fayetteville to witness. After graduating in 1956, Maxie attended the University of Arkansas, where he played in the big Razorback marching band and at gigs around Fayetteville with his five-piece ensemble. After leaving the university he played sax and clarinet with the Shep Fields orchestra and other big bands across the country. (Maxie continued to play gigs around his hometown and to run his family's dry-cleaning business until his early death in 1986. R.I.P.)

If Maxie was not cool in the conventional sense he was my idol nevertheless, and I hung on his every word and, well, his every toot out of that marvelous clarinet. I remember that he showed up one day in an unusual sort of sweater/shirt, black in color with the thinnest of orange vertical pinstripes, black buttons, and two little pockets near the bottom hem. I coveted that shirt to the point of violating a key clause in the Ten Commandments; I had to have one. But when I eventually located one in town just like it, I was crestfallen to learn that it sold for $9.95, an impossibly high price for any article of clothing, perhaps even a sport coat, in 1956. But then, happy day, no one else in town could afford it either—or perhaps would not be caught dead in such a bizarre affair, and when it ultimately went on sale at half off, I pounced, throwing away, still, a tidy sum for it. But I was closer to being just like Maxie!

If Maxie could play the clarinet, why couldn't I, my thinking went. Both Maxie and I had been bowled over by two Hollywood musical biographies, almost unwatchable now but essential pop culture in those days: *The Glenn Miller Story* in 1954 and *The Benny Goodman Story* two years later. Both films celebrated wonderful music and exceptional musicians and brought about a kind of mini-revival of their Big Band sounds. Maxie's clarinet, played an octave higher than the saxes, emulated that golden sound that Miller invented, and I can almost still hear Maxie's rendition of "Moonlight Serenade" with its glissando opening that only a master clarinetist can pull off.

Fig. 32. Maxie Gundlach. Courtesy of Mrs. Judy Gundlach.

I had not one but two clarinets during my brief career in music. The first, purchased for about $40, maybe less, at Beaulieu's Hardware Store, where one expected to find not musical instruments but fishing tackle, monkey wrenches, and bolt cutters, was nothing but a piece of junk. A clarinet is a beautiful thing, with seemingly a hundred keys, a thing of exquisite precision. But this one's metal parts seemed to have been made of lead that bent with little or no urging; it existed in a constant state of becoming. And it sounded awful when I tried coaxing music out of it. Within a few months I received stern advice to get another horn if I was really serious about music. So we did, and the day my new clarinet was ordered remains one of my most cherished memories of my Dad.

A young instrument salesman, who no doubt had been alerted by our school's band director that a live customer awaited him on South Thirteenth Street, called at our house one summer day ready to sign us up. Told that Dad was working on a job nearby, the salesman started off to find him and I tagged along to witness this momentous transaction. When we arrived at the construction site, Dad, dressed in carpenter's bib overalls and straw hat and, thank God, in a good mood that day, greeted the young man cordially and sat down with him to go over the paperwork. The clarinet this man was selling was priced at about $250 (or what would be a little over $2,000 today). Then and there, amid the sawdust and wood shavings, and without a moment's doubt, hesitation, grimace, or groan, but rather with a confident sense that it was exactly the right thing to do, Dad signed a contract to "pay out" the cost over a couple of years. It was a breathtaking moment. And that was not to be the last time that Dad was to vote yes in favor of his arty son.

We had a big high school band (in our official yearbook photo, fronted by our drum major Susie Baker, the ensemble filled the entire front steps of our school) and was led by the estimable, dignified, and *tiny* figure of Mr. George Fentem. Mr. Fentem—he was the kind of fellow who deserved, and needed, the otherwise redundant title—had been the school's band director for as long as anyone could remember, perhaps even forever. (Fig. 33) He was also very probably the smallest man, size-wise, in Arkansas. It was as if Mr. Fentem, on an expedition to the jungles of the Amazon, had been captured by a tribe of headhunters who had then shrunk not just his head but his entire body. He stood only a little over five feet tall and weighed perhaps a hundred pounds, yet he carried himself with a sort of fierce gravitas that demanded respect. When he raised his baton in band practice he glared at us as if to say, "I believe music is serious business and you'd damned well better think so, too." I have tried and tried but I cannot for the life of me picture Mr. Fentem with a smile on his face.

Fig. 33. George Fentem, Band Ditector

But I can see him in his Rogers High band uniform leading us in "The Star Spangled Banner" on the sidelines of our football field, or in the gym while we sawed away at "Pomp and Circumstance" for graduation ceremonies, or as we marched down Walnut Street in our Friday afternoon Homecoming parades, trying to stay aligned, in step, and play Sousa more or less together. Turned out in his quasi-military outfit, the same one that made us kids generally look like dorks, Mr. Fentem looked great. He was proud of his profession. I can readily bring to mind a picture, and almost the sound, of Mr. Fentem taking us through a rehearsal of some piece for the umpteenth time in the basement-level band room. With both arms extended outward, he'd intone, "Ready, one, two, three—play," and then lead us through the piece while whistling the melody, or, rather, not exactly whistling so much as expelling air through his lips on pitch. If he grew impatient with us, he might single out one section or another for chastisement. Once, memorably, he urged our trombonists to play with greater vigor: "Now, skin it back," he commanded, much to the amusement of us clarinetists.

But he seemed worn down by the lackluster human material he was perennially saddled with. Year after year he patiently led one generation after another of half- hearted musicians who honked and shrieked away while he dreamed, perhaps, of excellence just over the horizon, of another Maxie Gundlach who would emerge from the ranks, but was forced once again to settle for a bunch of musical mediocrities.

Just how very bad we were as a musical ensemble was driven home each spring when Mr. Fentem took us to Fayetteville to take part in district (or perhaps it was state) band competitions. At these affairs each school band was given a shot at playing its strongest piece. With this we generally did fairly well, since we'd probably practiced it for six weeks. Next, cruelly, the judges would distribute sheet music to each of us, the score to a piece of moderate difficulty that we had not seen before, and allow Mr. Fentem the laughably short time of ten minutes or so to read it, lead us in practicing it as best we could, and then guide us as we tried to plow through the damned thing. Since we'd only gotten to preview thoroughly only the opening bars of the arrangement, we did all right as we began but as we got more deeply into the score, one after the other of us overmatched musicians would drop out, hoping against hope that Mr. Fentem would not know which of us had thrown in the towel. Then whole sections, the trombones perhaps, would pack it in, and as the piece blessedly neared its end, only two or three of our best musicians—and I'm afraid I was probably not among them—would still be going at it, although perhaps not at the same point in the score.

Mr. Fentem, stoic as always, would put on a brave front, but we must have realized already that we would not be receiving the blue ribbon that year. But since grade inflation was not unknown in those times, our band usually went home with a third place or an honorable mention.

Today, more than a half century later, and after a thirty-year career of my own in which I often felt like a preacher before a deaf congregation, I am in awe of the dedication and stubborn optimism of teachers like George Fentem, who year after year for perhaps four decades continued his tireless campaign of trying to wring music out of a bunch of knuckleheads. Nor was he by any means alone on our faculty in his patient willingness to take on still another generation of high school students and to do his part in making us a little smarter.

But this recital of our band's shortcomings does not do justice to the value of the experience, to the sheer joy of playing music with other kids, to the guilty pleasures of mostly un-chaperoned teenagers on long bus trips to Podunk towns, to marches and gigs in faraway places. Like to Joplin, Missouri, just over the state line, where we marched in a Christmas parade one year when it was so cold that all the wind and brass instruments, full of our spittle, froze up and left us marching with only the rattling of our drum section and the ding-a-ling of our glockenspiels to accompany us. Each fall we hit the big time as our band joined those of a dozen other high schools on the field at Razorback Stadium to offer a rendition, not quite in unison, of our national anthem. And then there was that memorable summer when we played our indispensable part in "Rogerama," providing the musical accompaniment to the low-budget, underwhelming pageant celebrating the seventy-fifth anniversary of our little town's founding (see the film *Waiting for Guffman* for a hilarious send-up of this quintessentially American genre).

And there were even more satisfying moments for me in music. Although I was a willing and decent, if undistinguished student of the clarinet, I could do a reasonable rendition of "Peg O' My Heart" and "Moonglow," for example, numbers requested on occasion by Uncle Fred: "Play us a tune, Hoyt," he'd say. (In a takeoff on my middle name he enjoyed calling me "Hoyt, Loyt, Doyt," a nickname I didn't mind, since silliness is a necessary component of the good life.) But the high notes—and the clarinet can in good hands really soar—were impossible for me, and the longed-for vibrato of the great Artie Shaw was simply not forthcoming, try as hard as I might to get it. Excellence lay forever just beyond my reach, and if it wouldn't come to me, or at least meet me halfway, I was not willing to reach it by practicing conscientiously.

One moment in my brief musical career that has stayed with me took place when I was a junior in high school. Stuart Wilson, the son of our doctor and a friend since grade school, played the cello in the Fayetteville Youth Orchestra. Unlike me, he was a fine musician. (Stuart would go on to become an ophthalmologist and, after retirement, a sculptor. At least one Renaissance man came out of Rogers!). Stuart, after getting the director's permission, invited me to join him at one of the orchestra's practices. I sat among the wind instruments in the center of the orchestra as we had a go at Sibelius' *Finlandia*. Thankfully, my part was not that difficult and I joined in with increasingly confident pleasure. Surrounded by bright, gifted young people who obviously really *did* practice, I had an epiphany similar to that I experienced with my first pair of glasses—*I can SEE!*—and this time it was all about hearing how great good music can be, especially when it sounds as grandly *loud* as it did that Saturday morning in Fayetteville, and what a thrill it could be to help make that music.

But as time passed the clarinet came out of its case less and less frequently. By my senior year I was ready to quit the band and move on to other interests. A consistent, long-term application to just about everything I dipped my toe into—football, music, theatre, the Boy Scouts, the DeMolays, the church— seemed beyond me. I had—and still have— my "enthusiasms," as my mother-in-law once disapprovingly observed, which I pitch into with brio and then let gradually fade away. Attention-deficit disorder (as yet not identified in the fifties) or just plain laziness? I prefer now to think of it as simply a search back then for something that I was good at, or at least something that I was less mediocre at. My meandering course towards that goal took its sweet time, but by my senior year I was getting warm, as a few things just seemed to fall into place naturally: I got a couple of book reviews published in our local newspaper, I was picked to be editor of the school newspaper, and I appeared a few times on a Saturday morning radio show, where we played a few records and chatted about high school events and personalities. If I have had a gift or a "calling," it was for the written and spoken word, and I began to realize that, and to practice it, by the time I was about seventeen.

13

⬤◆⬤

THOSE "MISTER'S AT THE VICTOR"

AND NOW IT'S TIME TO go to the movies—or, as we always put it in our proud Arkansas patois, "Goat th' show!" And the "show" was on South Second Street between Walnut and Poplar, to me the classiest, most cosmopolitan part of town, because the Victory Theater was located there. (Fig. 34)

Our movie palace, which opened its doors for the first time in 1927 and closed them in the 1970s, was my gateway to the rest of the world and to the whole of history. Hell, I learned more there about the Bible, thanks to Cecil B. DeMille, than I did in Sunday school at the Presbyterian Church! Even today, when making that little extra effort to head for my local cinema—which means leaving my house and my 42-inch, HD, surround-sound television on which I can dial up 250 channels or watch 23 new movies On Demand—I experience the same pleasure I first felt at about age six at the Victory, the pleasure of settling into a special place and seeing movies the way they were meant to be seen: on a big screen and with other people, friends and strangers alike, around me, all of us rattling around in our popcorn bags and sitting back to enjoy the show together.

Before television began competing with Hollywood for our entertainment dollars, we went to the Victory sometimes two or three times a week, and if we *really* liked a movie we'd go back and see it several times over. I believe I saw *The Greatest Show on Earth* ten times, enough to develop a serious crush on the incomparable Betty Hutton and to fuel my fantasies of becoming a rugged, no-nonsense circus manager like Charlton Heston, or a handsome, sexy acrobat like the Great Sebastian, played by Cornel Wilde. Kids got in for a dime in the early fifties, and adults paid only 45 cents, and for those few shekels you got perhaps two to three hours of entertainment. My parents would send me off to "the show" with perhaps a quarter, and then 25 cents could be stretched a long way—I could get my ticket, a bag of popcorn, and a candy bar with that quarter—and I was in hog heaven.

Fig. 34. The Victory Theater in 2010.

Sometimes I bought the candy bar, or perhaps a package of Doublemint, outside the theater from a sidewalk vender who hawked his wares from a garden wheelbarrow season after season, wind, rain, or snow. Tracey Lockhart (Fig. 35) was a fixture on Second Street, familiar to generations of moviegoers and kids like me who heard him sing his signature jingle a thousand times:

Chewing gum and candy,

Right here handy,

Taddle, daddle da-a-a-h-h.

Tracey warded off the cold in winter in an olive-drab army overcoat several sizes too big for him and a matching wool cap, and in summers he'd appear more nattily garbed in white shirt and tie and straw hat. Tracey lived in a shack south of town where he cared for his invalid brother and supported both of them through the proceeds from his sidewalk business. Amazingly, he did well enough to contribute $500 toward the construction of Rice Memorial Hospital at Walnut and South Thirteenth streets, a display of generosity that must have (or should have) shamed a lot of people in Rogers.

Fig. 35. Tracey Lockhart. Courtesy of the Rogers Historical Museum

You might buy from Tracey, but were careful not to get too close or to prolong the transaction, because the old man wasn't "right in the head," and such conditions might be "catching." But according to a town legend, he knew the names and birthdays of many of the young customers who spent their nickels on his gum and candy bars.

Tracey's little cart wasn't the street's only source of goodies. As the years went by, and our discretionary spending increased, we'd drop by the Rexall Drugstore on the corner of Walnut and Second streets for a lime Coke or strawberry milkshake, or pop into the Snack Shack across the street for a quick bowl of chili before show time. And right next to the theater stood Dean's Bakery, whose window displays laid out before our eyes a virtually pornographic cornucopia of treats—chocolate doughnuts, bear claws, and Danish pastries (an uptown word we wouldn't have recognized then), whose swirls of sweet dough were covered with a white, sugary substance and daubed in the center with generous globs of goo related, however distantly, to cherries, apples, or pineapple. And each of those little sweeties cost a mere nickel. The Candy Kitchen, just opposite the Victory, also housed an abundance of luxurious temptations, such as candy by the bag or, when we were older, Sen-Sen, those little drops that were the fifties' version of Tic-Tacs. (Fig. 36)

Fig. 36. The Candy Kitchen in the 1950s. Courtesy
of the Rogers Historical Museum

The Candy Kitchen was also my prime source of comic books, and a trip
to the Victory was often paired with a brief visit to the shop's metal racks
placed strategically up front near the plate-glass windows, where I could
peruse the latest offerings. If I just looked and didn't buy, the short Greek
owner, Tom Mulos, our town's only evidence of ethnic diversity and a man
who seemed perpetually pissed off, would shoo me away. But if I had a spare
quarter and did buy, I'd usually walk out with one of the several magazines
published under the misleading banner of "Educational Comics," or E.C.
Comics for short, a company that specialized in a boy's favorite lineup of
genres: horror, fantasy, suspense, science fiction, and war.

Much is made these days of graphic novels, and the stable of superheroes
from Marvel or D.C. dominate the steady stream of summer blockbuster
movies. But most authorities on the history of comics—and there are a lot
of experts out there—agree that the real golden age of comics was the late
forties and early fifties. Like most kids, I collected and traded comics; the
colorful magazines, with their lurid stories punctuated by sound effects and
screams in bold-face type ("**ARRGHHH!**"), were a form of capital for us.
I had a powerful addiction to *The Haunt of Fear, The Vault of Horror, Tales
from the Crypt* (later the basis of a movie series on HBO), *Weird Science,* and

Two-Fisted Tales, the latter devoted to combat stories from the whole history of warfare.

E.C. could justifiably boast of its superb stable of artists, and, perhaps in an early foray into stylistic analysis, I grew to recognize each artist's hand and personal sense of design. My favorites were Jack Davis, Will Elder, Wallace Wood, Harvey Kurtzman, and John Severin. The stories weren't much; the plots, with their quirky or ironic surprise endings, were the type that would also be trotted out repeatedly in thirty-minute TV dramas on *Twilight Zone* or *Alfred Hitchcock Presents.* For me it was always about the art, the powerful draftsmanship, the shading, the composition, the color.

And then, around 1954 or so, there were no more E.C. comics. A publicity-seeking psychologist named Frederic Wertheim went on a national crusade to "clean up" the comic book industry. In his book *Seduction of the Innocent,* in widely read articles in *Readers Digest,* and in testimony he gave before a Senate committee, Wertheim charged that there was a direct link, a cause-and-effect relationship, between my favorite comic books and the rise of juvenile delinquency. Basing his conclusions on shoddy, unscientific "research" (studies that would never have passed muster among professionals in his field), he asserted that violent and frightening material in comics twisted young peoples' minds. With public opinion turning against them, publishers agreed on a code that, among other things, forbade the use of the words "horror," "terror," and "crime" in all future comic books. What fun was that? E.C. owner Bill Gaines said to hell with it and took his staff in a new direction, one that resulted in *Mad* magazine, a satirical comic that was a hit and is still around.

But we were headed to the movies ...

Yes, an afternoon or evening at the Victory was always an occasion to anticipate and savor. For one thing, attendance signaled one's relative sophistication in a town where such a distinction was in short supply. Under no circumstances would we have considered going to the Rogers Theater around the corner and just a few steps west on Walnut. Known as the Stinker—not necessarily for the clientele who kept it in business but for its unpleasantly fragrant toilets that were the quickest triggers of the human gag reflex in our part of the state—the Rogers got by on a staple of westerns, trashy melodramas, B movies, serials, and recycled films from the 1940s or earlier turned out by the bottom-feeders of Hollywood studios, like Republic

Pictures. Almost inconceivably, admission there was even cheaper than at the Victory. Its patrons were working people, farmers, and other country folk, many of whom might only come to town once a week to stock up on groceries. Among the regulars at the Stinker were Effie Johnson and her one-armed husband, Harry, who would come trooping into town on Saturdays from their home in the greater Avoca area to catch a Roy Rogers "oater" and to cheer on their hero, loudly and lustily, from their seats up close to the screen. Effie wore a ragged straw hat and toted a small toy rifle. One day someone standing in line at the ticket window in back of Effie sought to get a rise out of her by shouting out, "Roy Rogers is a coward!" whereupon Effie rose in defense of her hero and physically attacked her tormentor. This colorful, middle-aged girl, along with Tracey Lockhart and Buddy Harris (see below), rounded out our town's complement—our troika—of oddballs or "crazies" and, like them, got her fair share of ridicule and teenage nastiness. I'm slightly embarrassed to admit that an expression I still use, may the good Lord forgive me, is "cob Effie," a bit of nonsense that over the years evolved into a kind of equivalent to "Holy Toledo!" or "Laws a' mercy!" Its distasteful origin lies in the notion that country people wiped themselves with dried corncobs. Hence, "cob Effie!"

The Rogers was the theater that screened the most controversial film of the day: *The Outlaw,* a steamy black-and-white western produced by Howard Hughes that introduced Jane Russell to the town's heavy-breathing boys as well as the bluenoses among us who were always on the lookout for threats to the public morals. First introduced in 1943, this film, nominally about Billy the Kid and Doc Holliday, was really all about Ms. Russell's breasts, the contours of which were said to have been enhanced by a complicated bra designed by Hughes himself, putting to use his expertise as an aircraft engineer. Denounced as sinful and dirty, the film was withdrawn from general release soon after it first appeared, only to be re-released a decade later after much of the "good stuff" had been excised.

But such shocking stuff would never have been featured at the Victory. No, the Victory was a classy place, a family-friendly theater. And it was also roomy, unlike the Stinker. Its two long aisles led down to the proscenium arch, in which a gauzy curtain remained closed until show time, at which point it parted dramatically for the beginning of the selected short subjects. High up on the side walls, flanking the screen, small box seat sections, decorated with their own set of curtains, lent a gaudy, luxurious note to the theater's interior design; they sat there unused year after year, but ever ready in case Queen Elizabeth II and Prince Philip paid a visit to town. Oh, and near the entrance to the theater, just to the right as you walked in, stood a drinking fountain in its own little niche, a fountain that delivered to us the sweetest and coldest water to be had in all of Rogers.

Today's multiplexes can't hold a candle to yesterday's movie palaces, of which the Victory was a worthy small-town example. But, I'll yield the floor here to the great film critic Roger Ebert, who has seen a million times more movies than I have: "What I miss … is the wonder. People my age can remember walking into a movie palace where the ceiling was far overhead, and balconies and mezzanines reached away into the shadows. We remember the sound of a thousand people laughing all at once. And screens the size of billboards, so every seat in the house was a good seat."

(Indeed, the experience of seeing a movie with hundreds of other people is different from the one you have when it's just you and your wife and maybe three other people. Recall how much more terrifying *Jaws* seemed when you screamed or covered your eyes with seven hundred others. I remember the evening we joined a big audience of other Saturday-night moviegoers in a large theater to see *Pan's Labyrinth* and how a truly magical moment occurred when this crowd—and such an unusually huge bunch turned out for a Spanish film with subtitles—continued to chatter and crunch popcorn and noisily open candy wrappers until we all settled into a kind of trance induced by the utterly compelling, dream-like imagery and the evil workings of both men and beasts. In fact, my worst movie experience was when I went to a late showing of *The China Syndrome* and was the *only person in the theater*. About halfway through the film, the curtains closed over the screen, the lights went up, and the projector ground to a halt. I sat there stunned, thinking this was surely a mistake, before getting up to seek out someone who could get things rolling again. Reaching the lobby, I found the concession booth abandoned, not a soul in sight. Next I began to pound on a locked door labeled "Authorized Personnel Only" and was beginning to think I was approaching the Twilight Zone. Then I heard the movie start up again and returned to my seat.)

When the Hollywood studios were pumping out dozens and dozens of films each year, much as General Motors hurled Chevys and Buicks into the world, the Victory offered up a varied and briskly changing selection of films to suit almost everyone's tastes. As I write this, in the summer of 2011, the one and only movie theater in Taos, New Mexico, where we spend a part of each year, is offering five films in its tiny viewing compartments: *Captain America: The First Avenge*r (an adaptation of a Marvel comic book series aimed at kids of all ages); *Friends with Benefits* (a "date movie" for young adults featuring the latest hotties of both sexes); *Cowboys and Aliens* (a western/science fiction big-budget special effects hybrid), *The Smurfs* (a kiddie cartoon), and *Harry Potter and the Deathly Hallows, Part II* (the final installment of this franchise aimed at young teens who will text and check their messages throughout the show). In short, nothing, or at least not much (the cowboy movie sounds like fun) for anyone looking for a serious film with an adult theme. And the movies listed here will be at that theater for weeks. Maybe all summer.

But at the Victory you could see as many as five different movies a week, and the next week there'd be perhaps five new films on the marquee. If you missed a movie, you might go to another town to see it, but, as a rule, films would have their few days of life then slip into obscurity and you wouldn't see them again. Television didn't start showing old movies until the sixties, and certainly there were no VCRs, DVDs, or DVRs and no American Movie Classics or Turner Classic Movies to dial up on the tube—not yet.

The weekly lineup at my movie palace went something like this: on Tuesdays, Wednesdays, and Thursdays you could expect to see a double feature (another nearly extinct dinosaur) that might pair a B-movie film noir, maybe something with Jan Sterling or Glenn Ford, a police drama or mystery (what Aunt Ethel called "a mister' at the Victor')—with a "woman's picture," like a Bette Davis vehicle about love gained and lost and found again and then a slow death with musical accompaniment from a chorus of angels. Fridays and Saturdays were generally understood to be for us young people, and the bill of fare would spotlight a Gene Autry, Roy Rogers, or John Wayne western. You were either a Gene Autry or Roy Rogers kind of guy; you couldn't be both. My tastes leaned more toward the actor Charles Starrett, better known by any guy approaching three score years and ten as the Durango Kid, who, though a good guy, dressed entirely in black and wore a black bandanna to preserve his identity. Lash LaRue, who sported a bullwhip, was strictly beneath us; for Lash you had to go around the corner to the Stinker.

Or perhaps you'd be treated to a Bowery Boys movie, featuring the estimable stars Leo Gorcey and Huntz Hall. Or maybe a tacky, low-budget horror or science fiction schlock-o-rama like *The House of Wax*, starring

Vincent Price, or *Them,* in which giant ants, mutated by atomic fallout, bring out the army to save mankind. If you were unlucky that weekend, though, you might have to sit through a Jungle Jim black-and-white featuring an aging and ever-expanding Johnny Weissmuller, then well past his svelte days when he played Tarzan. Or perhaps you'd be stuck with a double feature beginning with a Francis the Talking Mule comedy, starring the superb dancer Donald O'Connor forced in this awful series of films to play straight man to a mule (voiced by Chill Wills), and winding up with the latest installment of the wretched Ma and Pa Kettle series, with Marjorie Main and Percy Kilbride. But we weren't proud; we'd watch anything.

Sundays and Mondays were given over to family oriented, classy, "cultural" stuff, like musicals (*State Fair, South Pacific,* and anything featuring Fred Astaire and Cyd Charisse) and biblical epics like *The Robe* or *David and Bathsheba.*

After buying your ticket, picking up your bag of popcorn, and taking care of the obligatory socializing, you'd settle back to participate in what was essentially a ritual; you knew the evening's program would unfold in a time-honored, predictable order. The selected short subjects preceded the feature presentation. First you got a glimpse of the news, brought to you by Pathé Films (whose signature logo, a squawking and flapping rooster, signaled the start of the evening's entertainment), which was usually something about the christening of a ship by Mamie Eisenhower, say, or a bathing beauty contest or a football game that was played sometime in the near past. But it was all stirring and uplifting, especially as narrated by the enthusiastic Dan Herlihy, the familiar newsreel voice of the fifties. Next came the treat, almost as anticipated and delicious as that bear claw at the next-door bakery: a cartoon, one featuring Tom and Jerry (the older ones were by far the best) or Sylvester the Cat and Tweetie Bird. I was less happy to have to settle for Mr. Magoo, voiced by the detestable Jim Backus, or the Roadrunner and Wile E. Coyote, because I always rooted for the coyote and he never prevailed.

Cartoons were followed by the previews of coming attractions (we never called them "trailers"; they were, after all, the *pre*views), but we'd still be settling in for the show and wouldn't give them much mind. Then, always greeted by moans and whistles from the rowdy sections, there was a two-minute pitch for donations by the March of Dimes or the Screen Actors' Old Peoples' Home "hosted" by some well-known celebrity. This lineup was usually augmented on Saturdays by a Three Stooges short or with a serial. (The latter is a genre familiar to anyone over sixty. But for the woefully uninformed, a serial was an ongoing drama or adventure story broken up into chapters or episodes, each one of which ended in a cliffhanger from which there appeared no chance of survival, a stagecoach containing our hero hurtling off a bluff, for example. And you had to come next Saturday to find out what happened.)

Then, finally, what we'd really come for: 90 minutes of blessed escape from our colorless, small-town, everyday lives. And how desperately Hollywood sought to give us what they thought we'd like, not only throwing at us a rich variety of movie genres pitched on an ascending scale from crap to quality in an imaginative range of technical inventiveness. And with joy and eagerness we greeted it all! As more and more Americans in the fifties parked themselves in front of televisions to get their entertainment free, the big studios started trying to tempt us back—or keep us loyal—by messing around with the old film and projection formats that had served us perfectly well for a half-century. First there was the novelty of 3-D, seen in such a non-classics as *Bwana Devil*. But that craze didn't last long. I always felt and looked like a fool—and still do—in those stupid glasses. The whole affair you just knew—or hoped, perhaps—would be as ephemeral as the hula hoop. The enormous success in recent years of James Cameron's *Avatar,* however, has convinced Hollywood that the medium is where the really big money lies, and the 3-D summertime blockbusters—aimed principally at the international market— are now back with a vengeance.

And while we'd been content with the nearly square 35mm picture aspect (actually 1.37 to 1) that had been around since 1900, Hollywood said, "Wait! We can give you *more!*" And they did: Cinerama, which debuted in 1952, required three projectors casting their images on a huge, curved screen to form one, humongous picture; Vista Vision gave us a wider, sharper picture with one projector; Cinemascope used a special lens in both camera and projector to create a picture nearly three times its height; and Todd-AO used a new, super-wide (65mm) film.

With these fancy, presumably more expensive formats came pricier tickets and even advance, reserved-seat sales. When I saw *Ben Hur* for the first time, I bought my ticket a couple of days ahead, showed up in a jacket and tie, and was ushered to my seat as if I were at the Metropolitan Opera. We were awed and grateful to be offered such an important cultural—and religious, of course—experience.

But the Victory wasn't just a public auditorium in which to watch movies; it was also a handy meeting ground in our teenage social lives, a place to get together away from school, a destination for a date, for which it might serve as a flimsy (and impatiently slogged though) prologue for the serious business of going parking after the show. We had our own special rows where we'd gather, a section on the left about halfway down. And as we moved up through the years, from one high school class to the next, from freshmen to, at long last, seniors; as our lists of laurels grew longer, from letterman in basketball to National Merit Scholar; and as our social skill sets increased from near zero to the almost acceptable—as we matured, I say—we grew not less rowdy but, emboldened by our virtually mythical sense of self-importance, our notion of ourselves as Masters of Rogers, if not Masters of the Universe, we could and often did make colossal asses of ourselves. We'd talk during the movies and move around constantly, like bees or hummingbirds making their rounds. We'd sprawl out in our seats, rest our feet on the chair backs in front of us, and toss popcorn at one another. Assembled in a darkened hall and poised to enjoy the most democratic art form ever conceived, we could relax and enjoy ourselves and one another. (Fig. 37) (As the scholar Neal Gabler has pointed out, no one would ever dream of eating, much less throwing, popcorn at the Metropolitan Opera!) Naturally, such boorish behavior required curbing, and, luckily for the other patrons, the official curber-in-residence was the Victory's manager, ticket-taker, usher, and self-appointed enforcer, the dreaded Ollie Nichols.

Nichols, a stern, middle-aged, dignified man for whom the hyphenated adjectives "hawk-nosed," "beetle-browed," and "long-suffering" may well have been originally minted, was the ultimate law-and-order man of the Victory Theater, and he took his responsibilities very seriously. Always dressed in white shirt, jacket, and tie—albeit the same shirt, jacket, and tie year after year—he'd take our tickets without uttering so much as a single "hello" or "enjoy the show." Then, after the screen's curtain parted, he would cruise the aisle nearest us just to let us know he was there, on full alert, and as unwilling as ever to take any sass from us smart-ass high school kids. After years on the job, he'd probably grown to hate any boy under 20; his manner signaled his firm conviction that we were a lower form of life. Just a slow-burn look from

Ollie was usually enough to settle us down or to remove our loafers from the seats in front of us. If more persuasive force was called for, Ollie was ready to deliver that too. One night after he'd angrily told my friend Lowell Harris two or three times to shut up and stay in his seat without reforming the behavior of our class cutup one iota, Ollie sneaked up behind Lowell and delivered a sharp-knuckled noogie to the back of his skull. Although today a kid could probably press charges for such an attack, Ollie's nuclear option back in 1959 had the desired effect: Lowell was as quiet and still as a statue for the rest of that evening.

Fig. 37. "Senior Night" at the Victory Theater, May 1960. Left to right: Karen Russell, the author, Margaret Marlowe, John Martfeld.

So, yes, we assembled at the Victory to hobnob, misbehave, and congratulate one another on being cool and young and on having our whole lives in front of us. But when the MGM lion roared or the big WB logo flashed onto the screen, accompanied by Warner Brothers' signature brassy musical intro, or when Twentieth Century Fox's trumpet fanfare blared those staccato notes we can all still play in our heads at will, we didn't need Ollie any longer to tell us to sit back and be quiet; we were ready to be transported.

Interesting how I can't recall one whit of information I learned in high school trigonometry; I don't remember a shred of enlightenment I garnered from one poem I encountered in English class (well, maybe the opening lines of Whittier's "Snowbound") or one enduring principle from any of Mrs. Price's art classes. But I can tell you plenty about the movies I saw at the Victory Theater: plot, studio, director, cast, black-and-white or color, most-moving scenes, key phrases and dialogue, costumes … Not only is my head still cluttered with factoids connected to the films I saw then, but I also gathered important lessons about style, attitude, the intricacies and nuances of romance, useful strategies for seduction, interior design, foreign accents, and on and on. And no one in Rogers, maybe no one in Arkansas, was a bigger movie fan than I, the kid who never missed any show, whether a classic or unquestionably awful or anything in between. If it had a great story loaded with bigger-than-life characters and possessed the scale of Hollywood blockbusters, like *The Greatest Show on Earth* and *Giant,* I'd go back again and again, perhaps just to see that stupendous train wreck and richly deserved death of Lyle Bettger or to watch James Dean steal every scene from Elizabeth Taylor and Rock Hudson.

My movie-going habit began in the late forties when I'd accompany (as in be dragged off by) Patsy and Phyllis to the Victory and squirm through some "woman's picture" or squeaky-clean musical, or to cower in my seat, hands covering my eyes, during a science fiction or horror film I shouldn't have been taken to see in the first place. Although I can't recall my first exposure to *Mighty Joe Young,* a 1949 film about a giant ape transported from Africa to Manhattan, a kind of *King Kong* II, I'm told that seeing it turned into a traumatic experience for little Ben Lloyd: I walked in my sleep for weeks afterward and was one night rescued from who-knows-what form of self-mutilation when I climbed onto the bathroom sink in search of razor blades in our medicine cabinet.

Hollywood wasn't so interested in our mental well-being back then; rating systems keyed to age groups were still years in the future. So I was allowed—no, encouraged—to witness all sorts of terrifying spectacles in my childhood. I recall one especially awful movie called *The Beast with Five Finger*s, starring Peter Lorre, in which a concert pianist's personal secretary, left out of her employer's will, chops off one of his gifted, pianistic hands. The only memory I retain of this gothic tale is the image of a disembodied hand running over a piano's keyboard, the very thing I did not need to see at age six or so. My nights were haunted by that damned hand for weeks thereafter.

And why did my parents allow their kid to see such terrifying spectacles? Search me. People just didn't think that much about the sensitive souls of little boys back then, I guess. If they had given the matter any thought at all, they would have spared me the agony of *The Thing* (or *The Thing from Another World*). This tale, set in the Arctic and dealing with an alien found locked in the ice who when thawed out proceeds to rip apart one unlucky scientist after another, damaged my tender psyche as well. I had never seen anything so terrifying. Not until *Jaws* did a movie again feature so menacing a creature essentially unseen until the climactic moments; the film encouraged you to conjure up its horrible form in your own head. If I'd known at age ten that the alien "thing" was portrayed by James Arness, later to star as the saintly Matt Dillon in *Gunsmoke,* that might have lessened my terror a bit, but I couldn't have known that at the time.

The curious thing is that while I was so slow to outgrow this childhood vulnerability to horror, I went back again and again for more of the same. I saw *The Fly* in 1956 when I was 14, but one or two terrible scenes in that movie turned me to jelly and caused a lot more sleepless nights.

To put it mildly, I was a very suggestible youngster, and one who was no less vulnerable to the tender and romantic than to the terrifying. Love stories could also hit me like a well-thrown brick. I was swept away by movies that dealt with love promised then denied, frustrated, or otherwise sent spinning down the tubes. I was in agony when Montgomery Clift, one of Hollywood's most beautiful men, saw an enchanting future with Elizabeth Taylor exchanged for a trip to the electric chair in *A Place in the Sun,* that gauzy, dreamy, but utterly convincing depiction of two young people in love. In the doomed-love department, that movie has never been surpassed. And when Clift, playing Private Robert E. Lee Prewitt, dies of a knife wound in *From Here to Eternity,* a World War II film set in Hawaii, I went back to the Victory to see it perhaps eight more times, rooting for Monty to pull through and have a future with his dance hall girl Loreen, played by Donna Reed.

Or did I camp out at the theater just to see Deborah Kerr one more time? Oh, that Deborah Kerr—so British, so dignified, so refined, so incredibly busty! She was one of the two Hollywood actresses I obsessed over in my early teens. I loved her in *King Solomon's Mines* when she co-starred with the equally British and beautiful Stewart Granger—why couldn't God have chosen *me* to be Stewart Granger?—and then in *Quo Vadis,* one of the better of the umpteen religious epics Hollywood threw at us in that decade. Deborah looked terrific in her toga as she played a Christian maiden in love with a Roman centurion (Robert Taylor) with whom she escapes the nefarious and ridiculous doings of the Emperor Nero, played by Peter Ustinov in a hilariously campy performance. But as Karen Holmes, the neglected wife of the base commander in *From Here to Eternity,* Deborah was cast against type as a chain-smoking middle-aged American woman in a tight skirt. She is more than a match for the athletic, tough-guy Burt Lancaster. When she and Burt hit the Hawaiian beach for a nocturnal swim date and a sexy roll in the surf, the scene got everyone's attention, especially mine, and I would have my own nocturnal events while under the prolonged influence of that memorable scene. And when Burt calls at the commander's home, knowing the wife is alone and ready to invite him inside, Deborah does her best American accent as she murmurs: "You're doing well, sergeant. My husband's away, it's raining outside, and we're both drinking." Wow.

But around 1955, a platinum-blonde, velvet-voiced, and incredibly beautiful graduate of the drama department of the Chicago Art Institute entered my days at the Victory, and I forgot all about Ms. Kerr. That Kim Novak made her debut on the screen around the time I was emerging from puberty probably made her hold on me all the stronger. She wasn't much of an actress—Alfred Hitchcock, who cast her opposite Jimmy Stewart in *Vertigo,* reportedly said of her, "You think you're getting a lot, but you're not"—but she did a perfectly wonderful job of portraying the sexiest blond in America, and that was fine with me and about ten million other American teenage boys. I first saw her in *Picnic,* the film adaptation of the William Inge play, in which she played Madge Owens, the prettiest girl in sleepy old Salina, Kansas, who gets swept away by William Holden, the penniless, ex–football star Hal who arrives in town on a freight car. In the film's most memorable moment, the two discover their remarkable sexual chemistry on the dance floor to the tune of the picture's theme music (written by Steve Allen), a variation on the old Benny Goodman standard, "Moonglow." In the months after seeing the movie I must have played that record on every jukebox in town. I was in *love.*

Picnic is almost unwatchable now. For one thing, William Holden is about fifteen or more years too old to believably play a dense ex-jock. But for a movie made in 1955, it was downright daring. Even a thirteen-year-old

Presbyterian boy could see that the two principals consummated their love the night of the picnic. That the "old maid," played by Rosalind Russell, was also sexually attracted to Hal went right over my head back then, however, probably because it was inconceivable to me that anyone over twenty-five would be interested in sex.

Another of her movies, *Vertigo,* which I thought simply strange in my younger days, has gotten better and richer with each viewing since then. In the film, Hitchcock demonstrated his genius as he transformed the modestly talented actress into two memorable characters. The plot, centering on one man's obsession, is as complicated as a Verdi opera, so suffice it to say that Novak is simply compelling as the haunted, "possessed" society woman Madeleine Elster, who appears as an ashen figure in her tailored, grey suit and platinum hair and later, after the Madeleine character dies, as Judy Barton, now with a completely different, rather tawdry appearance. In the first role Novak is the very embodiment of a lady; in the second, she's the tramp. Hitchcock brings to artistic life his fantasy of a female type who is, as he once put it, a lady in the drawing room or at a dinner party but "a whore in the back of a cab." *Vertigo,* a film as powerful and disturbing as a recurrent dream, remains a perfect example of a "classic," when that word is applied to any work of art that holds up over time and never loses its impact.

Inevitably, my Kim obsession weakened, then disappeared altogether, as I got interested in real, flesh-and-blood girls. But I could also be bowled over by the great actors of the fifties. I was mesmerized by James Dean, for example, and, after seeing *Rebel Without a Cause,* would not rest until I'd found a red nylon jacket just like the one he wore in the movie. But, oddly enough, the actor of that decade who impressed me above all others was Cary Grant, a classic figure one usually tends to attach to an earlier era. The guy began making movies in 1932! By the late 1950s he was an icon, to use once more that overused cliché—smooth, suave, stylish, the perfect gentleman or rogue, or both, depending on the role. At age 18, that's what I wanted to be, a debonair, dynamite dresser who was always perfectly turned out, a challenging task for a guy who made, at most, a dollar an hour at the time.

In Hitchcock's *North by Northwest,* Grant plays Roger Thornhill, a Madison Avenue ad man thought by spies to be an American secret agent. He is chased cross-country to the Black Hills of South Dakota, and at one point strafed by a crop-dusting plane while running through a cornfield.

Throughout this hide-and-seek pursuit, Grant appears in an immaculately tailored blue wool suit and never looks less than perfect, not a hair out of place. (One movie critic, in an offbeat take on the film, remarked that the movie is really *about* the blue suit!) When Grant finally enjoys a shower and a brief respite in a Rapid City hotel, a CIA agent brings him a fresh change of new clothes—white shirt, black slacks, black loafers, etc.—and he looks perfect in all that, too. Teenage Ben, on the verge of high school graduation and ready to say adios to Rogers and see what the rest of the world was all about, soaked up the valuable sartorial lessons Cary Grant taught him. It's important—damned important!—to look good. And, twenty years later, when I could finally afford one, I returned from a preppy Cleveland men's store clutching a hangar bearing a perfectly tailored blue wool suit.

I took in my last movie at the Victory during my college years, in the early sixties, when my mother and I went to see the first Bond movie, *Dr. No,* starring the greatest 007 of them all, Sean Connery. By then a ticket had shot up to something like $1.50, and the old entertainment center of my younger days was on its last legs. In the mid-1970s, the Victory, a casualty of changing times and the rise of the multiplexes, was converted into a flea market. Today the Victory is a dinner theater that serves a new important role in the admirable attempt to keep alive the "historic district" of my hometown. On a recent trip back to Rogers I paid a sentimental visit to the place and my jaw dropped when I saw how the interior had shrunk over the years. I had remembered the old place as a vast hall! But now, it was as if a new owner, sick of heating such a massive interior, had built a kind of partition on which to hang the screen and to wall off the back two-thirds of the space in a move to economize.

I'd hoped that the fiftieth reunion of our high school class could have been held there, but the place was already booked. Too bad. It would have been like old times.

14

Workin' for the Man

We Americans need to work. It's in our DNA. We need to make a living, and we need work to give our lives structure and meaning. The fortunate ones among us have been able to combine the two purposes. I have. Although I did not, over a teaching career that spanned three decades, make a lot of money, my family and I enjoyed a good life, and I made what I consider to be a meaningful contribution to society and to my profession. And, I hope, I was able to fulfill my dad's admonition to "make something" of myself.

One element necessary for a happy life—perhaps the most important one—is finding work that combines your natural gifts, education and training, social skills, creative abilities, and desire to make a positive contribution to others with your own rather selfish need to be successful, to "be somebody."

Not everyone is so fortunate to realize such a wonderful mix in his or her working life. And here I come to the good news/bad news part. For each of us there is good work and there is bad work. From our first to our last, we're inevitably going to experience both kinds of jobs. And what we might think the absolute pits someone else will find fulfilling. Hard, physical labor requiring little education or brainpower is fine for some people but not everybody. I've done it but I hated it, primarily because I've lacked the strength and staying power for it. Recently, the widow of a victim killed in a West Virginia coal mine explosion proclaimed proudly that her husband loved the mines and looked forward to returning to work each day. That same miner might have thought that talking about art in a darkened room for thirty years was a ludicrous waste of time, and all those years spent earning advanced degrees could have been better used to earn a decent income.

Bad work is basically work you hate and can't wait to move on from, whether to the next job or retirement. And you hate it for a variety of reasons. You're not suited for it. Or maybe you're out of your depth. Or perhaps you're overqualified and find it boring, without challenge. Or you're forced to work with people you can't stand, and you have to be with them seemingly forever, or at least from 9 to 5 on a strictly enforced schedule. Or perhaps an overbearing boss is constantly monitoring how you spend your time. Conditions in the workplace have improved since the Victorian era, when 12-to-14-hour days six days a week was the rule, but that's little comfort to today's unhappy employee. Maybe your boss or supervisor is a detestable tyrant who lords it over you, making your life miserable when you know you're much smarter than he or she is. Or perhaps it's a dead-end job with little or no chance for advancement and only the most grudging hikes in pay. Or it could be that you're sure you are being paid less than you're worth (a consistent leitmotif in academic bitching). Or you may have found yourself in a job that overwhelmed you with all these miseries and was also physically exhausting. (There's no better portrayal of a soul-crushing workplace, the meat packing industry, than Upton Sinclair's novel *The Jungle*.)

Too often those stuck in jobs they consider pointless or beneath them have limited opportunities to change their situations: there might not be anything better available, or they can't relocate, or perhaps, by education or ability, they can't improve their lot. Or maybe they're in debt and can't afford to lose the job they've got. We've all encountered people mired in these kinds of jobs. They're the TGIF crowd that spends much time during the week leading up to their Friday liberations talking about and looking forward to their "breaks." The workday, then the week, is something to get through, survive. They are the cashiers who never smile and don't see you and are remarkably capable of the most creative reasons to be late or to leave early. Their moaning and groaning about the job becomes a pain for their fellow workers, unless they, too, join the chorus.

Good work is the kind you want to find and stick with because you love it. It's fulfilling and rewarding. Who you are and what you do become one and the same. It's great work because it brings out the best in you. The happy worker might also be one who believes he can make a contribution to society. He wants to be useful, to ask "how can we make things better" or "how can I help this company/office/college succeed in its mission." Essentially, you're being paid for something you might do for free. The ultimate example of a happy worker was Winslow Homer, the American watercolorist who was paid handsomely for works of art that celebrated his life on the Maine coast and his travels to the woods upstate and the Caribbean. For Homer, there was no distinction between work and vacation; his work was pure pleasure.

Dad worked a five-and-a-half- or six-day work week from his mid-teens until he was nearly seventy years old. And was glad to have the work, not just because he needed to support his growing family but also because he appeared to like carpentry and being the man who could be depended on to get the job done well. He took pride in each house he built, and he built dozens in Rogers. Pride of workmanship served to sharpen his critical eye to the work of other builders, most of which he found lacking. The worst thing he could say about a slip-shod piece of construction was that it resembled "a widow-woman's job." He worked for little pay and had no real job security or prospects of ever being able to amass a nest egg so that, at the end, he could take it easy. He never belonged to a union—Arkansas being a right-to-work state, meaning that no union could lock out a nonunion workman—so he pretty much had to work on his boss's terms. During his 50-plus years as a builder of houses, he never enjoyed a vacation (unless you count the days when he was idle because there was no work or because work was suspended when it got too cold). Despite his lot, Dad was no complainer. He took his work seriously and gave good service for his $2.75 an hour. Adjusted for inflation, Dad's $2.75 hourly wage in 1958 would be $20.22 today, or $889.68 a week (a 44-hour week; he worked Saturday mornings), $3,558.72 a month, and $42,704.64 a year before payroll taxes. That seems like a lot, but even today I think of a dollar still having its 1950s value, when gasoline was a quarter a gallon and a hamburger was a dime.

Implicit in Dad's no-nonsense approach to work was a belief that working was honorable, was the decent thing to do, while idleness had the smell of sin and corruption about it. He would not have been out of place in the front pew of a New England meetinghouse where the preacher spoke of God's blessings flowing to the industrious and the thrifty while the idle were only a drag on society. And what was true and right for Dad should apply to everyone, and most immediately to the people in his own family. In the Bassham household, it was never a question of working or not working; you worked, period. We're not talking about a breach of child labor laws here. We guys were allowed to finish our boyhoods and to go to school. But as soon as we hit our teens and school recessed for the summer, it was "get to work."

From the age of 14 until well into college, I worked every summer. I liked earning my own "walking around" money. I got no allowance, and I hated asking my parents for money. And I needed money—bad! I remember one time in particular when I was caught short of money. On a church trip to Oklahoma City with Bob Moser and other fellow Presbyites, I took a whole roll of color film with my new camera. When I returned to the drugstore where I'd dropped off the film to be developed, I learned that my little packet of memories would cost about $6.50. *Six dollars and fifty cents!* (Adjusted for inflation, that's about 50 bucks today.) I didn't have it. Or, more precisely, if I'd had it, I wasn't about to spend it on twenty lousy color photographs. So I just left the packet of photos there, saying I'd be back later when I'd saved up the cash, and thereafter I'd drop by and, as nonchalantly as a 16-year-old can, ask if I could just take another glance at my pictures, go through them once again, and take my leave, promising to be back soon to settle up. Bless their hearts, the girls behind the cash register could not have been nicer or more accommodating.

So, making my own money was important, but mostly I worked because I did not look forward to spending my summers having Dad roust me out of bed every morning and shove me out the door to find a job. (Recently I had lunch in Rogers with five classmates—four women, one guy—and asked them what summer jobs they'd had in their teens. To my astonishment, not one of them recalled working during summer vacations.)

Bill and Bud worked with Dad on construction jobs every summer while they were in high school, and even earlier, as boys, they had hired themselves out to work farmers' fields behind a horse and plow. Bud especially hated manual labor and vowed early that he would not spend life outdoors as "somebody's mule." He was the first in our family to go to college, determined to use his brains and not his body to earn his living; he wanted to become, in the words of a later acquaintance of mine, "the man other people go to see."

Thus, for Bud, work had been a valuable, alternative form of education: He learned what he did *not* want to do. And work can teach a few other valuable lessons as well: how to get along with other people; how to know when to speak up and when to keep your mouth shut; how to follow directions, even from a boss you're convinced is an idiot; how to learn from mistakes; how to find out what you are good or hopeless at; and how to handle money. In short, the whole enterprise is a course in reality.

I entered the wonderful world of work and learned my first bitter lessons at about age 11 or 12, when I joined the newspaper business. I became a paperboy. I was only at it for a few months, but that time seemed like an eternity to me. John Buckelew, a classmate from earliest childhood both in school and at Sunday school, passed on his paper route, which he also had for only a few months. It had not taken him long to find out that the arrangement by which he made money delivering papers was a recipe for disaster, and he welcomed the chance to pass his business on to an eager young recruit like me. You see, the circulation manager of the newspaper—either the *Northwest Arkansas Times* out of Fayetteville or the *Arkansas Gazette* from Little Rock, I forget which—sold the papers to us deliverers at a discount and then encouraged us paperboys to collect the higher subscription fees from their customers, thereby earning a profit. In other words, capitalism in miniature. It was not an enterprise for the faint of heart. Delivering the papers was actually kind of fun; collecting was pure torture.

John was the only son of two pillars of the Rogers community. His father, Dr. Hollis Buckelew, one of the town's most respected physicians, passed away from heart disease at a relatively young age. John's mother, Hazel, was a nurse and, when I knew her, sang a sweet, quavering soprano in our church choir (where I sang bass-baritone). She was a splendid lady and a fabulous mother to her boy John. And she could surprise townspeople and John's playmates with her independent thinking. She was one of the first, if not the very first, driver in Arkansas to purchase a Volkswagen Beetle, for example. She also had the originality to stage a Sunday-afternoon tea dance in her home so that John and his friends, and some invited girls, could rise above our customary savagery to learn how to negotiate a social occasion. That kind of thing hardly ever happened in Rogers.

John and I often played together, at my house or his. We each had hordes of plastic army guys along with supporting tanks, artillery, and fighter planes to fight our wars on the floor or bed (wrinkled blankets formed nice mountains and valleys). We paid close attention to military "stagery," as we used to call it (a George W. Bushism long before its time). Our engagements would invariably end in arguments and harsh words concerning whose army had the most firepower or whose forts could withstand the other's bombardments more successfully. We would sometimes part in an ill-tempered way, perhaps ordering the other to leave the premises and never return, but then we'd soon make up and resume our wars.

We also played touch football or, later, tennis together and took our squabbling onto the field or court. With my childhood hotheadedness, John's calm and somewhat aloof demeanor sometimes sent me around the bend. But we got along pretty well during our high school years. The guy I had once pigeonholed as a softy when he was little developed into a big, tough guy in his later teens. He became a brawny and aggressive member of the football team—he played lineman and was the placekicker—and, in his senior year, won an appointment to the Naval Academy, where he earned the rank of lieutenant in the Marine Corps. And, as an officer, he then served with distinction in Vietnam.

So, thanks to John, I found myself, in the middle of winter, rising before dawn and riding my bicycle, now equipped with an enormous basket, the mile or so from South Thirteenth Street to the circulation manager's drop-off point downtown, where I picked up my stack of papers. After 10 minutes or so spent ingeniously folding each paper into a compact missile in a variation of origami taught by my mentor, the aforesaid Buckelew, I set off to attempt the only fun part of the job: launching the papers onto front porches with a satisfying thwack. I made my rounds that winter in a getup so absurd that I deeply regret that no photographs preserved my appearance. I wore a wool-lined, leather, World War II Army Air Corps helmet to keep my head warm (despite the small holes located over the ears for airmen to hear their earphones through); my recently acquired eyeglasses, which doubled as wind goggles; jersey gloves (the only kind I could afford); and a rubber band around my pants cuffs to keep them free of the bicycle chain. My coat was either a thin jean jacket or my prized suede jacket I received as a quite unexpected gift one Christmas. I had so few customers that I could complete my deliveries in less than an hour and head home for breakfast and a bit of the *Today* show (featuring Dave Garroway, Frank Blair, and their staff chimpanzee) before heading off to school. On mornings when it rained or snowed, Dad would drive me on my rounds. Once when I was sick, or pretending to be sick, he even uncomplainingly made the deliveries himself.

But my newspaper business was a money-losing proposition. Deliveries weren't so bad— any job involving a bicycle has some redeeming features—

but collecting was a huge hassle. When, before taking over the route, I asked Buckelew what collecting was like, he sang the praises of the process and painted a rosy word-picture, with all the charm and artifice of a master. He conjured up portraits of grandfatherly, pipe-smoking clients with soft spots in their hearts for hard-working youths and of aproned housewives ready with fresh-baked cookies for their darling delivery boy. "Only fifteen cents today?" they'd ask. "Here's a quarter tip, dear boy, for always putting it on the porch." I *do* exaggerate a bit. Instead, my customers wouldn't be home (even though it was collection day!), or I wouldn't have change for a ten, or they wouldn't have money at all. Frequently they would want to argue over the bill: "Weren't you just here?" they'd ask. I learned it was always a mistake to wake someone up, or hit them on a day they were suffering from a massive hangover. It was also a bit depressing to get glimpses into the chaotic, foul-smelling interiors of some of my customers' homes and then be met by the words, "Sorry, boy, I just ain't got it today." Some of my customers were so decrepit they sometimes made it to the door and sometimes didn't. One was said to be a veteran of the Spanish-American War. Then there was the task of trying to keep proper records of all of this, who had paid, how much, and when. Maybe I *had* collected twice from the same customer that week. It was not long before I found another mark and began singing my own version of the Buckelew siren song. And with that, my first and only foray into the free enterprise system ended.

Throughout my teenage years, oddly enough, jobs fell into my lap; I never needed to apply or interview for any opening. My "agents" were Phyllis and Dad. Phyllis would begin working in a place first and then whisper my name when the boss happened to mention that he needed a boy for this, that, or the other. And Dad was seemingly always on the lookout for openings for me, whether I was qualified for them or not.

(Fast forward about 15 years. I returned home from graduate school for the summer to the family's new home in Tulsa. At supper my first evening back, Dad says, "Well, boy, I found a job for you, starting tomorrow." "Oh, what kind of job?" says I, fearing the worst. "You'll find out, starting at 8:00," he replies to me, a lad accustomed to rising two hours later. When he drops me off at my post the next day, I see before me a waking nightmare: a tractor trailer loaded with concrete blocks. "Just unload these blocks and stack them over here," Dad says, a little smile playing on his face. And so I went from studying the influence of the High Renaissance on Italian Mannerism to this back-breaking labor in the Oklahoma sun. Today they use fork-lifts for jobs like this; then they used budding art historians.)

I was thirteen when I landed a morning job at the Rexall Corner Drugstore downtown, and this time the job was fun and even led to something more important. Again, Phyllis had worked there behind the fountain, pouring coffee, making milkshakes, and dispensing cherry cokes to groups of businessmen in the morning or to the preshow crowds in the evening (the drugstore was situated equidistant from both of the town's movie theaters). My duties were to sweep the sidewalks and wash the plate-glass windows each day before school; I think they paid me 35 cents an hour for work that took perhaps thirty minutes each morning. "They" were the store's owner, head pharmacist and chief grouch Fred Applegate and his assistant, the more affable Kenneth Petway. When Phyllis moved on to her next job at the Munsingwear plant south of town (now a single mother of a toddler, she needed higher pay, though she still lived at home), I moved into her old job behind the fountain counter in charge of drinks, sundaes, and milkshakes, in which capacity I distinguished myself. I became a master of not only the conventional concoctions but also such creative treats as cherry phosphates, pineapple milkshakes, and lime cokes. I also sold cigarettes, cigars, and pipe tobacco as well as chewing gum and magazines, including the *Police Gazette*. My job description also included a regular mopping of the linoleum floor every Wednesday night, a task I didn't look forward to.

Rexall was a classic small-town drugstore, rather like the drugstore where Jimmy Stewart worked in *It's a Beautiful Life*. It was proudly old-fashioned. Its perimeter interior walls were covered with dark-stained wood cabinets below and beautiful glass-enclosed cabinets above; the place was as dark and gloomy as a mortuary. Glazed cabinets displayed boxes of candy, camera equipment, patent medicines, and sundry other items. (Sometime after I moved away, the drugstore's interior was stripped of its beautiful woodwork, cabinets, and beveled glass and remodeled into a more up-to-date, gleaming white space similar to today's "big box" drugstores in a move calculated to show that Rexall was no longer anchored to the past. All that beautiful carpentry went into a dumpster.) The pharmacy was at the back, decorated with the customary glass containers of green and red mystery liquids that symbolized the arcane science of pill dispensing. This was Mr. Applegate's domain, and

I was not welcome there. Behind the counter were, among other things, that product no one dared mention in public: contraceptives. "Rubbers," we called them (or, as one of my classmates referred to them, "proto-plastics"). Only Applegate and Petway were allowed to sell them. The same was true of certain "feminine products." If a lady came in to purchase sanitary napkins, we were to immediately refer her to our white-jacketed professionals in the back. What if it was an emergency, I wanted to ask.

There were six or so booths on the fountain side of the store and they, too, were like relics of the early part of the century. In the main these were occupied by a morning crowd of clerks and managers from nearby stores who would come in for a cup of coffee and a smoke. As a tall, skinny, four-eyed adolescent, I became a handy target for their gentle joshing. One morning the father of a girl I had a crush on came in for coffee and, fully knowing that I liked his daughter, complained that his coffee wasn't hot enough. "I could stick my dick in it and it wouldn't get burned," he observed, and I was sent back to fetch a fresh cup. I thought that this seemed an odd way of determining the temperature of a liquid; I didn't wait around to see if he tested it.

At Rexall drugs, I had a broad and illuminating view of the pulse of life downtown, such as it was. I got to know a lot of people who had made the fountain their hangout for years. The younger clientele were for the most part characters from the fringes of society; the tonier crowd and the elite of Rogers High School hung out across the street at the Rose Pharmacy, where, after school, they could lounge noisily in the booths, consume Cokes and grilled cheese sandwiches, and shoot chewing gum–tipped straw wrappers at the ceiling, which accumulated there like stalactites for years. Perhaps Rexall's was associated by the snobbish set with other establishments that clustered on the south side of Walnut between South Second and Third streets, a pool hall and the Rogers Theater. A couple of greasy spoons, a barber shop, and the ice cream parlor on the corner rounded out the block.

One of our regulars, a guy who seemingly never missed a Sunday-afternoon stop at the fountain, was a retarded man whose parents owned a fruit and vegetable stand on Highway 71 on the way to Springdale. Once each week he'd hitchhike to town to stop by for a Coke, a visit of an hour or so, and the inevitable teasing. I recall—or wish to recall—that I didn't take part in the teasing; I simply talked to him, loudly, as if he were a child. We called him—and if there is a God and a Heaven I'll have to answer for this someday—"Ick." His real name, or at least his less insulting name, was Buddy Harris. He could speak only a little and that with difficulty, but he could understand us and respond mostly with nods and grunts. Sometimes other people at the counter would get too rough with him or ridicule him with mocking laughter, and then Buddy's eyes would well up and he would leave, letting us know by his expression and body language that he was hurt and angry and of a mind to avoid our company in future. The irony is that physically he was a formidable, well-muscled man whose body had been shaped by hard work and heavy lifting at the vegetable stand. He could probably have killed any of us with his bare hands. He was a good person with the mental age of a child of five or so. This was all 55 years ago, and I always wondered what the rest of his life had been like. Only recently did I learn that he was hit by a car and killed several years ago while making one of his many trips into town.

Business at the drugstore was not brisk in any season or at any time of day; it was one of four pharmacies in town, after all (there was an Applegate Drug Store on South First Street run by Fred's nephew). So my job at the fountain was not a taxing one. Occasionally, in the evenings, Mr. Petway would bring out his guitar and sing a gentle song or two for the help and our few customers. He also liked to regale us with lame jokes; there was more than a bit of the entertainer in him. He was a wonderful, good-looking man, soft spoken and agreeable; he could have been one of the recurring characters on *The Andy Griffith Show*.

Mr. Applegate was another matter: I never saw a smile on his face. He was a boss that you didn't want to tangle with. When I woke up in the middle of the night at our big rented house on North Fourth Street remembering that I'd forgotten to turn off and clean the coffeepot back at the drugstore fountain, I was certain that I was a goner. But when I arrived at work later that day, I found that the place hadn't burned down and the coffeepot, now with a brown residue baked into its bottom, had been put to right by Mr. Applegate, and I received only a mild rebuke.

Sadly, Fred Applegate, after his retirement and the sale of the store, lost his wife, Margie, to cancer. Inconsolable, he essentially drank himself to death. Kenneth Petway, who eventually bought the drugstore from Applegate, still lives in retirement in Rogers, where he writes and publishes his poetry.

I left my post at the drugstore the fall that I entered my freshman year in high school, whether by my own volition or because I was gently let go I can't recall. But I was not through with the service industry, for the next summer, 1957, once again Phyllis, who had left the sweatshops of Munsingwear to begin waiting on tables at the Lakeside Café, suggested to her boss, Cactus Clark, that I was the perfect candidate for the job of dishwasher, which required minimal training and no brainpower whatsoever. The job paid $20 a week with one meal a day thrown in. (That 20 bucks a week would have $154.90 of buying power today.) I washed dishes in a big plastic basket that I shoved into a machine that blitzed them with high-pressure soapy water jets and then rinsed them; the rinse water was so hot the dishes dried themselves. In addition, I was given the duty of filling bowls with precut salad fixings prior to the evening rush hour.

I really liked my job at the restaurant. We had a talented and good-humored cook—we didn't know the word "chef" then—and he kept the mood in the kitchen upbeat and cheerful. I have tried my best but can't recall the man's name. He had a small café downtown, west of the Rogers Theater, where he was said to serve a dynamite bowl of chili, and he either moonlighted there and worked full time for Cactus or spent most of his time at his own place and moonlighted at Lakeside; I never could determine which. But our cook was a true mensch. When leftover T-bones were brought in with only two or three bites taken out of them by probably some dainty female diner, he'd say, "Sure, go ahead, what the hell, help yourself," and another kitchen gofer and I would dig in and finish it up.

The Lakeside was the town's most prestigious restaurant, known for those steaks, and it attracted good crowds from both Rogers and the surrounding area. The place had something of an air of a country club in a town that lacked such a tony amenity, for it was part of a complex that also included a heated swimming pool on an outdoor terrace that diners could sit beside and watch the bathers or look out onto Lake Atalanta. The restaurant was the brainchild of J. D. "Cactus" Clark and his wife, LaVonne. Cactus was the oldest of three brothers who were active in Rogers businesses. Harry Vance "Buddy" Clark owned the Horseshoe Café downtown on North Third Street, and Ernest ("Buck") ran a Phillips 66 gas station on South Fourth across the street from the Presbyterian Church. (Fig. 38)

Fig. 38. Cactus Clark (far left) and Buddy Clark (center), ca. 1951.
Courtesy of LaVonne Clark

(Establishments such as Buck's service station and its ilk in the 1950s were run not by cashiers whose dealings with the public today extend hardly further than selling them lottery tickets and beef jerky but, rather, by people like Buck, who would actually come out to your car, dressed in a shirt and a cap with the company's logo prominently displayed on both, and fill your tank—or give you a dollar's worth of gas, my usual limit then—and ask you if he could check your oil and maybe your tires, clean off your windshield, and answer a query about that strange noise coming from under the hood. He also had an actual mechanic's shop, where he repaired engines and changed tires.)

Cactus was a terrific guy and a good boss, but he wore his heart on his sleeve. When business was booming, he was upbeat and fun to chew the fat with; but when things lagged because of cool or rainy weather that chased customers off the terrace, he got sullen and closemouthed. One of the few times I ever saw him grow testy was when one of the waitresses got too familiar once too often by asking him at closing time, for the hundredth time that summer, how much we'd taken in that day. Finally he'd had enough:

"None of your goddamned business!" he replied, stalking off in a huff. (It was said of Cactus that he was the town's most successful businessman who never made any money.)

Unfortunately, because of an incident years later, after I'd graduated from the University of Arkansas, Cactus and I did not part amicably before his death. A few of us in my family—Bud, Phyllis, some others, and I—went to the Lakeside for those delicious steaks (which by that time Cactus had started dousing with Lawrie's Salt, whether you wanted it or not). In my snide manner, I whispered to Phyllis that I thought Cactus should give me my meal as part compensation for that lousy 20 bucks a week he'd paid me way-back-when. Phyllis thought that was so funny (and maybe true) that she repeated it to Cactus, who, understandably, was not amused. He didn't say anything; he just fumed, deservedly so. For my part, I was ready to dive under the table. But because of my stupid, unthinking remark, our once-friendly relationship frosted over and never thawed.

During a brief period in my teens I also washed dishes at Buddy Clark's Horseshoe Café, though I can't recall exactly when and for how long. I liked Buddy even more than Cactus; both were very likable fellows. Buddy was a short, compact, handsome man with a lively wit and joie de vivre that made him one of Rogers' most popular and attractive characters, especially with the ladies, or so it was said. I know his waitresses adored him and even seemed to compete with one another for his attention. He was always fun to be around. In the kitchen, where Buddy doubled as both café owner and cook, he would point at me as if he had some important directions or ideas to share, pause dramatically, and then break into an upbeat rendition of "Cement Mixer, Putty, Putty," a popular ditty of the 1940s. He was a man who adored life while also giving the impression that he thought most of it was a kind of joke.

Sadly, this very vital man was shot and killed by the woman reputed to be his lover during a hot July night in 1958, thereby setting off probably the biggest scandal and the most sensational criminal trial in our town's history. The woman, Virginia "Queenie" Rand, a tall, slim beauty who, beneath a wide-brimmed straw hat, worked on her tan almost daily at the Lakeside Pool, was the wife of J. O. Rand Jr., a prominent Rogers businessman who also served on the school board. With her regal (hence "Queenie') bearing and legs that went on forever, she was like someone who had been lifted up out of Hollywood and deposited plunk down in little ol' Rogers, where she stood out like an emerald in a bowl of grits. In retrospect, one could argue that she was accused not only of murdering Buddy but also of being too beautiful for Rogers. She was indicted, charged with second degree murder, and her case went before the court in Bentonville, the county seat. Her attorney argued that Buddy and she were not lovers and that she had shot him in self-defense that Saturday night because he was an intruder in her bedroom. Figuratively speaking, her fellow townspeople brayed in unison, "Riiiiiight!" Despite this dubious claim, for of course everyone *knew* they'd been carrying on a long-term affair, Queenie was convicted and sentenced to eight years in prison. Her attorney appealed, she fired him and got a new and presumably more expensive lawyer, the case was reheard at a new venue downstate, and Queenie was acquitted.

Buddy's death by gunshot both shocked and sobered a town unused to such dramatics, and the outcome of the trial left a sour taste in the mouths of many people in Rogers, rather like the unsatisfying verdict (to some) in the O. J. Simpson trial two generations later. First, how could it happen here, and then how could the jury have gotten it so wrong, many people asked? One clear lesson of the whole affair was that assumptions, what "everyone" absolutely believed to be true, didn't amount to a hill of beans in a court of law. The case is still sometimes hotly debated in Rogers more than five decades later, and theories concerning what really happened abound.

Back to work …

Dad, always vigilant on my behalf, and never content with any of his male offspring staying in bed past 9:00 A.M. when they could be out earning up to a dollar an hour, found me a job one summer that turned out to be a true disaster. Again, I can't remember exactly which summer—'58 or 59?—and neither can I recall how long I had this job, but I was so inept at it that it couldn't have lasted more than two or three weeks. A fellow named Harry Wesner had purchased and refurbished an old hotel, the Arkansas Traveler, at the corner of Walnut and North Third, and right next door he built a café, Wesner's Grill. (Fig. 39) Harry was a nice guy, a popular figure in Rogers' business circles and one of the town characters. He had kind of rubbery, funny-looking face that made him resemble one of those journeymen wrestlers we were all watching on TV in those years. I mean it as a compliment when I say he could have joined Moe, Larry, and Curly as the fourth stooge.

The summer I worked for Harry was the café's debut; everything in it was brand new, including the fry cook—Harry—and his all-purpose, all-around … me. Wesner's Grill was a small establishment, with a counter, six or eight counter stools, and maybe four booths; when full it might have held 20 people. Harry wasn't going to get rich there, but as the head cook and coffee pourer, he could chew the fat with the handful of regulars who stopped by while providing a handy dining spot for visitors staying at his hotel next door.

Fig. 39. Travelers Hotel and Wesner's Grill, late 1950s.
Courtesy of Rogers Historical Museum

We served breakfasts, burgers, the full high-cholesterol bill of fare. And Harry had one tried-and-true specialty of the house: chicken-fried steak served on a platter with coleslaw and enough french fries to feed six people, the entrée of choice then and now anywhere south of the Mason and Dixon Line. (If you haven't had one you haven't lived life to the fullest, and if you've had a lot of them you probably will not live very long. Here's how you make it: take a piece of beef, one that has been cut to a standardized oval shape, then tenderize it by running it through a machine that punches a thousand tiny holes in its hide, a kind of pre-mastication step; process it, in other words, until it retains a mere trace of the donor steer's D.N.A. Next dip both sides of the meat-like substance in a batter of egg, flour, and spices and lower it in a basket into a vat of super-hot cooking oil. Cook like, oh, I don't know, forever. Serve then stand back to watch Wesner's *pièce de résistance* consumed with gusto. Everybody loved it. Actually, it does sound pretty good; I wish I had one right now.)

And, always, you had to keep the coffee coming, gallons of it. My friend Jerry Patterson's dad would come in every day and drink coffee for an hour, it seemed. He'd always say, "The hotter the coffee, the more it cools a body down on a hot day like this." (He worked at the ice plant.) This morsel of Ozark wisdom was one I could never quite grasp. The physics of it all eluded me.

I'm not quite sure exactly what I did, or was supposed to do, at Wesner's Grill. I know I peeled potatoes and cut the fries. We had a device mounted on a counter in the back that you put the potato in, standing it on one end and then pulling down on a handle that pushed the spud through a grid of blades. That was fun, but I couldn't have done that for eight hours at a stretch. Did I cook? Harry would never have trusted such an important job as that to me. I guess I waited on customers, took orders, rang up the money, cleaned off the counter, made coffee. Most of the time I just walked around in a fog. I have sharper memories of the things I did wrong, though, and one such screwup sort of sums up my whole, miserable time at the Grill.

We had a big stainless-steel refrigerator behind the counter in which we kept the milk. One day when milk had run out, I had to replace the canister. These containers were equipped with a rubber tube that was perhaps eight or 10 inches long. You put the canister in the cooler with the tube at the bottom; then you pushed up on a handle with its heavy stainless-steel ball on the end and put the tube in back of the handle, so that when said handle was lowered the weight of the ball pinched the tube tightly. You then cut off the end of the tube. To dispense the milk, you lifted the handle, unpinching the tube, so to speak, and let it flow. But the one and only time Harry let me renew the milk supply, I stretched the tube toward me to cut off the end, and, sure enough, the tube, as if withdrawing into itself, made its way slowly past the pinch zone, the point of no return, and milk—pints, if not gallons of it—began flowing everywhere. Harry went into a full panic mode. Not only was this expensive, messy, and embarrassing (the café was full at the time), it was inexcusable idiocy. Not many days afterward, Harry took me aside in the back room and there gently, quietly, and tastefully fired my ass. He said:

"Ben Lloyd, I'm not firing you. I don't want your daddy to hear that I'm firing you. But it just didn't work out. I'm just letting you go. You're a good boy, but you're probably not cut out for the restaurant business." This was the one and only time I ever got fired, and, let it be said, I richly deserved it.

I was not particularly happy in Harry's employ, but I looked back on my job at the café with a bitter nostalgia when I joined my dad as a carpenter-laborer-gofer on constructions jobs in the weeks that followed. Problem was, I could not be fired when the boss was my father. (To escape his clutches, I discovered, I would have to grow up, go to college, and become a professor, which is exactly what I eventually did.)

I suppose I could have opted for another summertime employment opportunity dangled before us high school kids: picking watermelons in Texas. This was touted widely each year as a chance to make big bucks by working long hours at a dollar an hour in the Texas sun and at the same time "building yourself up" in preparation for the upcoming football season by heaving the big melons up onto trucks. The boys from Rogers were bused down to the nether reaches of the Lone Star State and housed in barracks during the weeks of the harvest season and fed at the contactor's expense. Most returned with neat rolls of dollars and some with another souvenir of their trip, a certain communicable disease acquired in sundry haunts south of the border. I passed on both experiences, the watermelons and the nighttime revels.

I look back with very conflicted feelings on the summers I worked in construction with my dad, and I'm sure my brothers also viewed their days as Dad's subordinates with mixed feelings. Bud, especially, found throughout his life that getting along with Dad was almost impossible for him, and he did everything he could to escape Dad's domineering presence and control. (Toward the end of his life, Bud had stopped speaking to our father.) The trouble for all of us was that Dad had basically two faces that he put on to confront the world. He could be genial, companionable, even charming a good deal of the time and then, without warning, become combative, furious, frustrated, and angry with the world and everyone in it. To be in the sights of this frustration, to be the target of his out-of-control anger, could result in a frightening and unpleasant experience. At "the job," as we always called whatever house we were building at the time, he, as both foreman and superintendent of construction, might be hesitant to ball out one of the other carpenters, but his sons got no such pass, and we often caught hell from him in front of all the others.

And there were also the Arkansas summers to contend with. I had then and still have now almost no tolerance for heat and humidity. (As I write this, I am in the high desert country of New Mexico, where both rain and humidity are strangers and where the mountain air during all seasons of the year should be bottled and sold for $1,000 a unit. I live the rest of the year in northeast Ohio, which has its own hot and sultry summers, but the region is blessedly visited perhaps a dozen times each summer by cool, dry air imported from Canada, nature's air conditioning.) I recall one day in the mid-1950s when the thermometer hit 111. It got so we were always careful to keep our tools out of the sun whenever possible because otherwise they could get too hot to handle. One summer I worked with my brother-in-law, Joe Mathew, a masonry contractor, when my assignment was to mix mortar, carry it to the bricklayers in a wheelbarrow, and tote bricks up ladders to scaffolds. It was maybe 90 degrees that morning, and by 10:30 I had folded up like a cheap suitcase. Taking pity on me, Joe, with tact and understanding, sent me home.

On the plus side, working construction jobs brought me more money than dishwashing or working behind a soda fountain. In 1959, my labor brought me a dollar an hour, and I could take home, after payroll deductions, around $35 a week (about $276 in 2012 purchasing power). Sometimes I'd earn a bit more if we worked Saturday mornings. The cash came in handy for clothes, dates, and the like, and when I started college in 1960, I saved my earnings to pay for tuition. I didn't own a car (and wouldn't until I was 27), so I had no debt, no insurance payments. Room and board was taken care of. Come to think of it, I was, financially at least, on easy street (and we actually had an Easy Street in Rogers).

The two luxuries I allowed myself were a Zenith high-fidelity phonograph and a subscription to the Columbia Record Club. I bought the record player "on time" from Rogers Radio and Electric, the downtown establishment not coincidentally owned by Cedric Watson and his brother-in-law Scotty, the very businessmen who also doubled as the builders who employed Dad and me. I paid about $15 a month for an attractive little affair about the size of an end table. (I paid, that is, until I just sort of stopped paying, after which no one said a cross word, or any word at all, despite the obvious fact that I was shafting Cedric and Scotty on the deal. Perhaps they figured they'd made their cost and a little more and just let it go.) My little hi-fi brought all of us a great deal of pleasant evenings. I listened to my recordings of Mozart's 40th and 41st symphonies, my many Four Freshmen records, and Nat King Cole. And Dad and Momma loved our LP of Harry Bellefonte's calypso songs.

So, working with Dad during the summers of my teens—and those summers all run together in my memory—was both agonizing and satisfying, the feeling that comes from doing the few things you like doing and doing them well. I liked framing, for example, that aspect of raising a house that involves hammering together the skeletal structure, the flooring joists, the two-by-fours of the walls, and the ceiling joists and rafters. All this happened surprisingly quickly; the frame of the house would seem to rise like the pop-up paper structures in children's books. I also enjoyed roofing the house, when we hammered down tongue-and-groove boards, covered them with tar paper, then topped it all with the overlapping shingles. (This reminds me of a joke. An out-of-work English professor applies for a job at a construction site. The foreman says, "I can't hire you. You don't know a girder from a joist." The professor replies, "I surely do. The first wrote *Faust,* the other one wrote *Ulysses.*")

Other aspects of construction were not such fun. The digging for the footers, for example. We had to dig ditches with picks and long-handled shovels, a technology dating from the time of the Egyptian pyramids, so that a concrete base—the footers—could be laid down to support the foundations. Apparently the backhoe, which today can accomplish the task of digging ditches for the foundation of a small house in two to three hours, had not yet been invented. My workmate and indispensable companion for this back-breaking duty was a perfectly stereotypical hillbilly named Hickory Williams (I never knew his real name), a good-humored, stoical bachelor who worked for Dad for years, perhaps because he had a knack for lightening the load of every workday by entertaining all of us. (If you know the character actor Arthur Hunnicutt from long ago, you'd recognize in him a rough approximation of Hickory.)

I'd known Hickory since I was a boy of seven or eight, when I begged Dad to let me come to the job at least for part of the day. There I'd busy myself in the sandpile I could always count on being there, along with the sand-covered turds the neighborhood cats had left behind for me to discover.

I'd also collect scraps of two-by-fours and two-by-sixes to nail together in rough approximations of battleships. Once at the jobsite, I received a bitterly painful wasp sting on one of my ears and underwent a form of folk first aid from Hickory, who held a strong conviction that his loose cigarette tobacco would lessen the pain when applied directly to the wound. It didn't. I recall that my ear swelled up and seemed to weigh about a pound. Wasps and bees seemed to seek me out of all the targets—did they sense my fear of them exuded through my pores?—and were the terror of my boyhood.

Hickory—and Dad liked to call him "Hardwood"—perhaps in his forties or fifties, was skin-and-bones, and he always showed up for work in bib overalls and a sweat-stained and much-abused slouch hat, and a roll-your-own cigarette perpetually dangled from his lips. As he worked the rocky, red clay Arkansas earth, talking constantly, the sweat dripped from his nose and down onto his cigarette. Hickory handled the long-handled shovel with a delicate, even elegant touch, the way a master surgeon might manipulate a scalpel. As if to amuse himself, or to lend a certain style to the task, he enjoyed picking up the smallest stones with the tip of his shovel and then flicking them aside. (Mark Twain said that he hated "a long-handled shovel. I never could learn to swing it properly." And I hated that particular tool as well.)

Hickory loved to tease me about my love life, or the lack of it, and colored his commentary with the most disgusting references to whatever girlfriend I was going with at the time as well as similarly unprintable lovemaking "moves" he advised me to adopt. But he was so funny and over-the-top that I didn't object too much. From time to time he'd rise up from his digging, take off his hat, wipe his brow, and exclaim with great conviction, "Oh, thank you, Lord, for that cooooooool breeze." At other times, he would let out, apropos of nothing at all, a perfect imitation of a braying donkey. His reconstruction, during the noon lunch hour one day, of a radio announcer's description of the 1959 Floyd Patterson-Ingemar Johansson prizefight, in which the Swede floored Patterson seven times in the first round and won by a TKO, was one of the funniest monologues I've ever heard. It went something like this:

> There's the bell. Ol' 'Hansson comes out like a goddamned
> bull moose. Hits Patterson with a right, another right, and
> Patterson's *down!* He's *hurt!* Up again, and Joe 'Hansson's all
> over him. Down he goes again! The refs a' countin' … one,

two, three ... but Patterson's up. He looks like he was in the worst kinda accident—maybe got hit by a truck! 'Hansson lands another right. He knocks the black'un into next week. Patterson looks awful ... he's-a spinnin' around ... eyes all dazed and shiny. And then that's it! The ref calls it off... Patterson don't know where he's at ... 'Hansson's the champ ... 'Hansson's the champ ... It's all over, folks.

It was better than being ringside. Hickory was an original folk performance artist whose dependable presence at the job lightened the eight grueling hours each weekday—plus the four hours on Saturday mornings—I spent there. I hope his retirement was long and happy after all those years spent digging footers. I can imagine he spent most of his sunset years in a rocking chair on the front porch of the rooming house he lived at on East Walnut, where I'd see him waving as I drove by on my way to Lake Atalanta on weekends.

Laughing at Hickory's antics kept me from moaning and groaning. My arms got so sunburned that summer of '59 that they looked like raw hamburger, and there was no option but to suck it up and go back out the next day. Silently I'd beg God for a thunderstorm to cool things down and give us a few moments of divine idleness. We did get a few of those blessed rainstorms, but breaks more often took the form of running errands to fetch needed materials. I looked forward to "quittin' time," when Dad would signal the much-anticipated moment by clanging a couple of metal tools together and quoting himself from yesterday and all the yesterdays before that one: "Well, boys, we didn't do much today, but we'll give 'em hell tomorrow."

(For as long as I can remember, each workday would begin around 7:30 A.M. with Dad on the telephone in the hallway about six feet from my bedroom, where invariably I was still in bed steeling myself for the day ahead. He'd be making his daily calls to the lumberyard to order all the boards and other supplies needed that day. Speaking at a volume that might suggest he was not telephoning but yelling his order out the window to the guy downtown, he'd say: "HELLO, THIS IS BASS-HAM. THAT JOB OVER ON DIXIELAND, WE NEED 14 TWO-BY-FOURS, 12, 20 TWO-BY-SIXES TEN, 10 SHEETS OF THREE-QUARTER-INCH PLYWOOD GOOD ONE SIDE, SIX ROLLS OF NUMBER-SIX TAR PAPER," and so on and on, while I groaned and rolled over toward the wall, muttering to myself, "Oh Lord, how much longer?")

Getting supplies, or doing anything precisely as Dad wanted it done, meant heading down a road with many potential pitfalls—and I fell or leaped into almost all of them. One day he sent me to the lumber yard, saying, I thought at the time, that we needed a box of 16-penny nails. When I got there, the guy taking orders asked me if I wanted box nails or common nails. (For readers unacquainted with this fine distinction among nail categories, common nails are thicker than box nails, as the thumb is stouter than the pinky finger.) No one had ever informed me before of any distinction, so of course I replied, "Common nails." Weren't they the most commonly used nails of them all? And, just as naturally, when I arrived back at the job with the wrong nails, Dad threw a fit, firing off some of his most powerful expletives, and, after denouncing me to all the other workers as the idiot that I was, sent me back to correct my error.

(My friend and boss, artist Elmer Novotny, liked to point out that is was okay to make a mistake but a very bad thing to make the same mistake twice. Yes, Elmer, so true, but given how life presents us with so many first-time opportunities to make mistakes, there's no point in worrying about the rare second-time screwup!)

The dollar-an-hour servitude of ditch digging was topped on the pain scale only by the efforts involved with anything connected with concrete. Instead of building foundations out of concrete blocks, the method used almost universally today, we took the extra, more complicated, step of building forms, or molds, into which we poured concrete, rather as if we were casting concrete sculpture. When the concrete delivery truck arrived, everyone had to snap to attention and pitch in, because the task of pouring had to be done *right now*. This urgency, the heavy mud—which required some poking and pushing around, raking, shoveling, and so forth—and 90-degree temperatures all made for wickedly hard physical exertion. But I did what I could when the concrete arrived; after all, there was nowhere to hide.

And it didn't help that during those hot and physically demanding episodes Dad had many workplace rules that you were forced to live by. One in particularly seemed especially irrational and irksome at the time: the dress code. I asked Dad more than once if I could wear Bermuda shorts or cutoffs to better adapt to the baking heat of July and August. But, no; that was out of the question. "I don't want to see anybody on this job in short pants," he'd reply, and he meant it. This thinking was almost certainly based on his philosophy, one developed over four decades of experience in the construction trade, that there were certain unwritten but no less authoritative rules of decorum anyone working under him had perforce to observe. In this respect, he practiced what he preached, always showing up in pressed khaki pants or bib overalls, work shirt, and a straw hat during the summer months and a felt fedora the rest of the year. (In later years, when I supervised six to eight men and women in an office setting, I learned the value of a dress code by experience: Allow "dress-down Fridays" and that slippery slope leads to other informalities that become hard or impossible to reverse.) And on one memorable occasion I overheard him telling an older laborer who lived far back in a hollow near the White River to take a bath, if need be in the river, because he didn't want the man to show up again and "stink the place up."

There were other rules. He did not eat a big meal during the midday lunch break because he believed that a full stomach slowed you down and dulled the mind, and, because he frowned on pigging out, he discouraged me from doing so, no matter how starved I was by noontime. Of course this rule didn't extend to anyone else. (It almost goes without saying that you absolutely never went out to McDonalds or some similar fast-food place to get your lunch, as is so common today. Rather, you brought your lunch in a modest, metal lunch box, as self-respecting workers had done since the beginning of time.) And he never allowed a radio to be blasting away at the construction site; we were supposed to be working, after all, not being entertained. Today, every Lowe's and Home Depot stocks a DeWalt radio designed specifically for hard-hat duty; it looks as if it could survive a nuclear attack and come out unblemished. Dad would not have approved.

(As I write this, two very good men are working on a bathroom re-do in our home in Kent, tearing out the old fixtures, ripping up the tile on the floor, etc. It's not glamorous work, but they take a good measure of pride in their performance nonetheless. Around 10:00 each morning, they put everything on pause, no matter how pressing the circumstances, get out their thermoses and maybe some other light refreshments, sit down on whatever seat is at hand, drink their coffee, and visit for 15 or 20 minutes, as if this little break is guaranteed in the Constitution. In my recent experience, this custom appears to be widespread in America. And it's no big deal. But such a coffee break would have been out of the question in the fifties under my Dad's administration. Coming of age in an era when one could have been fired summarily for such presumption, Dad could never have imagined taking such liberties.)

Finally, it was strictly verboten to do any task on the job while sitting down, even if that might have made perfectly good sense to work in that position. Dad considered sitting to be an insult to the carpenter's profession; it just didn't *look* good. I think he pegged me early (and correctly) as a lazy guy reluctant to give his all to such time-honored activities as ditch digging. "You couldn't build a chair without having to set in it," he told me more than once.

Interestingly, Dad cut me considerable slack in other tasks common on a construction project, and the son of the foreman received special treatment that would never have been extended to any of the other workmen. I was then—and still am today—very uncomfortable with heights, so Dad never required me to perform a task that required climbing high ladders. (When he was 64 and I was 23, he took all the high ladder duties on a painting job we did one summer in Tulsa.) And I didn't like table saws or circular saws (Skil saws, they were called) for the very good reason that I did not want to lose a finger, or any part of a finger, in one of them, as I was certain I would eventually do. (We had an experienced carpenter named Bill Kirk who lost the end of a thumb in a table saw; the first joint wound up stuck on the ceiling.)

Did I ever feel sorry for myself that I had drawn the straw that condemned me to a life as the low man on the totem pole of the construction industry? Yes. Why couldn't I have had more glamorous employment like John Buckelew, who sold popcorn and occasionally took tickets at the Victory Theater and therefore had one foot in the entertainment business? Or like David Stiegler, who sold MacGregor shirts and fancy ties and men's clothing in a tiny shop on First Street in air-conditioned comfort? Or Chris Hackler, who got to shine cars and linger around the latest models of Olds and Chevys at his dad's dealership? Why did God appoint me to play the role of the sweaty, stinky day laborer? I did sometimes pity my lot, but never more bitterly than that day one summer when, perched on a scaffold above the sidewalk in front of the old Rogers Theater, chipping away at ancient bricks and mortar as we deconstructed the old building to turn it into a spanking new retail store, I spied Hackler, accompanied by a host of cute girls, drive by in a new convertible and give me a smile and a wave, as if to say, "We're all going to the pool, sucka! See ya!" Groan!

So you do have to start somewhere. I started as paperboy, soda jerk, failed short-order man, and carpenter, working every summer from the age of 14 on. At these assorted callings, I did only okay. But if I never hit one out of the park with any of these forms of wage earning, I landed my dream job in the winter of 1959–60, and that was to be very good work indeed.

15

HIGH SCHOOL: HELL OR HEAVEN?

IN FRANCIS FORD COPPOLA'S CHARMING, underrated film *Peggy Sue Got Married,* the title character, played by a very winning Kathleen Turner, attends her twenty-fifth high school reunion and, after being crowned queen of the evening's affair, mysteriously loses consciousness and awakens in the spring of 1960 just before her class is due to graduate. To follow her adventures there and to learn what she finds out about love and life in the process, rent and watch the movie. But before doing that, ask yourself whether you would want, in your heart of hearts, to go back to your senior year in high school. Would it be a dream or a nightmare?

If you were the valedictorian of the Class of 1960, the president of the student council, the quarterback on your undefeated varsity football team, a National Merit Scholar, the recipient of a full ride to Stanford, the guy going steady with the Homecoming queen, the guard on the conference-winning basketball squad, then maybe you'd have to say it would be a dream to return.

I was none of the above, and, while I can't say that high school was a disaster for me, I would not relish going back to those halls of Rogers High. Insecure, feeling vaguely guilty a lot of the time, though guilty of exactly what I hadn't the slightest idea; not knowing the answers to life's big questions, not even knowing what the big questions *were;* slouching through courses taught in antique, underequipped classrooms by worn-out, underpaid teachers; wanting for it all to be over.

The whole thing took place in that aging, creaky structure on Walnut I earlier called one of the town's nicest architectural landmarks. But during the years I was required by law to show up there and be educated, 1954–60, it was a noisy, hot, dark building with a fragrant interior owing to the daily presence of hundreds of kids, big and small, for it housed grades 7 through 12. Imagine throwing together hoards of shrieking pre-pubescents with the fully grown proto-adults we'd become by our senior year! In the late summer, when school began, or in the early spring, we sweltered inside the place, cooled as it was not by air conditioning but by classroom windows raised to the max, and you dearly hoped that the kid sitting next to you had showered after phys. ed. The old high school, in fact, would be shuttered, then consigned to the wrecking ball following our graduating class of 1960, and everyone moved the next year to a sparkling new "campus" south of town.

Put that many kids ranging in ages 12 to 18 in an old building, trying to keep them under control solely by use of the carrot-and-stick of grades, and anarchy is just barely under the surface every single day. This was the age of juvenile delinquency, after all. We didn't have gangs, drug problems, concealed weapons, or security guards, nor were we required to have metal detectors at the entrances. But there was a lot of testosterone roiling around. We had some tough, unruly kids—I saw more than one fight break out during the noon lunch hour or in phys. ed. classes—and even those of us who weren't tough (meaning me), presented school authorities with disciplinary problems that had to be dealt with almost daily. Our principal and his minions kept order and maintained morale through a two-pronged approach: the iron hand of corporal punishment and, if that failed, expulsion. But if you promised to be "good," the school sort of agreed to become a partner with you in promoting "school spirit," the purpose of which was and still is to make school more fun. From the outside, high school life must have seemed to be *mostly* about school spirit.

Rogers High School presented us with a bewildering variety of extracurricular activities that extended far beyond the usual array of athletic activities, though football and basketball, for both the players and the spectators, did outrank all others in importance. All hail blessed sports, the ultimate symbol of school identity and unity! There was our band, which was bigger than probably some college bands, and a large coterie of girls in the school's cheer squad, the Blue Demons, "sponsored" by our art teacher, Mrs. Price. Varsity sports, however, were not in the cards for the school's girls; theirs was solely a supporting role for us jocks. And there were more clubs than you could shake a stick at, clubs representing every conceivable—and some not so easily imaginable—student interest, academic discipline, avocation, or future field of employment, some eighteen clubs in all. What these clubs actually did, how often they met, or what they were for is difficult to say; they were just clubs to be *in*, to list on your resume, presumably. (What the devil is a Latin Club all about, for example?)

We also had assemblies, another device to give us a sense of being a part of a larger, somehow vaguely grander community. How often we gathered in Kirksey Gymnasium for these all-school affairs I can't recall, but they were big deals involving motivational speakers, awards presentations, or student-organized variety shows. I recall being appointed to head up one such variety hour and the pains I took to put it together. Whom could we coax and cajole to sing, play, recite, or perform anything—God, *anything*, please!—just to get the damned thing over with? I vividly remember getting my classmate Karen Snyder on the phone the night before an assembly I was helping put together:

"Karen, could you please play something on the piano at assembly tomorrow at 10:00?"

"Sure, I'd be glad to."

"Oh, God, thanks. I've called seven people already and you're the first person who's said yes."

Yes, I actually said that to Karen Snyder.

One assembly is especially memorable because it marked the debut of a singing group built around the very talented Neal Bloomfield and backed up by Don Baker, Stuart Wilson, and me and accompanied on the piano by Betty Sutton, the wife of our principal who also doubled as the music director at the Presbyterian Church. Because we were varsity athletes of one persuasion or another, we called ourselves the Four Lettermen. After a girls' trio finished their act to enthusiastic applause, we walked onstage and tore into a spirited rendition of "The Banana Boat Song" ("Day-o, daaaaaay-o, daylight come and me wanna go home") and brought down the house. Neal had a splendid, natural singing voice (and went on to have a career as a singer after graduation), Stuart possessed a passable bass, and Don and I were in the group because in our absence the ensemble would have to be called the Two Lettermen. Before the four of us graduated, we sang—always with our arranger, Mrs. Sutton, at the keyboard—before a number of audiences, like the Odd Fellows, the Lions Club, etc. At a student banquet leading up to commencement ceremonies, we sang the Four Freshmen hit "Graduation Day," featuring a very nervously rendered solo ("Now we leave in sorrow all the joys we've known ..." Sob.) by me. (Because I had sung in her choir at church and could read music after a fashion Mrs. Sutton had earlier persuaded me to take voice lessons with her and put me on the program of a recital by some of her students. I was to sing "Danny Boy," but I got stage fright and begged off at the last minute, thereby nipping in the bud a promising career in show business.) So by encouraging school spirit and staging events that gave us a sense of being part of something bigger than ourselves, the Powers That Were held any threat of anarchy at bay.

And they also plied us with food. While many kids sought noontime nourishment at one of the two fast-food places near the high school, at Rife's, for example, whose nickel hamburgers and Frito pies were a big draw, most of us opted for the school's cafeteria located on the lowest level across from the faculty lounge, where are teachers hid and smoked. There we stuffed ourselves on government-subsidized lunches prepared by a staff of middle-aged, hefty, hair-netted women whose culinary strengths leaned heavily toward the "Sloppy Joe" food group, except on those days when a chicken-based casserole was thought more appropriate to the season. (If you want to get a sense of what the cooking was like in that cafeteria, hurry down to your local Cracker Barrel and order the meatloaf special with mashed potatoes, brown gravy, and green beans, the latter right out of the can, soft and juicy.) The cafeteria's specialty, in my memory, was their home-baked rolls, which the lunch ladies prepared on enormous baking tins, each portion measuring out at about nine cubic inches and containing perhaps 600 calories. The top of each luscious bun, resembling a baby's buttock, gleamed with a glaze of glistening fat that seemed to say, "Momma's little baby loves shortenin', shortenin', momma's little baby loves shortenin' bread." To use my Dad's ultimate compliment, an expression reserved for only the most exquisite of dining experiences, "You come out of there *full!*"

And the milk we consumed by the gallons. A bottle of milk, again thanks to the Department of Agriculture's generosity, cost 2 ½ cents! For all intents and purposes, it was free—so we made free with it, engaging in informal competitions to see who could drink the most bottles in a sitting, our stomachs bulging and eyes glazed over with satisfaction. And, of course, on more than one occasion binge drinkers started to giggle, then laugh, until milk gushed from their nostrils and mouths, sending the rest of us into hysterics.

One day I was lunching in the cafeteria with a guy in my circle known for the joy he gained in mounting his high horse. I asked him a question when his mouth was full and he contentedly was in his masticating mode. He waited until he'd swallowed before scolding, "You might have waited until I'd chewed my bite of food before asking me a question." No sooner was the sentence out of his mouth than a gigantic fly landed on his lower lip. Hah! "Bite of food" indeed!

But a dark flipside to school spirit and the sunnier side of crowd control, calculated to keep mischief at bay by seeing that everybody stayed as busy and involved as possible, was the corporal punishment, the stick—almost literally—intended to bring rowdies into line. And when I say "corporal punishment," I mean that form of discipline long out of favor in our public schools: three, four, or five whacks on the ass with a wooden paddle. I caught it twice and can almost still feel it.

On the first occasion, the lashes were meted out following a field trip to the local dairy (or was it the town's potato chip plant?), after which I and Lowell Harris, our class cutup, were sent to the principal's office to take our medicine. Lowell was a special case: Perpetually mouthy, rude, loud, he was a clever, nonstop entertainer on his best days but a pain in the butt on most. That day, walking back from the dairy or the plant or whatever, Lowell and I got into a good-natured gravel-throwing duel, seeing who could most painfully sting the other with pebbles we picked up along the way. After we returned to our classrooms our teacher turned us in. What happened to Lowell I don't know, but I had to make the long walk to the principal's office alone. There, the head man, Fay Moore, the tall, hulking guy who was the father of my friend and Sunday school classmate Joe, the mournful old guy whom I'd seen for countless Sundays among the congregation in our church, sat me down and asked me to confess my crime. Then, after telling me we could not have such goings-on, such nonsense, at Rogers High—and murmuring something about how he hated, really hated, to have to do this, it hurts me as much as it's going to hurt you, etc.—he asked me to stand, bend over, and grab my ankles. Thereafter he took down from a shelf a wooden paddle, like the kind used in fraternity initiations and hazings. I then closed my eyes and took the whacking like a … boy. It hurt like hell.

Not surprising, then, that the next time I got into trouble—for blowing saliva bubbles in a kind of competition with my buddy John Dacus—the teacher sentenced me to another visit with Mr. Moore. Recalling our earlier conference, I took a calculated risk and went instead to the boys' restroom, where I killed time for fifteen minutes or so before returning to class, wearing what I hoped was a convincing expression of contrition. But my teacher smelled a rat and inquired at the principal's office if I'd actually shown up there. "Ben Lloyd? Nope, nary a sign of him." So it was back to the executioner. And do I still harbor resentment for such punishment? Does the bear make big doo-doo in the woods?

But there was also some learning that went on at Rogers High. My classmates and I took all the usual courses— history, government (or was it "civics"?), English, a smattering of languages ranging from Latin to Spanish (actually, *limited* to Latin and Spanish), typing (which I should have taken but didn't; I'm still a two-finger man), bookkeeping, shop, art, band, a full array of math and science courses, home ec., and phys. ed. Some of our teachers taught two, three, or more of these courses and with widely varying degrees of success on their parts and of receptivity on the part of the largely clueless student body.

I'm afraid that I was not a very good student. I was an underachieving student making not "gentlemen's Cs" but average-Joe B-minuses. I did fine in what I learned later to call the humanities, those subjects that involved reading, writing, and language, but I was a numbskull in the sciences and math, although I suppose I absorbed enough of those disciplines to avoid being a total failure, both in the courses and on the national college entry tests. I took algebra, geometry, and trigonometry and retain today the definition of an isosceles triangle and the method of determining square footage, but that's about it. I never moved on to calculus and to this day do not even know what calculus is, though I have been careful never to admit this around my math colleagues during a long career in college teaching. (Coppola's Peggy Sue character, in a memorable scene, shows up at her algebra class and, on learning that there is a pop quiz that day, tells her classmates that they will never, ever have a use for algebra the rest of their lives. So it has been for me, although I do suspect that my life of learning would have been enhanced had

I caught on to the mysteries and beauties of math. I continue to be charmed by references to "elegant" solutions to math problems, and I suspect that one's understanding of nature will always be just short of complete without a grasp of math.)

Anything having to do with the printed page, however, flowed right into me and, for the most part, stayed there, and for some reason certain forms of learning, like names, dates, and geographical or spatial concepts, came naturally to me. I furthermore possessed what I learned during a career in teaching that many students lack: a keen imagination and a powerful sense of curiosity. I read a great deal as a teenager, even though a lot of my reading material was junk, like E.C. horror comics (of course) and science fiction or whatever crummy paperbacks constituted the hot popular literature of the day, like *Peyton Place*. The joke around our high school was that you could toss in the air a paperback copy of Grace Metalious' sexy novel and it would land open to one or more of the book's "good" parts. ("Oh, darling, your nipples are as hard as diamonds!" Or was it "your diamonds are as hard as nipples"?) But I recall also reading Norman Mailer's *Naked and the Dead* (where I saw the curious word "fug" for the first time), James Jones's *From Here to Eternity,* and even Nikos Kazantzakis's controversial book about Jesus, *The Last Temptation.* I was also an enormous fan for a season or two of the novels of Thomas Wolfe. But how could a boy *not* want to read a book titled *Look Homeward, Angel?* I was irresistibly drawn to the tweedy image that Wolfe projected of himself, the handsome, forlorn, always-seeking author at whom wealthy and attractive women threw themselves.

I suppose I would have taken greater advantage of the town's library on Poplar Street but for an unfortunate incident that occurred when I was about twelve: I checked out *Bambi* and kept it out for months, maybe more than a year, then, fearing a chewing-out or some other humiliating scene when and if I took it back in, not to mention the enormous, unaffordable fines that had been amassed. And of course I didn't check out anything else during the period I was holding *Bambi* hostage. I finally slipped the cursed book in through the front door slot during a fines moratorium. I don't even think I read the damned thing.

No, I wasn't a distinguished scholar—despite, if I may brag, contributing a book review or two to the *Rogers Daily News* during my senior year—and I didn't get serious about school until well into college, where I elevated my performance to that of a somewhat-above-average-Joe B-plus. Hell, I'm still trying to bear down and be a good student, making up for lost time and lost opportunities, still hoping to make something of myself.

I'm sure I took the ACT and SAT exams—if we planned on college we had to—but I haven't the slightest recollection of having done so, though I'm told by classmates with more remaining brain cells than I that we assembled at the Masonic Youth Center for the ordeal. To see my scores on those exams today would, I'm sure, make me cringe. I recall that after the test scores came in I had a conference with Mr. Bartley, our school's guidance counselor, who assured me, and not unkindly, that I was definitely not Ivy League material but could probably make a go of it if I lowered my expectations to something like, oh, South Dakota State Teachers College, for example. We were also all subjected to the reigning national tests of the time to determine our IQs, our career interests as gauged by the Kuder Preferences Test (would you rather be a cherry picker or an atomic physicist?), and our personality types. I did pass the I.Q. exam, though I believe the results in high school are untrustworthy, since I took it again in college and scored thirty points higher. But, no, those scores shall go unrecorded here; actually, I've forgotten them. Let's just say that the scores fell rather short of the "genius" category, as you no doubt have surmised if you've read this far. And that call from the Mensa Society never came.

We had some outstanding teachers back then as well as a few other instructors who seemed to be just putting in their time before retirement, or were there only because they had to teach a class in order to coach one of our teams. Our best teachers embraced their jobs with dedication and what can only be termed joy. George Fentem, our esteemed band director, was certainly one of them. But I also had high regard for Leith Worthington, our august empress of the English language and the well-constructed sentence, for Mrs. Floraine Butt, the always enthusiastic and creative director of our little drama department, and for Mrs. Pauline Price, our vivacious art teacher with a seemingly infinite reservoir of ideas for class projects and a boundless devotion to her students, and finally, for the Reagan sisters, Betty Lynn and Mary Sue, who, with endless reserves of patience and forbearance, spent virtually their entire adult lives teaching history and government to the kids of Rogers. Those were marvelous teachers, indeed. (Fig. 40)

Fig. 40. Pauline Price, Betty Lynn Reagan, Mary Sue Reagan, c. 1960

Leith Worthington, who taught speech, journalism, and senior English, stands out in memory above them all. (Fig. 41) She was an exceptionally tough and demanding teacher whom you either admired, as I did, or hated, as was the case with many in my class. If you could not perform to her high standards, or got on her bad side because you didn't give a damn about writing or literature, you were in trouble. Mrs. Worthington was known to fail a student even if that might mean missing graduation with the rest of the class. At our thirtieth high school reunion, a photo of Mrs. Worthington was awarded as a joke to one of our number who'd had a celebrated tangle with the lady in senior English, and there was much good ol' boy guffawing about what a witch she had been. Admittedly, she could be intimidating, and while some students could rise to her implied challenges, others appeared to just crumble under the pressure of her gaze and aloof bearing. Once, one of my classmates attempted a recitation in her presence, and we watched—some with horror, others with amusement—as his face turned bright red and his words stuck so tightly in his throat we thought he might have a stroke or suffocate right before our eyes. But she was not a terror to all her students. As I'll explain later, she gave me an opportunity that boosted enormously my self-confidence and even set me on a path that led, in a way, to my life's work. It's not too much to say that I don't know what I would have done or where I'd be today without the influence of that formidable lady.

Fig. 41. Leith Worthington, 1960

And a lady she was. She did honor to her calling by showing up each day, her face nicely made up, her dress not showy but always neat and attractive; she might have passed for an elderly executive assistant of a corporate bigwig. (She would not have approved of dress-down Fridays, if such a thing had existed in the late fifties.) It must have been a torment for her during the week that she came to class every day while bearing the pain and the awful disfigurement of her face by an abscess she declined to seek medical attention for because she was a follower of Christian Science.

Mrs. Worthington retired after seeing off our class that spring of 1960, but her legend lives on. There should be a bronze statue of her standing on the grounds of Rogers High School, or at the least a photograph of her inside, and one not given as a lame joke.

Another of our teachers, however, fell far short of Mrs. Worthington. Mr. Bevers (pronounced "Beavers") taught mathematics, Latin, and psychology. By the time we were subjected to his ministrations, he was a veteran instructor well past his prime, and his major accomplishment seems to have been his embrace of the physician's admonition to "first do no harm." Mr. Bevers performed long, rambling monologues on whatever topics were rummaging around in his head that day. He lectured us at length once on the correct pronunciation of the clothing brand Van Heusen. "It's not 'Van *Hyoo*-sen, as most people believe," he'd intone, showing off. "It's a German name, so it's pronounced 'Van *Hoy*-sen!" And all during this little performance Mr. Bevers would be busy with the long pole, the one fitted out with a little metal hook at the end to use in raising or lowering the room's big sash windows. I can still see the old guy brandishing that long pole, which he used as a kind of stage prop. Pacing back and forth behind his desk, the wise professor would pay a visit from time to time at the wastebasket, which he used as his personal spittoon.

Not that at the end of the day it probably mattered to most students whether the teachers were good at their professions or not; students then and now appear above all to just want to get through the term and move on, to "get it behind me," as the saying goes. And our teachers surely realized that the majority of their students would end their formal education after earning a high school diploma. Looking back on those years, I can only be impressed by our teachers' dogged daily acts of endurance as they faced those timeless adversaries: massive indifference and apathy on the one hand and, on the other, the power of teenage culture, the folkways of American kids with their cliques, their tireless struggles to achieve and maintain status, their dating habits, the care and maintenance of an acceptable wardrobe, the imperatives of their libidos, the monitoring of the daily gossip, and the distractions of the marketplace—pop music, movies, and television. As our schools and teachers come under fire today for allegedly failing to educate America's youth, not nearly enough is said in their defense about their tireless enemy: the defiance of teenage culture that says, in effect, "school is not that important." Certainly to many seventeen-year-old minds, classroom learning is not as important as the daily doings of that little, isolated world they call home, a distinct society with its own do's and don'ts, its own values, and its own haves and have-nots. Anthropologists are born to study cultures like these.

After all, academic achievement is fine, in its place, but, in the seventeen-year-old mind, it can't compete with good looks, personality, and popularity. The president of your senior class can be a big man on campus before commencement day and might be working as a janitor at the plant four years after graduation. What matters above all are those short sweet golden years, when you're young, full of juice, and know where you and everybody else fits into your social hierarchy.

For some, that time is the high point of their lives, and the years that follow just a long slog down from the mountaintop. Class reunions are at least in part attempts to revisit that warm and fuzzy time when you were young and had yet to encounter life's hard knocks. It's interesting, but no surprise, that reunions can be stiff and disappointing affairs because classmates who didn't speak to one another in the halls of Rogers High continue to observe the same caste system that ruled "back then," and avoid eye contact with one another fifty years later.

Not particularly studious or electable to class offices or Student Council, and a washout in athletics and "horn tooting," I worked doubly hard at being cool, which meant listening to only the best music: the already dated big band sound of Stan Kenton or the upscale, modern sounds of the Four Freshmen, and, above all, the cerebral West Coast jazz of the Dave Brubeck Quartet, featuring the sublime improvisations of alto saxophonist Paul Desmond. Not for me the tacky, dirty-fingernails music of Elvis Presley and Gene Vincent ("Be-Bop-a-Lula"), the insane shrieks of Little Richard, or the airhead 45s of Frankie Avalon. How my parents must have suffered as I endlessly played my favorite vinyl LPs at home on my hi-fi, which reproduced at full volume the blasts of Kenton's crazy brass arrangements, Brubeck's seemingly aimless plunking of his baby grand, and the insufferable whining of the Four Freshmen, whose music has, shall we say, not traveled well through the decades.

But my buddies and I thought that the Four Freshmen were terrific back then, and we bought their records—what seemed like an album a year—and drove miles to hear them when one of their many singing tours reached our area. (Fig. 42) I went with several friends to hear them at the University of Arkansas during our senior year and sneaked backstage during intermission for autographs. Surprisingly, to us, the guys were very friendly, and each of them generously signed an album cover I'd brought along, as well as Neal Bloomfield's plaster arm cast, an emblem of a recent football injury.

(Some twenty-five years into the future: My wife and I are out with friends for an evening to hear the Ink Spots, the Four Aces, and the Four Freshmen present a trip-down-memory-lane show of oldies from the fifties. Even though, like the knife that's had three new blades and four new handles, in all of these groups the old guys have mostly been replaced by interchangeable parts. The Four Freshmen have had 23 different singers over the years. Bob Flanigan, the singer who'd supplied most of the original Freshmen's signature sound, that whining falsetto, was still going strong as he performed with guys half his age. During the intermission, I took the same album I'd schlepped to the college concert over to the bar where Flanigan sat on a stool enjoying his break and a Miller Lite. I mumbled stupidly, "Mr. Flanigan, you don't remember me, but years ago you and the other guys were nice to sign this album. Could I ask you to sign it again?" He growled back, "Jeez, can't you let me drink my beer in peace?" He signed it, then dismissed me without ever making eye contact. Jerk.)

Fig. 42. The Four Freshmen (Left to right: Ross Barbour, Bob Flanigan, Ken Errair, Don Barbour) c. 1956.

With my rarified tastes in music, books, and movies I was well on my way to becoming a snob. I put distance between myself and all the others, with the odd result that, way out there on the margins of Roger High School's brisk social whirl, I started to become invisible. At my fiftieth class reunion banquet I sat next to a classmate who turned to me and said, out of the blue, "You know, I have no recollection of you whatsoever." And, much as I wanted to say in reply, "Yes, we have had instances of early-onset dementia in my family as well," I got it: I simply didn't make much of a splash in the big scene that really mattered back then. As one of the cool guys, trying to dress like Joe College, wearing my thick, Brubeck-inspired horn-rims, I very much wanted to be different.

I was abetted in my ways by the other guys who made up the cool set, Chris Hackler, who could pull off the feat of being a high school sophisticate, a football star, a National Merit Scholar, and a big man on campus all at the same time; John Buckelew, a stand-out in both athletics and the classroom; John Dacus, a transfer student from Henrietta, Oklahoma, who had talent and wit to burn and with whom I enjoyed a long, simpatico friendship well into our college days; Steve Pelphrey, a relative newcomer from California and a studious, good-looking guy who was the school's best overall athlete; and Stuart Wilson, a quiet, proper kid but very much a part of this exclusive gang. Together we double-dated, played tennis and cards, traded insults and witticisms (at least we thought they were funny), and viewed the proceedings around us with a superior, ironic, cool attitude bordering on hauteur, not an easy stance for a bunch of high schoolers to assume. We were a little like, but considerably less neurotic, the ultra-self-aware clique that pushed their personalities on us on *Seinfeld*. And if we had someone reminiscent of the Elaine character, that would have been Martha Wesley, a cute, smart blond who had the sharp eye to see through our acts and poses. Martha was one of the priceless bonuses of Daisy Air Rifle's move to town. Steve Willis also came down from Michigan, and, even better, moved in just across the street from our house in Rogers Heights. Of course, being a Yankee, he did talk funny, but we liked him a lot anyway. On the whole, such newcomers as Martha and Steve, plus Judy Sanchez, whose father came to town to open Rogers' first bowling alley, were welcome anomalies. New faces and new friends settled rarely in our midst, and their small numbers made them all the more special.

A group of school kids who grow up together—a cohort, to use the technical term—is a bit like the passengers together on a cruise ship: they embark at the same time—at kindergarten, we'll say—then sail along through the years, seeing the same sights, sharing meals together, paying attention to their tour guides, calling at this port and that. They enjoy both smooth sailing as well as some bumpy weather along the way. Very few new people get on, and now and then someone disembarks, jumps ship, but, on the whole, the original passenger list stays pretty much the same. You're kind of stuck with one another. You all grow up together on this twelve-year voyage. On this journey you make friends, in some cases for life, and you lose some.

And along the way there are romances. A girl you first had a crush on in sixth grade grows up a little more, and you get a crush on her again. Maybe you start going out with her, and then she becomes your steady girlfriend. This is a very big deal, this "going steady" business. One or the other of the partners has to propose this arrangement, and there had to be a clear "yes" or "no" to seal the deal or end it. But it wasn't so much the "liking" part—forget love—as the need for a boy to have a girlfriend and a girl to be linked up with a guy. How else could you demonstrate convincingly that you were a card-carrying heterosexual? If you were not paired up, there had to be at least a little something wrong with you, and there were just too many important social occasions—postgame gatherings at the Masonic Youth Center, Homecoming Prom, those Saturday night makeout parties to a Johnny Mathis record—to be stuck without a girlfriend.

I had a girlfriend in high school, a tall, lovely, immaculately (if fussily) dressed maiden whom I will call Missy Landerkuchen (not her real name, because this is not a tell-all book, and the proprieties must be observed). I liked her in elementary school. I liked her again in junior high. And later in high school, after Missy had matured a good deal, and in the nicest way, I *really* liked her. She was an extraordinarily attractive girl and unusually photogenic; there probably exists not a single bad photograph of her. And her beauty was enhanced by a reserve rarely found in a high schooler of sixteen or seventeen. She was so pretty that I didn't like her so much as was in awe of her; I just wanted to be with her so I could look at her. Missy was blessed by good looks she won in the genetic lottery but cursed with a mother who, Svengali-like, tirelessly designed and manipulated Missy's wardrobe and public "look," picking out her accessories and maybe even her lipstick color as if preparing her daughter for one of those ghastly children's beauty pageants. The girl sported not only dramatic hair-dos, barrettes, and earrings but the ultimate fifties fashion touch: cat-eye glasses with sparkling rhinestones.

It was both a privilege and a burden to be Missy's boyfriend-of-choice— privilege because she was, you'll pardon the sexist term, gorgeous arm candy, but a burden because the implicit question was always out there, hanging in the air: "What the hell is she going out with *him* for?"(Coincidentally, this is a question I've frequently had to field later in life when acquaintances who admire my wife of forty-three years needle me by asking their annoying, rhetorical question, "Why on earth did she marry *you*?" My lame, stock response: "Well, I used to be a lot better looking.") The question must have crossed the minds of Missy's parents more than once, for it seemed every time I appeared in their living room to collect her for one of our big dates, her parents appeared to be suppressing chuckles, covering their mouths the way

Japanese girls hide theirs when they giggle. Perhaps the Landerkuchens were simply continuing to laugh about something that had amused them prior to my arrival? No, it had to be me. "Oh, Missy, that *guy* is here again," they'd shout to a back room, where their gorgeous daughter, not quite ready for the evening's proceedings, was busy equipping herself from her vast collection of barrettes and gold bracelets.

Even worse, Missy had a big brother, a heavily muscled monster who, later in life, might well have been a mob hit man. I'll call him Mace.

Mace Landerkuchen had an awful time dealing with the idea that a wimp like me was dating his little sister, and he made no effort to hide his contempt. We rarely spoke about this or any other matters, but when we did exchange words the conversation would go something like this:

Mace: "So, you like to play tennis." (This from a lineman on the varsity football team.)

Me: "Yeah, I like tennis."

Mace: "Tennis is a game for sissies."

Me: "Huh-uh."

Mace: "Oh, no? Want me to beat the shit out of you?"

It didn't help that Missy lived so damned far out in the country, way out on the Prairie Creek road almost to the White River. Driving to pick her up for a date always took on the scope of a scenic country outing requiring a fill-up before departure; occasionally she would take pity on me and stay with a sister in town.

(Distance was a fact of life with us high school kids then. Rogers was a consolidated school district, which means that its students came from an enormous chunk of northeastern Arkansas. School buses left early in the morning and covered dozens of miles on their routes. Some of my classmates came from areas that had their own zip codes; they might even have lived in different time zones, for it seemed some of them spoke in dialects strange to me and my townie pals. During our senior year the area was hit by a major snowstorm, a natural disaster that southern towns are woefully underequipped to deal with, and we enjoyed a long winter "vacation"—blessed days!—because the roads that dipped and curved through the hills and hollows of our buses' routes remained ice-covered for more than two weeks and the country kids couldn't get to school.)

My relationship with Missy was an on-again, off-again thing that extended from my childish, fifth-grade infatuation to our senior year in high school. During one of the extended off periods, when I was not dating "someone new," as the song goes, I found myself facing a major upcoming social occasion—the Valentine's Day dance perhaps?—without the faintest idea of who I would take as my date. Ol' Missy, maybe? She didn't appear to be going with another guy at the time, so I figured I'd ask her. I must have been feeling particularly forlorn and worthless in the days leading up to the necessary but dreaded phone call, because when I finally got up the nerve to ring her up, I was almost hyperventilating. When she came on the line, I dispensed with all the preliminaries and, in a quavering voice, asked her if she had any plans for the big dance. She might have come back with, "What business is that of yours?" but instead, as if on script, she demurely answered,

"Why, no."

"Would you go with me?" This in a tiny, barely audible voice.

"Sure."

And, then, God help me, I gushed, "Thank you, oh, *thank* you!"

So we went to that dance, though I have no recollection of the evening whatsoever.

There were other girls who figured in my love life, and I in theirs, both before and after that big night. In truth, Missy was those other girls, because she is, as friends who shared those high school years with me might have guessed by now, a composite of several young ladies I doted on and dated and who liked me as we all engaged in those rites of passage and passion that most teenagers have to negotiate, like it or not.

My last high school girlfriend was a pretty Presbyterian I'd met when we both worked the summer of 1960 at a church camp in Oklahoma. We corresponded the rest of the summer and one night in August, my serious crush on her inspired by the deathless, evocative prose of her letters, words that suggested she thought I was simply the bee's knees, I set out to visit her at her home in Enid, Oklahoma. My knowledge then of regional geography was imperfect, however, and I seriously underestimated the distance between Rogers and my sweetheart's hometown. I set out in Dad's Ford station wagon soon after work on a weeknight and drove and drove and drove the 209 miles to our rendezvous, arriving at about 11:00 that evening. The girl was glad to see me, her parents not so happy. After a half-hour or so, I had to start back, arriving home at about three in the morning. The next day Dad said, "You sure as hell put some miles on that car last night. Where'd you go?" "Oh, just here and there," I replied. Was that long drive into Oklahoma worth it? Yes, even though that little love affair didn't survive the summer.

And this is the point at which the question arises: "When do we get to the sex part?" To which I answer most soberly, in the 1950s we had no sex, and all our television programs were in black and white. For both sex and color television we had to wait until the 1960s to get what was coming to us. As a member of our Latin Club might have put it, perhaps ungrammatically, "coitus non exsistamus est!"

Of course, sex was very much on our minds. But before the great sexual revolution of the 1960s, we grew up in a very Puritanical, Bible-belt world that essentially forbade premarital sex. "Wait," we were soberly advised. "Save it." So we made out up to a point and then stopped. If a girl did It with one or more guys—serially, I hasten to add—word got around and she was branded "easy," or the school tramp. There were stigmas attached to promiscuous behavior; a girl had her reputation to maintain, after all. And woe to him who would dare to knock a young woman off the pedestal we all conspired to place her on.

Sex for boys mainly consisted of solitary sessions of "self-abuse" behind the family's locked bathroom door. Do that enough, folk wisdom had it, and you could go insane. But you'd go insane if you *didn't* do it! And everybody did. Woody Allen called such private activity "sex with someone I love." Dick Cavett, in a more sentimental vein, said it was like finding a friend for life.

If there was sex experienced by any of us high school juniors and seniors back then—*if*, I stress—then it was undoubtedly sex of the most amateurish, fumbling, desperate, and mutually unsatisfying kind that teenagers engage in. It was the kind of sex you'd do just to discover, finally, what all the fuss was about. Something you did to "get it over with" and to "lose your cherry," an expression so enigmatic that I'm still, at seventy, trying to figure it out. And afterward, your sixty seconds of backseat gymnastics would be followed by a month of funk, worry and disappointment—"So that's it?"—and shame and guilt, for, as everyone knew, premarital sex was wrong. It was a sin, and you were *supposed* to feel guilty afterward.

Sex was freighted with fear as well as shame, for if it led to an unwanted pregnancy, you could find yourself married at eighteen and could say goodbye to freedom and the plans you'd made for the future. Terminating a pregnancy in the fifties was possible but virtually unthinkable, since it was illegal, dangerous and socially unacceptable. "Abortion" was a word one hardly dared utter in public, and it was looked on by the church as a mortal sin.

I think my generation believed sincerely that marriage was *the* safe haven for intimacy between a man and a woman. We didn't "hook up," we didn't go in for one night stands. From this side of the great divide that was the 1960s it is all a bit breathtaking to reflect on how *good* –albeit repressed—we were during that decade we grew up in Rogers. We went to Sunday school at church, we attended classes from kindergarten to high school graduation faithfully, we absorbed the work ethic learned in odd jobs from the age of 14 onward, we watched "Father Knows Best" without a sense of irony, and we joined the Boy Scouts, if maybe only briefly in some cases. In his splendid, funny memoir, *Life Itself,* my contemporary (and my hero) Roger Ebert breathes a nearly audible sigh of relief that his coming of age occurred before the great sexual revolution of the sixties when most young people thought sex had its preordained place in the time-honored order in which the major events of life were destined to unfold: first education, then employment, marriage, a home, children, and finally, that reward for growing old, grandchildren. There existed a much different set of proprieties we were expected to observe faithfully in the fifties, and those who deviated from that norm were branded with stigmas almost as harsh at that "A" in *The Scarlet Letter.* Live together before marriage? Unthinkable. Continue attending class after getting pregnant? Are you kidding? Wear a T-shirt bearing an obscenity? Go ahead, but risk getting knocked down, expelled from school, or arrested.

(A brief aside to make my point: A friend standing in line at a Wal-Mart tapped the woman ahead of him on the shoulder then told her he was offended by the slogan on the back of her T-shirt that prominently featured the "F-word." She responded by giving him the finger. Imagine that happening in 1960.)

Perhaps Ebert and I make the mistake of sentimentalizing life and its strictures back then because we now view the time as a Golden Age, when, for we whites at least, life was ordered and full of optimism. Those of us born during the years of World War II came of age during an time of relative post-war peace and prosperity, eight years of which occurred during the administration of the grandfatherly, wise, war-weary Dwight D. Eisenhower, and while we faced significant challenges—the anxieties of the Cold War, the threat of Russian missiles headed for Rogers, the first stirrings of the Civil Rights movement— we were also lucky in many ways; we could look forward to the prospect of a happy, prosperous life in a country that was Number One in the world. And for my friends and I that meant first going to college in a period when higher education was virtually free to those smart enough to take advantage of it and willing to defer marriage and family to a later point in their lives. College could be our ticket to the future and to the good life that awaited us there. With astonishing naivete I just knew, despite the fact that in high school I had done only okay, that I was going to be a big hit when I got into a university.

Earlier that spring before graduation I attended some Presbyterian youth conference in Fayetteville where all the visiting students stayed overnight in the homes of local church members. After lights out, lying in a strange bed in a room much nicer and larger than my cubby-hole quarters back home, I heard singing coming from the nearby campus of the University of Arkansas. Fraternity boys were serenading the girls of one of the school's Tara-sized sorority houses, and it was lovely. It was a moment one imagined might occur only in the sentimental family films of MGM, featuring, say, Robert Wagner in a letter-sweater as he joins the singers and Spencer Tracey as the wise, kindly professor who pauses during an evening stroll to listen in. But it really happened that night, and I was smitten then and there with an impossibly golden ideal of college life that the serenading undergraduates seemed to celebrate. I was hooked, and this love affair, in which I've been jilted only a few times, has lasted a lifetime.

16

A "Stan the Man" Interlude

A DAY OR TWO AFTER my class had gathered in robes and mortarboards to walk across the stage in Kirksey Gymnasium to receive our high school diplomas, another semi-obligatory event, the baccalaureate service, was planned to occur, fittingly, on a Sunday. There was, however, a problem for me with its timing, for I and three or four other guys had been invited to go with a couple of our school's coaches on an overnight trip to see the St. Louis Cardinals. Our beloved Cards were scheduled to play a Sunday doubleheader against the Cincinnati Reds in the impossibly far-off city on the Mississippi River, a place as distant and mythical as the Land of Oz, the home of our beloved Redbirds. Not only was it to be my first live glimpse of a big league game, but it was also going to feature one of the greatest baseball players of the era, that superhero dearest to the heart of every sentient teenage boy in Arkansas: Stan the Man Musial.

Stan the Man. Stan the Man. It just feels good saying it.

A bit of background is necessary for the unfortunate reader possessing little or no familiarity with the life and career of the incomparable Stan Musial. (Fig. 43)

Stanley Frank Musial was born in Donora, Pennsylvania, a steel mill town near Pittsburgh, in 1920. His old man, a Polish immigrant, worked in the mills, and the Musials were also devout Catholics (Stan has attended Mass regularly throughout his long life). Known in his youth as "Stash," the diminutive of Stanislaus, he was an all-American boy. At six feet tall and about 175 pounds, he was an outstanding athlete who was excellent in every sport; he could probably have gotten a college scholarship on his basketball skills alone. As a teenager, he worked in a neighborhood grocery store; he later married the daughter of the owner (and they are still married).

Fig. 43. Stan "The Man" Musial after hitting five home runs
in a doubleheader against the Giants, May 2, 1954.

He was drafted by the Cardinals in 1939 as a pitcher, but the club soon moved him to the outfield, where, with his pitcher's strong left arm, he could fire the ball on a line back to the infield. And to say he could hit the ball is a little like saying that the Pacific Ocean is full of water. The first year Stan was called up, 1941, he got 20 hits in 47 at-bats, for an average of .426. He would hit well over .300 for the next 16 years until, beginning at age 39, he would have three straight subpar years at the plate before rebounding to hit .330. His lifetime batting average is .331.That means he got a hit in about every third official time at bat, an amazing feat given the fact that hitting major league pitching is one of the most difficult feats in sports. Oh, and in his last two at-bats on the last day of his final season, he hit two singles.

Stan spent his entire career with the Cardinals. His highest salary was $100,000, which he earned in 1958 (a measly $783,000 today. Hell, bench-warming, .211-hitting utility infielders make more than that today! The average salary of the 844 players on big league teams in 2011 was $3.3 million. Choke.) And, because he had a poor year at the plate in '59, Stan took a $20,000 pay cut for the next year—at his suggestion. What a guy!

Musial was on the National League All-Star team for the first time in 1943 and every year thereafter until he retired in 1963. He was also named MVP three times and played on three of the Cardinals' World Series–winning teams. (The Cardinals are second to the Yankees in World Series titles won.) He enjoyed the advantage of playing throughout his career on his home field, Sportsman's Park, which was tailor-made for him: an old-fashioned stadium with a short right field—310 feet deep at the foul pole—and a slight hill rising up toward the fence in left. Stan sent a lot of home runs into those stands in right and banked a lot of doubles off that hill when he "went to the opposite field" on outside pitches. But oddly, and perhaps significantly, of his 3,630 career hits, half were hit at home and half on the road in other National League parks. He also had the slight advantage of being a natural left-handed hitter, so when he made contact, he was already a step or more closer to first base than a righty. And it's said that he could reach his top running speed in only a couple of strides. When my brother Bud tried to make a baseball player out of me, he taught me to bat lefty so that I could become the next Stan the Man.

Musial's trademark was his unusual, even eccentric, stance at the plate: a coiled-up, spring-like pose that resembled a question mark in reverse, and one that's virtually impossible to mimic (but one he was happy to assume on request to please his fans throughout his lifetime). Like Ted Williams, whose stats are only a bit better, Stan had excellent vision that enabled him to see the ball as soon as it left the pitcher's hand. He's said to have cut his eyelashes shorter so he could see the ball better.

Oh, how we boys loved Stan the Man! We traded stories about him and coveted his baseball card, which, once secured, we'd keep in a special place, a sort of Stan Musial shrine. I remember the Sunday we were all abuzz because that day he'd hit *five* homeruns in a doubleheader. Then there was the tale we told and retold about how Stan had lined a drive—a sure double—off an outfield wall but was held up at first base because the baseball had hit the wall so hard it had rolled back to the infield. And the one about the All-Star game that went into extra innings, the players just wanting it to end so they could go home and get a rest. The legend is that Musial said as he went up to bat, "This has gone on long enough," and then hit a homer to win the game.

The man at the microphone, long before his days with the Chicago Cubs, was the great Harry Caray —"It might be, it could be…it IS…a HOME RUN!"— assisted by his "color" man, the former Cardinal catcher, Gus Mancuso (I thought his name was Gus "Man" Cuso, like Stan "the Man"). Caray was the voice for the Cards' games until 1969, when he left after a dispute with the Cards' owner, Augie Busch, which was widely rumored to have been over an affair that the announcer had had with Busch's daughter-in-law. If true, it turned out to be not such a good idea.

And those players' names! Enos Slaughter. Terry Moore. Marty Marion. Pepper Martin. Del Rice. Joe Garagiola. Whitey Kurowski. Red Schoendienst. Peanuts Lowrey. Vic Raschi. Alex Grammas. Lindy McDaniel (and his brother Von, a 17-year old pitching phenom who had one outstanding season in 1957 and then disappeared). Del Ennis. Harvey Haddix. Vinegar Bend Mizell. Ray Jablonsky. Rip Ripulsky. Wally Moon. Ernie Broglio. Gino Cimoli. Hobie Landrith. Ray Sadecki. (Hell, this sounds like the passenger list on a Polish freighter!) And, last but not least, Bud Bloomfield, a Rogers boy who played mostly in the Cards' farm system before being called up to the majors in 1963.

If you were writing a baseball novel you couldn't invent names as beautiful as those, and if you did, no one would believe you. Catcher Tim McCarver, the pitcher Bob Gibson, and shortstop Julian Javier (who named his son Stan in honor of his teammate), base stealer Lou Brock, and center fielder Curt Flood all came toward the end of Musial's career and helped St. Louis win two World Series championships in the 1960s.

So, was I looking forward to heading to St. Louis for my big doubleheader date with Stan the Man? You betcha! But first, I had to get out of going to that damned baccalaureate ceremony.

I brought it up earlier that week with Dad, who, of course, told me to go ask my mother, and she, sentimental to a fault and so proud of her baby who'd be off to college in the fall leaving her with Dad and an otherwise empty nest, would be no pushover. Surely she would want me to get all dressed up and show up at school to be preached to so she could be proud of me in public one more time. But, as expected, Momma, who loved me dearly, though she and other members of our family could never bring themselves to declare such a personal sentiment to another, saw the big picture—Cardinals vs. boring ceremony—and gave the trip her blessing.

And so I was off to St. Louis. About the long car ride there I recall almost nothing. We must have left Rogers soon after supper on a Saturday night, the two coaches up front where they would share the driving and the three or four of us boys in the back seat of the station wagon. As we motored east on Missouri's still-new I-44 (the old Route 66), we boys flipped the back seat down and tried to stretch out and sleep through the night. I know I slept for a while, because I distinctly remember waking up at one point with a companion's stinking feet in my face. We probably reached St. Louis around dawn, had some breakfast, and headed for the city zoo, where we spent a long Sunday morning before going to the ballpark. Sportsman's Park was an ancient affair that dated from the early years of the twentieth century. Over time it had also served the needs of the St. Louis Browns (before that team departed for Baltimore to become the Orioles in 1953), the old St. Louis Cardinals NFL franchise, various college football teams, and assorted local soccer leagues. It was a very old-fashioned stadium of the type much emulated by recent ballpark architects seeking that nostalgic link with the early days of baseball. It was constructed in a true bandbox style that power hitters, especially left-handed hitters, adored. But visiting shortstops not accustomed to the potholed gravel quarry of its infield terrain did not share the sentiment. My dim memory of the place tells me that all the grime, its countless layers of paint, and the decades of chewing gum on its concrete steps meant the park was old, *real* old, in 1960. (Fig. 44)

(Augie Busch, the St. Louis brewer, bought the Cardinals and the park in 1953. He wanted to name the place Budweiser Stadium, but the commissioner of baseball blocked that notion on the grounds that naming a park for a beer wouldn't look so good. So it was instead christened Busch Stadium, and later its owner brought out a beer named Busch. A colosseum-style stadium in downtown St. Louis (designed by Arkansas-born architect Edward Durell Stone) became the new home of the Cardinals in 1966, but it was recently razed, and a new Busch Stadium built near the same grounds, opened in 2006.)

I was thrilled with my first glimpse of the big league diamond and that expanse of spring grass, as well as that distinctive mix of ballpark sounds and smells: the special crack of bat on ball, the massive hum of the big crowd, the calls of vendors, the delicious aroma of boiling hotdogs. Even today, as the allure of baseball dwindles for me, nothing beats the wonderful rush that comes in those seconds when I emerge from the stair tunnel to see the impossibly green field and hear the big crowd.

Fig. 44. Sportsman's Park, St. Louis. Courtesy of Gary Townzen

The first of the day's two games against the Cincinnati Reds began at one o'clock. Hotdogs, Cokes, and Cracker Jacks in hand, we took our seats. Of those two games, I still retain only the faintest of memories, mental pictures that have faded to sepia: we sat high up on the third-base side, looking directly out at the far right-field stands; and Don Newcombe, the huge, black Cincinnati pitcher with his distinctive high leg kick, started and won the second game. Though I can't tell you much that happened that day, the baseball almanacs can, for, incredible as it seems, that reliable source retains the box scores for virtually every baseball game ever played. The Cards won the first game 5-4, and the Reds came back to take the second game 5-3. My man Stan, then an old baseball player at 40 and no longer the fleet-footed youth from Donora, was relegated to first base in game one, and St. Louis manager Solly Hemus benched him in the second game. Stan rose from the dugout to pinch-hit late in game two but only flied out feebly to left. His teammates that day included Joe Cunningham, Daryl Spencer, Bill White, Ken Boyer, Curt Flood, and Alex Grammas.

In 1960 probably even I realized that Musial was getting old and that perhaps he was just holding on for the big salary. After nearly twenty years of stellar play, he was no doubt losing a step or two and not seeing the ball as perfectly as he had in the past. As play began that Sunday in May of 1960, Stan was hitting a mediocre .247, and the Cardinal manager was on his case and grousing about being saddled with this expensive old-timer. In fact, there was even talk of trading Stan. No one was more disappointed in his performance during these down years than Musial, who would go on to hit .275 that year and improve "only" to .288 in 1961 before he realized he needed to get in better shape if he wanted to continue his career and go out in style. He worked out seriously during the 1961–62 off-season and rebounded to bat .330 in 1962 before deciding to pack it in the next year.

But all this is from the historical annals of baseball, factoids unavailable to me and my pals seated high up in Sportsman's Park that Sunday.

But the highlight of the day—the event that trumped that baccalaureate thing going on that very moment back in Rogers, the very best baseball memory a kid of seventy could possibly have—I have not forgotten.

Musial comes up in the bottom of the eighth inning of game one to face the Reds' Jay Hooks. By virtue of two home runs—one by Frank Robinson— in the seventh, Cincinnati leads 4-3. Stan goes into his signature stance, looking like, as another player described it, "a kid peeking around a corner." Hooks delivers, and Stan sends a high fly ball toward the foul pole in right, but the ball has too much "English" on it and fades foul and into the stands perhaps eight feet to the right of the pole. He takes his stance again, crouches, and lashes out at the very next pitch. This time the ball takes virtually the same high, arcing path as the previous fly but this time it's *straight*, and the baseball lands on the roof of the right field stands and bounces and ricochets this way and that, far from the hands of souvenir hunters. Two virtually identical line drives, both shots that exploded off Stan's bat, rocketed to right, one foul and the second just inside the pole. In the moment, Musial was like the golfer who takes a mulligan, recalibrates his second shot just so, and then hits a perfect 3-wood right onto the green.

And did Stan pause dramatically there at the plate, arms and bat outstretched, admiring his handicraft (a feat he accomplished 475 times over his long career) before beginning a slow, deliberate, home run trot, with a smile and body language that seemed to say, "Up yours, Cincinnati"? Did Musial, in the manner of Manny Ramirez and dozens of other self-regarding masters of the universe at large in the game today, take the opportunity to say, in effect, "Yes, it really is totally about me." No. He put his head down and loped around the bases with class, his loose-fitting home whites flapping and fluttering in the air.

As long as I live, I will remember the flight of the ball Musial hammered that Sunday to the roof in right. The ball had a bright, white highlight on it, about the size of a quarter, the entire length of its flight. And that's the best part of the memory: the baseball with its little dot of reflected sunlight ripping out there and then rattling around on that roof.

Musial tied the game, and Spencer won it for the hometown guys with a walk-off homer in the bottom of the ninth. And we boys, sunburned and sick on too many peanuts, sat through the disappointing second game before heading back to the car and home.

But hold on: there's an epilogue to this story...

Many years later, in the 1990s, a former Kent State University administrator named Ron Roskins took a group of teenage boys to St. Louis for a ball game. Because Roskins had met Musial when both men had served on the President's Council on Physical Fitness and become friendly, he asked Stan (now long retired but a kind of all-around ambassador for the Cardinals organization) if he'd stop by to say hello, meet the kids, and sign a few autographs.

(Well into his nineties, Musial always graciously gave a signature, as he put it, to "anyone who'd say hello to me." If he was in typical form that day, Musial would have peppered his remarks with his affable infield chatter—"Whattaya say! Whattaya say! Howya-doin'?"—a nervous habit said to be traced to a boyhood stutter brought on by being forced in school to write with his right hand.)

Stan agreed to meet Roskins' party, and, clad in his bright-red blazer, he came around to their section, where Roskins introduced everybody. Stan shook hands all around, signed a few baseballs, and wished the boys a pleasant afternoon. "Enjoy the game," the handsome old star no doubt said he before he walked away.

After Musial was out of earshot, Roskins heard one of the boys say to another: "Who the hell is Stan Musial?"

Sic transit Gloria mundi ("So pass the glories of this world").

So it goes for all of us.

17

CUB REPORTER EARNS OWN BY-LINE

AFTER 11 YEARS OF FORMAL education, most of which I was only informally engaged in, I found myself at the beginning of my senior year. I was a seriously unfocused 17-year-old. I had dabbled in this and that without managing to distinguish myself in anything.

I had flopped in sports. I was too skinny for football and unwilling to endure the tropical Arkansas heat of August practice sessions. I was content to watch my more macho classmates take the heat and the hits, as well as the glory. (And glory there was: Our team went 9-0 and won the district title our senior year.) And basketball, a game I had dearly loved and longed to prove that I was good at from the time I had been cut from the team in the eighth grade, had been a colossal disappointment. After a promising beginning marked by my making the varsity team as a sophomore (and not many high school players did that then), I had fizzled, fallen out with the coach, and decided that my love/hate affair with the game simply had to end. Today, I can hardly tolerate the sound of a basketball being pounded on the hardwood. I like to think that I failed at basketball because, aside from the fact that I lacked most of the basic skills (like the ability to dribble, for example), I suffered in games from what has since been given the distinction of a true psychological syndrome (if not, God help us, a disease) called performance anxiety. Stage fright, in other words. One or two major league baseball players have retired in recent years because they were terrified at the prospect of playing before crowds. Funny how I could shoot the lights out in pick-up games when the bleachers were empty and nothing important was on the line, but put me before a crowd and I seized up. "Don't throw the ball to me," was my motto, as I lingered in the corner of the court near the exit. Probably I was anxious mainly because I didn't want lots of people (such as former and present girlfriends) to know how lousy I was as a player.

So with no great returns as an athlete to look forward to, I'd given music a go—but for all the wrong reasons. Though I mainly wanted to be like my hero, Maxie Gundlach, I found out quickly that I couldn't play as well as Maxie. The clarinet is hard to play; it apparently takes a lot of practice to master. It has a huge range and the high notes on the scale are difficult to play. Add to that problem that all composers write clarinet parts with an overabundance of little notes running rapidly up and down and up again all over the scales. I may have been somewhat comfortable with whole, half, and quarter notes, but semi-quavers and semi-demi-quavers were beyond me. And, finally, you can practice and even practice some more, but in the end, if you don't have it, well, you don't have it. Maxie had it. I didn't. I packed up my horn at the beginning of my senior year and never took it out again. I hope someone is getting some use out of it now; it was stolen in a burglary of our house around 1980.

My chronic inattention to my studies also provided lots of time for me to try my hand at another extracurricular diversion: theater. (These days our daughter Marianna is establishing a name for herself as an actress in Boston, and people occasionally ask, "Does she take after someone in your family?" Without risking the appearance of false modesty, we can honestly answer, "No.") We had a theater group in high school named the Sock and Buskin Club ("sock" and "buskin" mean comedy and tragedy, respectively). In mounting our productions, we actors were advised and directed by Mrs. Floraine Butt.

(Wipe that smirk off your face. Mrs. Butt was a fine teacher and a lot of fun and the kind of teacher who never burned out after thirty or more years at Rogers High. But if you like that name, I've got more. There was Mr. Bevers, who was finally put out to pasture before our senior year. And we had a Mr. Measeles, who taught mathematics and was married to Mrs. Measeles, who taught science. We had a guy named Ken Necessary, an indispensable player on our football team. And I also went to school with Eldon Jump and with Robert Christ.)

I was in one Sock and Buskin play, a murder mystery that the group presented to a whole audience of tough theater critics: our high school class assembly. I played the manager of a hotel where the drama unfolded, and I had one line, which was, more or less, "Welcome to our hotel. We hope you enjoy your stay here." (Not exactly on a par with Samuel Beckett or Tennessee Williams, but the sentences do have the virtue of being grammatically correct, and indicated my character's ... uh ... welcoming attitude. But it was not the kind of role that would have encouraged me to explore motivation or imagine a back-story for the hotelkeeper: Had he been scarred by an abusive father? Did he wish someday to own a whole chain of hotels?) And that meager contribution, spoken probably with a little nervous quaver, begs these questions: Why didn't my abilities merit a better line, and a lot more of them. Did I lack talent? Presence? Good looks? Or had Mrs. Butt overheard me making fun of her name?

Even then I thought I'd be better as a monologist than a member of a cast (my wife, my daughters, probably everybody think I talk too much), and I can see now what was not obvious to me at the time: I needed a calling that would afford me a chance as a solo act.

As I've suggested earlier I prepared myself for that moment by spending a good deal of time and thought on what I wanted to look like. Sartorially, I tried to affect the look of those Joe College types who worked in the better men's clothing stores. On a limited budget this wasn't easy, but I gave it a try: button-down shirts, crew-neck sweaters, and those khakis or cords with the little belts and buckles in the back. Hell, I even had a pair of shoes that had little buckles in the back, and if Jockey briefs had had buckles in their backs I would have bought those, too. After years of combing my curly hair so that as much as possible fell over my forehead in what was then called a "waterfall," I opted now for the straightened, close-cut look inspired by Craig Stevens, a kind of small-screen Cary Grant who starred in *Peter Gunn*, a television detective series. I had my look so was now ready for whatever came my way. And, as luck would have it, in the first few weeks of my senior year I got a wonderful opportunity that led soon afterward to something even better: I was named editor of the school newspaper, *The Mountaineer*, and Joan Bender became co-editor. (Fig. 45)

Fig. 45. Co-editors of *The Mountaineer*, Joan Bender and the author. 1959

For the life of me I can't remember one story or editorial I wrote for *The Mountaineer,* and very probably copies of the paper, if anyone tried to keep them, have crumbled to yellow tea leaves by now. Even if the paper had been saved, I wouldn't want to revisit it. Who knows what kind of sophomoric blather I'd find there. But as such publications go, it must not have been too bad, for, as I just recently learned, the paper tied for third place in a statewide competition for high school papers, and my editorial writing tied for fourth. The news piece I read on this did not mention how many student papers were in the running or how many others tied for third and fourth places.

My head swelled even more when I was contacted by a couple of out-of-town newspapers, including the *Tulsa Tribune*, to make me one of their many stringers to report football scores in my area after the Friday-night games. When I made those collect calls to Tulsa, I thought I'd truly hit the big time. I think I was paid maybe five dollars for each phone call, but the important thing was that I could henceforth think of myself as connected to the larger profession of journalism outside Rogers. I was happy I'd traded the world of athletics for the more glamorous brotherhood of newspaper reporters. After all, there were forty guys on the football team and only one recently minted sportswriter! I could now attend our football games in the capacity of *Mountaineer* editor. And I began to dress according to my notion of the part. My sister Phyllis, who then worked as a waitress at the Lakeside Café, brought home a London Fog raincoat some long-ago (two weeks?), absent-minded customer had left behind at the restaurant. Turned out in this dashing coat, I strode about the sidelines as if on a serious mission. So convincing was this important new look, in fact, that one evening at an away game, some guys asked me to join them in the press box and serve as their color commentator during a radio broadcast. I didn't blink an eye and pitched right in, like somebody born to do this very thing.

My big break came later in the fall. For reasons lost to memory, someone at my school nominated me as the Junior Rotarian of the Month, an honor that required me to attend the club's weekly luncheons in the grand dining room of the Harris Hotel. This was a very mixed honor for me, for with it went the obligation to share a table and engage in intelligent as well as good ol' boy conversation with some of the town's movers and shakers and then, at my final guest appearance, make a little thank-you speech about what being with the club had meant to me, my hopes and dreams for the future, etc. At some point, either in conversation or in my farewell talk, I must have mentioned my ambition to be a newspaperman. One of the Rotarians, Robert L. Brown, managing editor of the *Rogers Daily News*, heard this and, a few weeks later, called me and offered me a chance to work for his paper, starting in January 1960. He offered me a job as feature writer and sports editor. *Hallelujah!!* I could not have been happier. To loosely quote Winston Churchill, I was like a drowning man who was pulled from the English Channel only to be told he'd won the Irish Sweepstakes!

The Roman philosopher Seneca wrote that luck plays a role in one's life when preparation meets opportunity. Getting this job at the *Rogers Daily News* was a great break for me, but I was ready for it because English grammar had been drilled into me from grade school (where we were taught by diagramming sentences), and I could write a coherent essay. I knew the language. Moreover, I was familiar with sports from having participated in football, basketball, and track since the ninth grade. And I was just cocky enough to know that I could do the job. Later in life, my friend Don Strange, a Kent businessman, preached the gospel that you hire the person for whom the job will be both a life-enhancing and career-advancing opportunity. That's certainly what Mr. Brown offered me, for my employment at the paper was the best job I'd had up to that point and one of the best ones I've had in my life. Basically, I got paid while I learned to write, and, with only a couple of dreary exceptions, I enjoyed every moment of the experience. I can't remember how much I was paid, although it couldn't have been very much; in truth, I should have paid Mr. Brown, as if I were paying tuition.

At first I covered home basketball games, writing in longhand in lined notebooks after the games while the details and the drama, if any, were fresh in my memory. The next morning before school, I would go around to the paper's offices and, with my hunt-and-peck method, bang out the story. From the beginning, my articles appeared under my byline: "By Ben Bassham." Oh, the glory! Oh, the ego trip! Mr. Brown, that crafty managing editor, must have known that, however meager my salary might be, having my name in lights would probably be a headier form of compensation. However, one had to go about this with confidence mixed with caution, for knowing that what you wrote would appear in print for all to see focuses the mind quite sharply.

I had learned the basics of writing news stories and headlines in my junior and senior journalism classes, so I knew going in that you needn't be an F. Scott Fitzgerald to write for newspapers; you only needed to stick to the tried-and-true formulas. First you have to grasp the essential point of the news piece and then—and here is the only creative step—take a certain angle on it, or hang the article on a "peg." You then organize the story by putting the most important content in the first paragraph, facts of secondary or less relevant stuff in the second paragraph, and so on, so that the reader gets the point right away and can move on to another article without finishing the story. The last paragraph might have details about the wind direction or the color of somebody's shirt, facts you can do without. Journalists would say that such a story meets the "cut-off rule." Composing an article this way is very useful when the editor might find he doesn't have enough space to run the whole piece. I also learned the shorthand lingo of news writing, noting "stet" in the margins when I wanted something left in and proudly jotting "30" below the final sentence of an article, signifying "the end."

If I had other duties during the winter and spring before my graduation, I can't recall them, but I do distinctly recall opening up the *Daily News* office early in the mornings, being there alone before the handful of other staff members reported, and having a proprietary feeling about the place. I liked the way the place smelled; I wish I could smell it again. The paper's offices and printing plant were situated in an old building (now, sadly, gone) at the southwest corner of First and Poplar. (Fig. 46) I had my own desk in the large workroom where a couple of secretaries who handled subscriptions and classified ads, the copy reader (who doubled as the society editor), and a few other people toiled; Brown and the city editor, Don Garrison, who wrote much of the most important stuff and who laid out the paper, had their own offices.

When I began working full time that summer of 1960, I'd arrive in the mornings and the teletype machine back in Don's office would still be thumping and pounding out hard copy of the stories that came in over the wire, as it had been since the wee hours. On a typical morning there might be 15 or 20 feet of paper that I'd tear off the machine in order to find the two or three stories for our skimpy sports section; on some days we wouldn't run any sports at all. One of my other assignments concerned the copy editing of Drew Pearson's immensely popular column "The Washington Merry-Go-Round," a gossipy "inside the Beltway" feature we ran on our editorial page. For some odd reason, the column was sent out to subscribers printed in all-caps and without punctuation and therefore served as a surefire make-work project for each paper's lowest man on the totem pole.

Fig. 46. The *Rogers Daily News* building, Courtesy
of the Rogers Historical Museum

The technology used then at the *Rogers Daily News* was probably little changed from that used in the early part of the century. On my desk sat an upright, decidedly nonelectric typewriter that could have dated from the Taft administration; the thing no doubt would have required a forklift if I'd ever wanted to move it. Ingeniously, it had been fitted out with a do-it-yourself wire support for a thick roll of newsprint of stationary width and of prodigious length; with this contraption I could feed paper into my machine and write articles several feet long, if I'd wanted to, and sometimes I did. My other writing tools were an 18-inch ruler and a pot of white paste whose lid was fitted with a brush. These were my cut-and-paste supplies, quite handy for taking a long article, ripping the paper with the ruler, rearranging the paragraphs, and gluing it all back together.

After finishing the piece and having it vetted by Garrison, the typescript, folded this way and that, would be turned over to a girl who labored away on another human-powered machine, a huge typewriter (of sorts) that converted the text into a code punched out on paper tape that could then be fed into and read by the Linotype machines over in the composing room. The Linotypes were truly products of the nineteenth century (Mark Twain went broke after investing a fortune in a lousy machine intended to compete with them), and they continued in use by newspapers until the 1970s, when they were replaced by photo-offset printing. As a compositor typed on Linotypes, tiny metal molds dropped into a row, or matrix, into which molten metal was poured. A "slug" cast from this composite mold thus formed a "line o' type." Columns of these lines, along with photos (printed from Ben Day dots) and line illustrations were all locked together to form pages in reverse and were printed on a flatbed, motorized press in the relief printing process first used by Gutenberg in the 1400s.

Our offices were outrageously hot during the summer, and the press room, with all that molten metal, was like a level of Dante's inferno. But I preferred those conditions to working construction in the hot Arkansas summers, and I did not complain. Besides, few offices or shops or houses were air conditioned in Rogers in 1960. People relied on fans to push the hot air around. The handful of establishments that had installed air conditioning, or "swamp coolers," made much of these amenities, boasting on their signs "Refrigerated Air!" or "It's COOL inside!" with the words usually accompanied by a picture of a friendly penguin. There was much amusement among the males in our office—not me!—when the cute girl who worked the Linotype code machine would stand before a floor fan and, a little like the manner of Marilyn Monroe in that famous subway grate scene in *The Seven Year Itch*, lift the hem of her dress to enjoy the cooling breezes.

When that press got rolling in the early afternoons, the racket was so bad you couldn't hear yourself think; it made enough noise to wake the dead and set the entire building to trembling. (As Roger Ebert, another journalist from the old days, put it, something went out of the newspaper business when presses ceased to make buildings tremble.) But it was a happy moment: The paper had been "put to bed," as we old newspaper hacks like to say, and you'd produced something useful once again, a product that went out to a lot of people who had been waiting for it and hoping their pictures would be in it and their names spelled correctly. In the world of work, there are a lot worse jobs than bringing out a newspaper. Too bad that today the business appears to be slowly dying as it loses the battle with cable news and the Internet.

I enjoyed jawing with the old guys in the printing plant, where the minimum age requirement seemed to be about sixty-five, and they in turn were tolerant of me, if they noticed me at all. They couldn't have cared less what was printed in the paper as long as they continued to have a job printing it. And I liked working for Brown and Garrison. Bob Brown was not a local guy; he was an outsider, a Yankee who spoke with an odd accent. But when he spoke, people listened. Brown was all business. Unlike most managing editors of newspaper chains, Brown was a journalist, not an advertising man. A graduate of the University of Michigan, he had worked for United Press International in Taiwan before coming to Rogers. He was probably sent in by higher-ups in the paper's parent company to straighten it out and put its balance sheets in the black. With his wire-rim glasses and backswept hair, and invariably dressed in suit and tie, he exuded an urbanity that stood out in good ol' Rogers, with its relaxed, decidedly non-urban ways. Looking back, I wonder if he was Jewish, for he looked more like the son of immigrants who had risen to be first-chair violist with the New York Philharmonic than a man running a small-town Arkansas newspaper.

I made a number of bone-headed mistakes that summer, but Brown was the very embodiment of patience with me. He always corrected me in private and assured me that he would not tolerate a repetition of the error. From him

I learned a valuable lesson that I tried to apply later in life: praise employees in public, chew them out behind closed doors.

One of my assignments was to run over to Bentonville, the county seat, to look up all the recent legal transactions—bankruptcies, drunk-driving violations, etc.—for routine public postings in the paper. At the very least, it was an assignment requiring a high degree of exactitude, one might think. But on one of my visits to the courthouse, I was less than precise, and about a week after we published a list of marriages and divorces, a man and woman came around to the paper and let us know quite angrily that they, brother and sister, had certainly not been recently divorced. Mr. Brown was not pleased, and I was pulled off the courthouse beat.

Another of my assignments was to produce the daily "Yesteryears in Rogers" column. This meant going back through the paper's archives to find interesting material printed 10, 25, 50 years ago, to rewrite or summarize the notices, and to come up with three or four column inches of what we hoped would be mildly entertaining copy each and every day. After about six weeks at this boring and unchallenging job, one I thought was beneath me, I went to see Brown to tell him that I hated doing the column and wanted him to take me off it. If I could go back in time, I would tap myself on the shoulder and say, "Don't go in there. You're about to make a big mistake." But I can't, and I did. Very patiently, Mr. Brown set me straight: "You are an employee of the paper. We pay you to work here. I am your superior, your boss. When I give you a job, you do it—if not happily, then silently—and, I hope, you'll do it well. Any questions? Have a nice day."

Don Garrison became my mentor at the paper. Don was a local boy, a 1956 graduate of Rogers High School, and a guy you would not have expected to find at such a young age sitting behind the city editor's desk. But he was very good, and, all these many years later, I thank him for taking me under his wing. Of course, it was in Don's interest that my assignment to the sports desk worked out. He had been sports editor before I came on, so his elevation to city editor, with its presumably enhanced salary, would, in retrospect, appear to be a good idea if I did a good job. (By the way, he got his job at the paper much the same way I had: He, too, had worked on *The Mountaineer* and had been recommended by Mrs. Worthington.)

On one occasion, however, Don got me into another sort of hot water with Mr. Brown. I was assigned to write an article about the observation of an anniversary of our local hospital, Rice Memorial. Strictly routine stuff, mostly worked up from material supplied by the hospital with a few factoids garnered from a couple of telephone calls. After an hour or so of work on it, I turned my piece over to Don so he could give me his two cents. After reading it over, Don said, "Let me see if I can punch it up a little bit." No problem. Don rewrote it, and the next day it appeared on the front page under my byline. I was working at something at my desk when Brown called me on the intercom phone and asked me to step into his office. "What the hell is this?" he asks calmly and ominously at the same time. "What?" I reply. "Read the first paragraph of the hospital story!" So I did, much to my horror: "Since its founding in 1951 more than 14,000 patients have *went* through Rice Memorial Hospital." *Omigod!* Don had written these foul, ungrammatical words, and the copy editor had missed the error. If the paper had printed the mistake in capitalized, italicized, and underlined print it could hardly have been worse. What to do? Thinking fast for an 18-year-old who knew that pride and truth would have to be sacrificed on the altar of loyalty to my city editor, I sheepishly took the blame for the mistake and promised never to repeat it.

My youthful cockiness and readiness to make ugly situations worse—character traits that got me into all manner of trouble over the years—landed me yet again on shaky ground that summer when I was sent out to cover another story that, to this day, continues to be a source of both embarrassment and amusement to me.

Another person who worked for the paper, if only on a freelance basis, was our photographer, James Andrew Duty. (Fig. 47) (What better name for a newspaper guy! And you must understand that, like my southern double name, his "Andrew" was not so much a middle name as the second half of his first. We were always "Ben Lloyd" and "James Andrew.") James Andrew was a slightly overweight fellow maybe a couple of years older than I, a guy who was always in a hurry, as if what he was doing was of the utmost importance and it had to be done fast. (He did everything that way. One summer he served as lifeguard at the Lakeside swimming pool, where he was more a danger to himself than a savior for others. For example, he chipped one of his prominent incisors when he took too deep a dive into the shallow end of the pool and made contact with the concrete bottom.) He talked loudly and in the most melodious southern accent, like a minor character in a Tennessee Williams drama. And he could be very dramatic at times. One story is the case of the stolen bicycle. One day during his boyhood, James Andrew rode his bike to the Victory for a matinee, parked it on the sidewalk outside, and neglected to lock it (if he even had a lock; most people didn't). After the movie he discovered that his bike was missing, so he angrily marched around the corner to the police station, pounded on the desk, and, with an arrogance gained from being the only son of one of the town's prominent attorneys, shouted, "Somebody stole my bicycle, so, chop, chop, get out there and find it!"

Fig. 47. James Andrew Duty, ca. 1958.

He absolutely luxuriated in his role as the paper's photographer and sometime writer, as he had when he served in that capacity for our high school annual, in whose pages he can be seen posing proudly with his huge flash camera. He was like someone in a Dick Tracy comic strip. Hell, James Andrew thought he was *in* a Dick Tracy comic strip. His mother and father indulged James Andrew shamelessly. They had bestowed on him a four-door sedan, a Buick, I think, which James Andrew then equipped with a radio that picked up dispatches from the fire department and the police. The car had a huge fishing pole of an antenna on the back that swished comically as he dashed about town. It was fun to cover a story with James Andrew, I the wordsmith and James Andrew the photographer, both of us in pursuit of our own Pulitzer Prizes.

One morning James Andrew blew into the *Daily News* office to announce that something really big was going down on the west side of town. Don sent us both out to get the story. When we arrived at South Thirteenth Street, a fire truck and a couple of police cruisers were parked together. The scene suggested that something awful had happened or was about to—an eminent explosion, a homicide, a suicidal gunman holding hostages, perhaps. This could be the big story of the summer.

Instead, a woman in the neighborhood had called the police to report that a mongrel dog—not hers—had given birth to a litter of puppies in a culvert at the end of her driveway. She had insisted that the animals were in immediate danger, especially if we were to be visited by a heavy rainstorm whose flood waters would carry them all to their doom. She had not only called the authorities to alert them, but she seemed also to be directing the firemen's rescue efforts. The police, after trying unsuccessfully to coax the animals out of the concrete pipes, had fashioned a kind of ramrod and tried to push them out. No luck. Then the owner of a pet store arrived on the scene and took on the role of chief rescuer. She directed officers and firemen to dig up the culvert and get mama dog and babies out and to be quick about it. With this absurdity, I mounted my high horse and took it upon myself to set this woman straight. "This is a fiasco," I said. "The animals are not in imminent danger. If water floods the ditch and culvert, the mama dog will carry her pups to safety. What's the big deal?" Whereupon Mrs. ASPCA went absolutely ballistic and gave me a thoroughgoing tongue-lashing. "Don't you have a heart? Don't you care about animals, this poor, homeless dog and her precious puppies? Who do you think you are?" And so on.

I must have carried my indignation over this nonevent back to the office and vented to Mr. Brown, or perhaps James Andrew bore witness there to my unprofessional behavior. My boss was not at all pleased. Once again I was on the receiving end of another patient and gentle lecture from the managing editor, the theme of which was this: A reporter should be an observer and chronicler of a story; he should never inject himself into ongoing events and become a participant in them. In short, butt out and stay out. Then Brown took me off the story. My partner, not I, wrote the article, "Puppies Living in Culvert Evade Cops—Surrender," and got both the scoop and the byline.

James Andrew was also the author of not one but two follow-up articles on the fate of Penny and her two pups. Clearly he and management had a better nose for the articles that sell newspapers, and, in retrospect, I can see that they were right. Newspapers, especially those published in sleepy southern towns, need lighter, local human (or perhaps canine) interest stories as relief from the murder and mayhem and the tedious political news that dominate the headlines. Small-town newspapers live or die by entertaining, or by publishing pictures of local people, or, above all, by printing names, names, names. I just hadn't caught on to this yet.

Only one of my assignments took me out of town, and that trip was an experience that I was probably lucky to survive. Daisy Air Rifle, which had moved to town from Michigan in the mid-1950s, sponsored a baseball team made up of company employees, plus a few ringers, that played teams in other towns. Garrison thought it'd be a good idea if I went along with the team on a trip south to Nashville, Arkansas, where the Daisy crew would compete in the state semi-pro tournament and I would cover the game as a kind of nod to Rogers' leading industry. (My hometown worshiped Daisy, an enterprise that had put the small town on the map.) The players, ranging in age from their teens to about 50, set off south in four or five cars. I was jammed into a sedan with four other guys for a 480-mile trip that must have taken several hours each way in those days before interstate highways. As soon as the car left Daisy's parking lot, one of my fellow passengers broke out a pint of whiskey and began passing it around, and soon we were hell on wheels as we made our un–air conditioned way south. (I note that I did not partake.) Someone once remarked that when you get more than three men together on an out-of-town jaunt, the synergy of the pack brings out the "Homer" in each one of them. Thus it was that summer afternoon. Fortified by Jim Beam, we sped into very antebellum-looking southern Arkansas. We traveled far enough south to see black field workers, the women wearing colorful bandannas on their heads as protection from the mid-July heat, an exotic sight to an 18-year-old raised in segregated, white-bread Rogers.

By the time we got to the park and play began, our boys had sobered up enough to give a good account of themselves, even though the game was an amateurish spectacle filled with passed balls, wild pitches, fly balls arcing over fielders' heads, numerous strikeouts, twisted ankles, and bruised egos. The Daisy team did all right until the eighth inning, during which they committed five errors, and Nashville broke away to win 13-3. To be honest, there was not much material for a good story. Even though our team lost, nobody seemed to really care. Fueled by firewater, most of our guys had had a good time. I remember that one of the Daisy players, an older guy, had one leg that was shorter than the other; he wore a huge, black shoe on the foot of his short leg that must have had a sole six inches thick. He was one of our pitchers and quite a sight on the mound, especially during his wind-up, when he'd lead with that big shoe. I recall, too, that the game was played with florescent, orange baseballs to facilitate drawing a bead on fly balls in the night sky, not that they seemed to be much help to our boys.

We packed up the gear and left town as midnight approached, pulling into the Daisy plant just before dawn. After a couple of hours of sleep, I got to the office in time to write up the story and see it in that afternoon's edition. Mr. Brown, a stickler for both form and details, liked the story but chastised me for not giving it a dateline to show that one of the paper's reporters, at risk to life and limb, had been sent out of town on assignment.

James Andrew's nifty police band radio picked up another alert that summer, and this time we had a genuine story to cover. In July he drove around to the office to collect me, and we raced off to the countryside south of Rogers to the scene of a truly horrible accident. Several men had joined together to pull a length of pipe out of a well and had, quite innocently but ignorantly, leaned the pipe, some 20–25 feet of it, against the top limbs of a tree. Unfortunately, the tree had concealed from their view the high-voltage electrical lines than ran along the road near the well, and when the pipe they were holding hit the wires, one of the men was electrocuted and his companions were badly burned. We got to the scene shortly after the accident, probably even before most of the members of the men's families had been notified, and, despite the number of people already present—James Andrew and I, a couple of policemen, firemen, and others—there was a decided hush that prevailed. The pipe still leaned into the limbs and foliage of the tree, and the body of the dead man lay uncovered on the ground. I could see that the soles of his shoes were scorched where the electrical charge had made contact with the earth.

The dead man was the first I had ever seen apart from a funeral, where corpses were always prepared for presentation to the living and all traces of the circumstances leading up to death had been scrubbed away. The man's body was now only a husk, a mass of meat that had only minutes earlier been the vessel of his self. His eyes were still partially open, but there was no longer anyone "home." James Andrew took a photo of the uncovered body, and I kept an eight-by-ten black-and-white print of it for years afterward, although I can't say why. And, no, we did not use that picture when the paper published my story of the accident the next day.

Such dramatic news stories were the exception and far from the rule that summer of 1960. Most of my work was ho-hum. But I soldiered on and loved the feeling that I was beginning to be—or at least to seem—like a real, grown-up professional, a role I could play even with the routine stuff. I wore a short-sleeved, white, buttoned-down shirt to work, adorned with a necktie that, true to the style of the day, was about an inch wide at its widest. At noon I would walk across the street and lunch in the classy dining room of the Harris Hotel. No more sinks of greasy spoons where I'd earned 20 dollars a week washing dishes. No more ditches where I'd labored with a long-handled shovel in Amazonian heat to make a dollar an hour. I had at last come up in the world. I was a newsman!

With little local baseball to cover and with national sports handled by wire services, there wasn't much for me to do but choose a few items for the page or page-and-a-half section we devoted to sports, lay out the page, and write the headlines. To be honest, the sports page wasn't much. Frequently it shared half the page with the comics. But I like to think that I brought a new life to that modest page. I added graphic interest by including large cartoonlike profiles of prominent sports figures and publishing local baseball league standings as if they were on a par with the majors. And I jazzed up headlines as much as I could. Still, Garrison had to find other things for me to do. I wrote many of the obituaries that appeared in the paper that summer—all, that is, except for those of important local personalities, in which cases Garrison or Brown did them and usually put the tributes on the front page.

Writing obituaries is not as simple as one might think. Today many newspapers charge a fee to bereaved families to publish death notices, and the writers can say just about anything they want. In those cases the language can take on religious flights of purple prose not otherwise appropriate for straight news stories. Such submitted texts stress how the late and lamented have "gone home to Jesus" or how husband and wife are now "together again." I, however, was almost daily faced with the task of coming up with some neutral word or phrase to report that someone was no longer among the living. "Died," "succumbed," and "passed away" just about constituted my three-word repertoire. It was a little like the problem writing about a basketball game: How many ways are there to say that a kid made a basket? "Swished the cords"? "Parted the nets?" "Hit two from outside"? "Downed a jumper"?

My big summer in journalism wound down toward September, and I began making preparations to head off for my freshman year at the University of Tulsa, where I planned to major in journalism. Interestingly, when I told Mrs. Worthington, who could be credited with pointing me in that direction, she expressed surprise. Why on earth go to college to study journalism when I was already a newspaper reporter? (This was 1960, before there was a college major for everything under the sun and universities began to stress how college graduates earned hundreds of thousands of dollars more in a lifetime than mere holders of high school diplomas.) It seemed odd and puzzling that a paragon of the academic life like Mrs. Worthington would not have been more enthusiastic about my college plans.

Soon after beginning college, however, my interest in journalism began to wane. My swan song as a newspaper guy was modest but memorable: The *Tulsa World,* on the recommendation of my journalism professor, hired me to work the phones on that memorable election night of 1960. An easy job, since I simply had to give callers the latest vote tallies as the *World* received them. I stayed up all night and went to bed at dawn, as most of the country did, wondering what the verdict in Illinois would be and whether my beloved Jack Kennedy, on whom I had an avid teenage crush, would be the next president. When I learned Kennedy won, I felt that a little of the credit should rightly go to me, so ardently had I pulled for him that fall in a state that eventually went for Nixon.

Why, after such a great introduction to newspaper work and with the requisite skills to do okay in the business had I decided that I'd had enough? I can't help thinking that I didn't have enough ambition, I didn't possess that proverbial "fire in the belly" to be a successful newspaper reporter. To get what you need for a story, you have to be a bit of a nuisance, to be willing to stick your nose into other people's affairs, even to be something of an SOB "What were your thoughts while your children were burned alive in that house fire?" you might have to ask. James Andrew Duty would have; he had more than the usual human allotment of chutzpah, and before his early death he continued to work in journalism. I did not and still don't have that kind of brass.

I had a sense of this already that summer at the *Daily News,* when Garrison sent me to Bentonville to get a statement from a man who was running for governor and who was required to visit our county seat to deal with some inconvenient, personal, and now long-forgotten legal matter. I was instructed to hang out on the steps of the county courthouse, meet the guy after his business with the county judge was concluded, and, come hell or high water, get him to say something, *anything*, that we could put in the paper. My heart wasn't in it, but I was determined to do my bit in defending the public's right to know (and, to be sure, to please my boss). When the courthouse doors finally swung open and the candidate, wearing a Stetson hat and cowboy boots, emerged into the sunlight, I was ready. Stepping into his path, my notebook and pencil at the ready, I managed to get out, "Sir, could you … ? To which he replied, without benefit of eye contact, "Not today, sonny, not today."

Sonny? *Sonny?!*

I know that at age 18, and at six feet two inches and tipping the scales at maybe 145 pounds, my eyes peering through thick glasses, I was not the most impressive of characters to be representing the fourth estate, but I was dignified, not to say pompous, beyond my years, and I did not relish a future filled with a potentially infinite number of such humiliating kiss-offs. To be a good journalist, an annoyingly dogged pursuer of the truth, the story, and, not least, a good quote, you have to be not only persistent but thick-skinned. And I was not.

But I am grateful for the invaluable experience I gained at the *Rogers Daily News,* my hometown paper, which exists today only on microfilm in the town's library, and to Bob Brown and Don Garrison for giving me a chance to write one day and to see my name in print the next. Beginning that summer of 1960, I became addicted to putting words and, most of the time, grammatically correct sentences on paper.

AFTERWORD

———◆———

As the summer of 1960 ended I was bound for the University of Tulsa, a small, private school I had applied to for two good reasons: Bob and Doris Moser had relocated to Tulsa, where they ministered to that very university community and my brother Bud, who worked for the now-defunct DX oil company, had married, bought a house, and generously offered me room and board while I went to school.

Why didn't I just stay in Rogers and continue working as a writer of feature stories, obituaries, *Yesteryears in Rogers* columns, and covering high school football and Little League games for the local paper? Maybe I would have risen to the rank of city editor in time, or graduated to the Associated Press, and then, who knows, moved on to the *St. Louis Post-Dispatch*. Quite simply I was just ready to go.

Today, as the country struggles to climb out of the worst economic conditions since the Great Depression, many sons and daughters remain at home in the bedrooms they grew up in and continue to park their legs under the family dining table. But my generation was a fortunate one. The economy was growing, the bright, young John Kennedy was on his way to the White House, college was cheap—indeed, state universities were virtually free—and we had confidence that jobs were out there just waiting for us to fill them. I couldn't wait to leave and put the old homestead in the rearview mirror.

But the experiment of going away to school, even when it was only 125 miles away, turned out not to be such a good one. For one thing, I never made any friends during my one semester there, and I grew lonely and homesick, as if I were still a twelve-year-old at church camp. The Mosers were nearby, but I had lost interest in things Presbyterian and felt, perhaps foolishly, that I was beginning to outgrow them. In addition, my room-and-board arrangement with Bud involved sharing the premises not only with him and his bride, but also with the new Mrs. Bassham's elderly mother and father—she a countrified, opinionated battle-ax who thought the home was hers, the old man a rag-picker who lived in an outbuilding in the backyard.

One evening at the supper table a political discussion inspired by the heat of the Kennedy-Nixon campaign grew very intense. The old lady made a little speech in which she predicted dire things for America should Kennedy gain the White House, to wit: the Inquisition would be reinstated, Washington would take directions from the Vatican, the pope would begin imprisoning all Protestants, non-Catholics would be broken on the rack, and so forth. Finally, I had had enough and rose to Jack's defense. But my debating skills being what they were, I did not choose to rebut the lady's arguments point by point but simply went after the one who voiced them, challenging her intelligence, even her sanity. "That's the biggest bunch of hogwash I've ever heard! You have to be not only stupid but crazy to say such things! How could anybody believe such crap?! Only an idiot would …" and on, I'm afraid, and on. Well, you get the picture. I left the table in a huff. The old girl was crying. It was horrible.

The next morning there was a cold silence as we ate breakfast and headed out for the day. And that afternoon, Bud picked me up at school and calmly announced that we'd both been kicked out, the marriage was finished, and we'd be looking for an apartment that afternoon. Neither of us was to be granted a second chance. Oh, God, what had I done? Surely things could be patched up, I'd apologize, it could be worked out, I babbled on. But, no. Bud said that this hadn't come as a surprise, trouble had been brewing for some time. *Some time?* They'd just gotten married, it seemed. True enough, we were out of there that day and into a small, two-room apartment close to downtown Tulsa, where we shared a queen-sized bed from October until the end of the semester, an end, as one might imagine, that I dearly looked forward to.

Despite these unsettling events, I enjoyed my courses tremendously. The University of Tulsa was a private school with strong degree programs in engineering, geology, and other fields of study related to the petroleum industry, or what we in the region referred to as the "all bid-ness." But I recall with fondness the liberal arts and humanities courses I took that fall. One was American history, taught by a tweedy, chain-smoking professor named Ivy who sat on his desk and talked—not lectured—to us, without the aid of notes, for an hour three times a week. I was enthralled. I began to think,

That's what I want to do someday! In another course, three profs, in a kind of tag-team fashion, poured out a ton of fascinating stuff about classical music, the theater, and, best of all, art history, the latter by a man named Broad (BRO-ad), and *he* was terrific too. I was starting to get hooked on this college business. I even liked freshman English, although there I found that Tulsa, while a private school, was not necessarily an exclusive one. On the first day of class, the professor sought to size up her students by asking us to conjugate some verbs. One guy got "freeze" to work on, and with considerable pain he slowly worked his way through this progression: "Freeze … froze …uh … frizzen?"

With Bud and the car at his office, I spent a lot of time hanging around campus, and in the student center one day I saw an exhibition of abstract— "modern"—paintings that impressed me very much. In high school I had painted one or two oil paintings, and when I saw that show I thought, Hmmm… maybe I should take that up again and chuck this journalism major.

When not on campus I'd hang around our dismal apartment listening to jazz, writing bad poetry and forlorn letters to a girl from Rogers, and feeling very sorry for myself. Things would have been different had I lived in a dorm or a fraternity house, but I couldn't afford either, and Momma didn't raise her son to become a frat. I began to miss my high school buddies, who no doubt had more comfortably relocated to the University of Arkansas, and I seized on every opportunity to go back home for reunions, motoring over there with Bud or taking the snail-slow Arkoma buses back home, and on one occasion losing my suitcase down the black hole of their baggage-handling system (thereby having to say good-bye to my priceless black corduroy suit, the outfit intended to make the world aware of how very cool I was!).

At year's end it began to dawn on me that I'd better switch to the university in Fayetteville, a school where I'd be guaranteed a host of old pals, lower tuition, and a bed to call my own. And that's what I did. And what a good idea that turned out to be.

To belabor the obvious, the University of Arkansas was not, and still isn't, Harvard, Princeton, or Yale (those schools Mr. Bartley back at Rogers High assured me I was not destined for, perhaps not even as a visitor allowed on their campuses), but the education I received there would compare nicely to that available at the Ivies. What marvelous professors I had there, and how

I took to them! Although still not a stellar student—I finished with a 3.25 GPA, mediocre by today's inflated standards—I was an eager one, sponging up the humanities, history, biology, German, and art history. Soon I switched to a major in art and began attending classes in a striking, modern building designed by one of America's leading architects, Edward Durell Stone, and that housed art, art history, architecture, music, theater, and dance, a building in which twirled two or three mobiles by another modernist, Alexander Calder. There I was in my element. Dressing the part, I gave up my old Craig Stevens preppy look in favor of sweatshirts, paint-spattered jeans, and long, unwashed hair. Although we had some professors who were on their last legs, or who drank too much, or both, we also had some genuinely good artists—Neppie Conner, Dick Knowles, and Lothar Krueger, among them—who doubled as excellent teachers. Many of them were products of the MFA program at the University of Iowa, where that terminal degree in the fine arts originated and where, because of the presence on the staff of Grant Wood, the slogan artists supposedly lived by was "Pull up a silo. I feel a painting coming on."

At Arkansas I connected with my professors; I liked them and they liked me. At the end of my four years in Fayetteville, I received glowing recommendations from them to two graduate programs: painting at the University of Indiana and art history at Wisconsin. Both schools accepted me, but Wisconsin offered me an assistantship with a stipend of $2200 for the first year. Today, an institution would have to offer me a hundred times that amount to approximate the impact that figure had on me in 1964, but even then it wouldn't be the same, for that acceptance, and that scholarship, became the key that opened the door to the rest of my life.

In her splendid, heart-breaking autobiography *1185 Park Avenue,* Ann Richardson Roiphe says that all memoirs are finally and essentially stories about "escape." Yes, indeed: escape is just the right word.

*　　　　*　　　　*

This book grew out of a much more modest plan to give our daughters an account of my family and also some idea of what it was like to be a boy growing up in a small town in Arkansas back in the Middle Ages of the twentieth century. The idea for this project nagged at me for years before I finally sat down to begin work on it, and after I started writing, the damned thing wouldn't leave me alone. I found myself waking up in the night to scribble notes or whole paragraphs; some of the best ideas came to me while driving the three-day car trip from Kent, Ohio, to Taos, New Mexico, where we live a few months each year. I found myself jotting notes while trying to keep the car on the road. I think a couple of good sentences even bubbled up in dreams. In short, I became obsessed, and the xeroxed and stapled typescript I'd at first had in mind became this book.

I took some lessons from a painter not long ago who confessed that he actually disliked the act of painting because it was such a difficult art to master. He said, however, that what he really liked was looking at and taking pride in a painting that he'd *finished*. I can sympathize, because painting, like playing the clarinet well, is a hard and risky business. But, oddly enough, writing isn't; or at least, from my days at the *Rogers Daily News* to the present, it hasn't been work for me at all. I loved writing it and, were it not for the occasional phone calls from a publisher's agent anxious to know "how's it coming?" and the requests from my wife to use the computer, I might have continued on it for the rest of my life.

From time to time friends and acquaintances who knew about this project expressed to me a similar wish to write something about their lives and their family, and I would say to them, if not quite this rudely, "Well dammit, do it!" These things don't write themselves. My genuine regret is that I didn't begin asking questions and taking notes years ago when most of the leading characters in this informal history were still alive. If I could go back in time to Rogers, I'd take a tape recorder and a camera, and I'd make a nuisance of myself interviewing everybody and snapping pictures all over town. That would produce a different book, however. There's something a bit special, if not necessarily always factual, about drawing a set of "remembrances" from within.

So, finally, this: I once knew a woman in Cleveland who enjoyed a well-deserved reputation as a superb cook, a veritable wizard in the kitchen. But she was that rare bird, a chef who carried all her recipes around in her head; no cookbooks, no clippings from the *New York Times* food section for her. And she guarded these recipes as if they were state secrets; requests for recipes from relatives and friends alike were always politely but firmly refused. She was like Dickens' Fagin clutching his treasure box to his chest even as he faced the gallows. One day a friend begged her for her meatloaf recipe, only to be turned down for the hundredth time. "But Rose," he pleaded, "You *must* let me have that recipe before you lose your *mind!*" So, before I lose my mind, and the memories still stored in it, I offer this book.

And this: I forgive Coach Camfield for being such a jerk. I should have tried harder.

A NOTE ON SOURCES

As the reader will have gathered, this book was never intended to be a serious work of non-fiction or a scholarly history of life in Rogers in the 1950s. Nevertheless, I often consulted and quoted from sources that should be acknowledged here.

I am especially indebted to the work of writers in my hometown who have published useful and frequently entertaining histories of our great little burg. Marilyn Harris Collins' *Rogers,* in the Images of America Series (The Rogers Historical Museum, 2006), provides a comprehensive and nicely illustrated history of the town and its people. I used James F. Hales' two books, *Rogers, Arkansas, 1881-2006* and *The Fabulous 1960s in Rogers, Arkansas* (both St. Joseph's Ozark Press), a good deal. Hales is to be congratulated and thanked for the splendid illustrated records of landmarks and townspeople he has given us.

I often quoted or referred to Roger Ebert's very charming memoir, *Life Itself* (New York: Grand Central Publishers, 2011) because he touched on so many subjects—the movies, newspaper work—that have been so important in my life as well. And, although I borrowed only a little from Anne Richardson Roiphe, her brave and riveting memoir, *1185 Park Avenue* (New York: Free Press, 1999), strongly reaffirmed for me the value and importance of remembering one's life in print.

J. Ronald Oakley's history, *God's Country: America in the 1950s* (New York: Dembner Books, 1986), helped enormously as I re-visited the politics, television, movies, and the crazy, lovable automobiles of the era. Neal Gabler's *Life, The Movie: How Entertainment Conquered Reality* (New York: Knopf, 1998), provided interesting insights on how film can shape behavior in impressionable kids like the author.

The story about Arkansas's miserable roads and highways was lifted from an article in the Jan. 23, 2011, *New York Times*, "The State That Went Bust," by Monica Davey. And my account of Coin Harvey's "Pyramids" at Monte Ne is indebted to Henry Miller's *The Air-Conditioned Nightmare* (New York: New Directions, 1947.)

ABOUT THE AUTHOR

———➤◆◄———

BEN L. BASSHAM IS EMERITUS Professor of Art History at Kent State University in Kent, Ohio. He taught courses in the history of American art and architecture for thirty years. He received his Bachelor of Arts degree (with Honors) at the University of Arkansas in 1964, and then studied art history at the University of Wisconsin-Madison, where he received his M.A. and Ph.D. degrees, from 1964 to 1969. He was head of the Art History Department at Kent from 1983 to 1987 before becoming an assistant dean and later Acting Dean of the Honors College. He has lived and studied abroad in London and in Florence, Italy. He retired in 1999 to devote his time to his career as an artist. Bassham has exhibited his paintings nationally and in several one-person shows in Ohio. He is an associate member of the Oil Painters of America.

Bassham's book, *Conrad Wise Chapman, Artist and Soldier of the Confederacy* (Kent State University Press, 1998), won the Henry Timrod Southern Culture Award in 2000.

Finally, notwithstanding the soberly offered advice by a fellow art historian that he never mention a wife or offspring in his resume because his colleague thought such practice "sexist," it says here that Bassham has been happily married for forty-three years to Carlyn, and that they have two lovely daughters, Claire and Marianna. The Basshams divide their year between their home in Kent, Ohio, and a studio-home in Taos, New Mexico.